Freeing
Black
Girls

Freeing Black Girls

A BLACK FEMINIST
BIBLE ON RACISM AND
REVOLUTIONARY MOTHERING

Tamura Lomax

Duke University Press   *Durham and London*   2025

Project Editor: Liz Smith
Typeset in Portrait and Helvetica Neue by Westchester Publishing Services

Library of Congress Cataloging-in-Publication Data
Names: Lomax, Tamura A., author.
Title: Freeing Black girls : a Black feminist bible on racism and revolutionary
    mothering / Tamura Lomax.
Description: Durham : Duke University Press, 2025. | Includes bibliographical
    references and index.
Identifiers: LCCN 2024033378 (print)
LCCN 2024033379 (ebook)
ISBN 9781478028376 (paperback)
ISBN 9781478024774 (hardcover)
ISBN 9781478060550 (ebook)
Subjects: LCSH: Lomax, Tamura A. | African American feminists. | African
    American mothers. | Motherhood—Political aspects—United States. |
    African American women—Religious life. | African American
    churches—Influence. | Misogynoir.
Classification: LCC E185.86 .L624 2025 (print) | LCC E185.86 (ebook) |
    DDC 305.48/896073—dc23/eng/20250122
LC record available at https://lccn.loc.gov/2024033378
LC ebook record available at https://lccn.loc.gov/2024033379

Cover art: The author and her mother in a similar pose.
Syracuse, New York. Courtesy of the author.

For Alexa, Chela, Kacey, Ky, Jasmine, and Black girls everywhere

Contents

Author's Note

Consider those cringeworthy reality television shows where parents drag their kids into scenes for a storyline. Now couple that with antiblack vigilante violence and discrimination against Black folks for merely breathing, let alone talking back to white supremacist capitalist patriarchy. Before I'm anything, I'm a fierce protector of those I love. More, the aims of this book require a different path. That said, *Freeing Black Girls* and *Loving Black Boys*[1] don't use names, with the exception of public figures and on occasion in storytelling. In that case I change names. I highlight relationships or roles instead—for example, my former "pastor," "spouse," "sister," "brother," "momma," "daddy," and so on. And because I have two sons, I've changed their names altogether. This is especially significant in *Loving Black Boys*. When I began this project, they were in middle school. I wrote about them often and didn't think to request their consent. I remedied this misstep some years ago, however, and they both gave me their blessings and trust. Somewhere between their trust and the threat to Black men's and boys' lives and livelihood, I endeavored to find a way to honor them and the truth of the story in these perilous times. Not a single day passes without me engaging racialized and gendered angst about their lives and lack of access to safety. And while some may read this as antifeminist, my sons' welfare comes before my politics. Moreover, this book is written by a Black woman and mother in deep relationship with Black men, not estrangement. That said, "self-protective disinformation" is in order, especially for them. Truthfully, I sometimes wondered if I should include my own name. Writing about white supremacist capitalist heteropatriarchy and aspirational black patriarchy as a black feminist is no easy task. Apart from writing and research, such work demands a range of very real prediscourses on safety measures between my household, community, press, university, and otherwise.

Additionally, some feminists may wince at my deployment of the word *husband* throughout this text and especially in *Loving Black Boys*. I'm well aware of the history of the term and how it relates to household management, control of resources, labor, breadwinning, and the institutionalization of heteropatriarchy in the home, community, law, and otherwise. I'm also cognizant of how Black men didn't historically get to be husbands and fathers during slavery, within the welfare state, in media, and beyond, and aren't always respected as such. Naming those who are, unequivocally, in a positive light matters. Deletion, even when political, is debilitating for reasons beyond whatever the white heteropatriarchal familial structure means to America and empire. As Audre Lorde states, Black folks never had access to that dream, anyway. Further, two things can be true at once. My husband is my partner, and this book resists heteropatriarchal masculinity. That said, I sometimes interchange the word *husband* with *spouse, life partner*, or *partner*, though in life beyond these pages I predominantly utilize *husband*. On a similar note, an early trusted reader of the manuscript struggled with my referring to my father as "Daddy" in print. They thought it "felt disempowering." I appreciate this feedback because *Freeing Black Girls* will make us feel a lot of things, especially discomfort. That is the intention. Critical personal and political black feminist storytelling is meant to be felt. And not all will feel good. Life is complicated. So is lived black feminism. So is this book. But please rest assured, I use the term as an empowered Black woman. "Daddy" and "Momma" are what I call my parents. And so it shall be in these pages.

Finally, I prefer *Black* over *African American*. Blackness includes the African Diaspora and refers to a diverse yet shared history in the African continent, contact/conquest, dispersal, trade, freedom, and social movement. Thus, this book deploys a capital *B* when referring to Black people, specifically, women, girls, men, boys, mothers, fathers, children, family, enslaved people, and folks.[2] Consequentially, liberties have been taken to change *b* to *B* in citations. Additionally, I maintain the disciplinary capitalization of the Black Church. Concurrently, *white* and *whiteness* are lowercased not to suggest a hierarchical racial reversal but to resist how the *W* has historically and contemporarily stood for manufactured supremacy as well as realized structural, institutional, social, political, and other oppressions. Generally, I use *w* to refuse racial dominance, terror, and genocide—namely, as the *W* moves between ideology and practice, for example, when it's deployed by white supremacist activists and politicians, using three fingers similar to the "OK" sign, to express "white power," thus evoking violence. Conversely, the *B* or *Black* in *Black folks*, though raveled with our own intracommunal and intraracial oppressions, has never been an invocation for global violence, domination, or collective supremacy. Quests for supremacy and the fight for freedom from that supremacy are oppositional. These moves should come as no surprise in a book centered on Black folks in general and Black girls specifically and our collective survival against white supremacist and patriarchal violence. Still, discerning between *B* and *b* was difficult. This book doesn't capitalize *b* when referring to ideas, concepts, things, places, and so on—for example, blackness; antiblackness; or black humanity, body, male body, female body, motherhood, mothering, manhood, personhood, femininity, masculinity, gender ideals, communities, institutions, identity, experiences, endangerment, feminine-*ism*, feminine theology, feminism, gender ideology, "nuclear" family, genocide, death, captivity, oppression, bravado, life, love, music, culture, joy, freedom, thriving, consciousness, patriarchy, monster, sexism, and so on. My intention is to affirm Black people while fiercely critiquing oppression, whether deploying a *b* or a *B*.

Acknowledgments

Sometimes the ugliness of life propels us to something wonderful. Not because we need trauma to get to the good, a notion I vehemently resist, but because many of us refuse to accept the bad and/or despair. *Freeing Black Girls* presses through a lot of ugly. That said, I never planned to write this book, nor did I want to. I needed to. I am especially thankful for the many reviewers for both *Freeing Black Girls* and *Loving Black Boys* and to Duke University Press for pushing me there, to an incredibly uncomfortable and vulnerable space of storytelling. *Freeing Black Girls* came alive because of your critical and incisive generosity. I only hope it does the work you imagined.

I thank my institution for time away to finish "the book." That book was *Loving Black Boys*. Notwithstanding, "giving me back my time" provided necessary space for me to write myself into clarity. Who knew I'd write two books in the process. It's amazing what one can do with good health, research, and dedicated time and resources. Thank you for supporting my need for creative space. Additionally, I offer special thanksgiving for the feminist mentorship and camaraderie of Kristie Dotson and Zillah Eisenstein. I've learned and gained enough from Dotson to last a lifetime. Thank you for guiding, seeing, challenging, and inspiring me. Thank you for your black feminist brilliance, movement, example, and power. And thank you for curating a politics of insistence. I'm better because of you. This book is—because of you. I'm also forever thankful for my sister-comrade, Z. Nobody has nudged me "to get it done" with love and conviction as you have. I jostled through fear, sadness, fire, imposter syndrome, and stress because of you. You consistently drive me toward radical love and power in ways that are invaluable. But it was your words and demand, "Don't give a fuck about the academy while writing. . . . Get back to your creativity," that got me all the way together. I lifted it from our text stream and posted it to the top of my computer. That creativity continues to activate me forward.

To Momma and Daddy, thank you for giving me life, love, and a fierceness that only comes about with parents like you. Some of these pages will be hard to read. Many others will make you smile. The bottom line is that my voice is foremost because of you. To my nieces—Alexa, Chela, Kacey, Ky, and Jasmine—every day that I wrote about Black girls and freedom, I wrote with pictures of you in my mind. I insist on a better world for you than I had as a Black girl and for you to own your power better than I ever did. Finally, to my love, our beautiful sons, and Maxx and Jesse, I awake in the dark and light thankful for you. To B, without you there are no books. You saw my future long ago, spoke that vision, and hurried me here, kicking and screaming. You knew my potential better than I did. And you welcomed the journey and evolution with grace and coalition. To my sons, I "never knew love like this before." You energized my fighting spirit and made me think I could and must dream new worlds. Thank you for your unmatched support, understanding, patience, and love. "The book" is finally here.

Introduction: Toxic Literacies

Good Black Mothers, Endangered Black Boys,
and Invisible Black Girls

I wrestled Lee and Seth from the tub and began the ritual of dressing them in their Sunday best. In just two short years I'd mastered the art of getting ready for church with two toddlers. Typically, my spouse and I would double-team the duo, or he'd take the lead because it takes me much longer to prepare. Let him tell it, my morning cup of coffee along with hair, makeup, and fashion decision-making takes at minimum two hours, particularly for fancy outings. Truthfully, it's more like one hour—pushed to the very limits of the final second. In any case, Sunday mornings were left to me. And preparing the three of us for the public was nothing short of artistry. Just before we left, the home phone rang. It was my husband, saying, "Hey, babe. I know it's Mother's Day, but don't come to church today." He was in leadership at the church and heard the sermon at an earlier service. However, as a new mother born and raised in the Black Church, I'd come to anticipate the complex doting that happens on Mother's Day. The Black Church is in no way perfect. Frankly, it can be quite savage toward Black mothers. Still, the oppugnant love experienced there is at least better than the vulgar vociferation from the rest of the world. As the elders would say, "Sometimes in life you have to take a little salt with your sugar." So I thought.

The Black Church is complicated. It's a black world within a world that proudly cavorts in antiblackness, a weekly anchorage away from unrepentant racial bias and schadenfreude, a source for critical black information, and though not the sole social center, it remains a significant communal, political, and cultural site where Black folks assemble. The service was full and sublime. Smiling brown faces and glistening chocolate flesh, donning resplendent pastels and seersucker, filled the vestibule and sanctuary. All kinds of mothering and othermothering joys, sacrifices, and pains were acknowledged through jubilating songs and spoken words that day.[1] If I had a magic wand, I would've paused the gorgeous gathering of Black folks there, because though the service was blissful, the sermonic moment was catastrophic. Listening intently, I sat in the pew with eyes so piercing you would think they were fistfighting the dais. Refusing to extend a single "amen," wave of the hand, or even that forgiving smile folks offer to make others feel comfortable when things go awry, I raged by unloading a fiercely intentional unapologetic oppositional gaze.[2] More, I purposefully locked eyes with the pastor to ensure he bore witness to my unreserved defiance. To say it's unnerving to speak from a podium under a steady and unequivocal disagreeable peer within a context that historically centers ecstatic call-and-response is an understatement.[3]

Deploying 1 Kings 3:16–28 KJV, the pastor preached about "two hos" "fighting over a baby boy."[4] He placed emphasis not on biblical exegesis but rather on contemporary stereotypes of morally corrupt, hypersexual, aggressive, irresponsible, lying, and cheating "baby mommas," as a way of distinguishing between "good" and "bad" Black mothers and articulating the state of endangered Black boys in America. To drive home the point about diabolical black mothering and certain unmarried women being hos and temptresses, he jokingly chided Black girls for too easily "giving it up to brothers for a coke and a smile" and Black women for baring too much skin in the church house, therefore distracting the men and boys from the spiritual experience.[5] He preached, "Sisters, I know it's getting hot outside but please help the brothers out!" Congregants laughed out loud and eagerly said "Amen." As I've written elsewhere, the hypersexualization of Black women and girls in the Black Church is met with spirited approval across genders more often than not because it both resonates with internalized misogynoir and differentiates among Black women and girls.[6] Meaning, zealously shouting "Amen!" at the idea that sundresses and bare arms are so innately powerful that they somehow entice Black cisgender heterosexual men and boys away from a spiritual reckoning makes it clear one isn't *that* kind of woman or girl.

A less sexist and pornotropic hermeneutic might've read the passage as an example of Solomon's superior impartial, unprecedented wisdom and thus fulfillment of divine promise.[7] Others interpret the text as an illustration of a good mother and her unrivaled love for her child. A more subversive womanist or black feminist reading would've likely explored the ethnicity and culture of the two women and the relationship between them; social designations and industry opportunities for widows and/or impoverished single mothers; Old and New World laws and oppressions related to women and girls, marriage, consent, patronymics, and inheritances; and correlations between capitalism, gender, race, labor, and sex work.[8] Such a critical stance might argue that the bellicose patriarchal rules and norms of the state make being a girl and/or an unmarried woman difficult and mothering from the margins nearly impossible. Perhaps it would also conceive how patriarchy insists on violence, damages relationships, leads to untoward survival mechanisms, and may enable dead children. Ultimately, this was a terrible textual choice for Mother's Day, however spun, as well as a missed opportunity.

To create space for thoughtful yet incisive interrogation and agency and to disidentify with the vile sermonic representations, I waited and emailed the pastor later that week. This was 2003 and before social media and iPhones. I couldn't post a video or crowdsource support. While those mechanisms may do good work, I'm not sure they would've been the most productive in this scenario. It depends on the goal and whether it's embarrassment, freedom, thwarting behavior, deepened conversation, something else, or all of the above. To be blunt, I'm not above any of these outcomes as I've participated in all of them. And sometimes public humiliation is exactly what's needed. Nevertheless, I opted for one-on-one email conversation. In addition to calling out the misnaming of Black girls, women, and mothers and discussing the racialized gendering of the term *ho*, I suggested the pastor spend some time on the history of women, widows, and sex work should he preach that text or one like it in the future.[9] The mothers in 1 Kings 3:16–28 weren't inherently pathological. They were surviving the patriarchy and the state.[10] This isn't to say bad mothers don't exist or that harmful decisions aren't sometimes made by desperate mothers. It's to note that sociopolitical and sociocultural contexts often shape both options and choices.

More, we'd do well to consider the thorny conditions of black mothering in America, specifically. Categorically perverting all Black women, mothers, and girls, thus reducing them to historical racial tropes, let alone on Mother's Day, is playing with white supremacy.[11] I should pause and note I wasn't always this person. I'm a recovering semiconservative Christian who once maintained hegemonic black sexual politics and black gender ideologies.[12] And though

I questioned sex and gender power dynamics early on, I was no feminist. I might've previously joined the chorus in shouting, "Amen!" However, my husband and I were both new divinity students at this time. We were learning to question and resist harmful embedded theologies from our youth. And we were growing our family and our sociopolitical view of the world, together. Specifically, my passage toward radical black feminism, a politics and movement against sexism and patriarchy, was just beginning and as it happens is ongoing. This was a pivotal moment in my journey from black traditionalist womanhood and toxic femininity—draconian and exclusive adherence to heteropatriarchal gender ideals and performances—to brazen black feminist rebellion.[13]

It was the first time I had language to name and resist theological misogynoir, foundational to the making of America, American Christianity, and the Black Church.[14] Thus, this was the first time I directly attacked and deconstructed the heteropatriarchal antagonisms toward Black women and girls that occur from the pulpit. And though I'm a "preacher's kid," it was my first time having access to a pastor who had an openness to critical dialogue on sex, gender, and sexuality. He was on the front end of fighting for Black men's gay rights in the Black Church. And though male-centric, the pastor's commitment to preaching love and acceptance over homophobia against Black cisgender gay men and boys created space for me to pursue a theology of justice and eventually black feminist politics in my graduate studies. To the pastor's credit, he listened and engaged back and forth with me over the course of the week through a string of lengthy emails. The exchange wasn't pretty. We disagreed, pushed back, tumbled forward, and expressed anger. And though he loved and supported our family and promoted me and my husband to leadership positions in the church, the heated dialogue was risky.

My spouse had recently left corporate America to work full-time at the church while in graduate school, and I'd left corporate America to be a stay-at-home mom turned graduate student. The church was our sole source of income. Additionally, it was a budding Baptist megachurch in the early 2000s, a type of church commonly structured like mini-autocracies where the traditionally male pastor executed absolute authority. We'd seen other ministers get fired for disagreeing with the pastor. Further, many congregants were like family to us, offering support and childcare for our two toddlers that was unmatched. Still, neither the pastor nor I held back. A fresh sense of fearlessness took me over and some would say has never left. In the end, we found middle ground on some things and agreed to disagree on others. The debate didn't hinder our relationship as far as I could tell. I became the first woman deacon in the history of the church shortly after. Nevertheless, my spouse and I discontinued our membership and his employment later that year. The church's movement toward a more emancipatory sexual theology failed to translate into a critique of sexism and patriarchy; undoing the autarchical organizational structure; or addressing how leadership treated cisgender, transgender, gender-neutral, nonbinary, genderqueer, bisexual, or questioning women and girls.

Several years after I left the church, graduated from divinity school, and subsequently moved away and completed my PhD studies, which explored injurious representations of Black women and girls in the Black Church and black popular culture, my divinity school invited me back to honor my work as cofounder of *The Feminist Wire*, one of the first online publications committed to intersectional feminist, antiracist, and anti-imperialist sociopolitical critique and activism. I saw the pastor in the audience and thanked him. We clashed on many things politically, theologically, and organizationally, and his views on women and girls were repressive. Yet, he was part of the reason I was there. The pastor wrote my recommendation letter to attend divinity school and was willing to engage my critiques, thus igniting my course of parrhesia in the public sphere. After the ceremony we embraced and caught up on life. He was astonished to see that the two little baby boys he visited in the hospital maternity wing just after birth and once held to the sky in the palms of his hands during their baby dedications were now teenage high schoolers. We laughed at how I was using my doctorate in religion to mass-mediate black feminist politics to millions of readers online with the intention of normalizing equity.

The pastor shared that our emails "changed" his theology and how he preached about Black women, girls, and mothers. Although I missed the transformation, I was glad to hear it. However, I'd learned some things, too. While patriarchy and misogynoir are ubiquitous and vicious, the struggle against them is possible, powerful, and dynamic. We don't have to submit to or be held hostage to second-classness or vitriolic misogynoirist theologies or ideologies just because they're wrapped in religious or otherwise palatable dogma.[15] Inter- and intraracial structures of dominance, including the religious, cause harm and must be resisted.[16] And call-and-response can be a form of radical engagement when speaking truth to power. However, this requires audaciously, collectively, and directly talking back. *Freeing Black Girls: A Black Feminist Bible on Racism and Revolutionary Mothering* does exactly that. It's an insurgent black feminist love letter to myself, Black girls, women, mothers, and othermothers, which offers a critique of ideology, religion, and culture through a collection of personal stories about my journey from black girlhood to black feminist motherhood. This in mind, it's about calling out and responding to the devastating consequences of inter- and intraracial systemic misogynoirist toxicity and misrecognition; the righteous saving grace of black feminist politics; and the power of looking and talking back.

Thus, it's not only a radical dream for black feminist futures or a spell book for black freedom but also a revolutionary quest for calling forth relations, communities, and ways of seeing, thinking, and being that value and nourish whole persons. Such a venture notes Black girls, women, mothers, othermothers, and black feminist mothering as essential to the black freedom project, and religio-cultural tropes, misogynoir, sexism, patriarchy, and discourses on black female and maternal insufficiency as toxic. Going forward, this introduction situates the backdrop against which the stories will unfold. First, it discusses the pursuit of defining "good" black mothering in black religion and culture after North American slavery, why this definition was needed, and why we need new literacies. Second, it puts forth a theory of collective endangerment across genders. Third, it engages what this book hopes to undo. Fourth, it states why I've called it a bible.

Mining the Religio-Cultural and Political Landscape on "Good" Black Motherhood

Mother's Day 2003 was neither the first nor the last sermon or commentary I'd hear on reckless and immoral black mothering, or how Black girls and unmarried Black women and mothers are especially promiscuous and threatening to Black endangered boys.[17] We're served a leitmotif on how negligent and/or licentious (particularly "single") Black mothers harm Black boys from a range of cultural sources.[18] The Black Church, with its political and theological commitments to black heteropatriarchal normativity and respectability, is one of many. To be clear, as the Mother's Day sermon indicates, there are dueling anxieties here: the desire to establish what a "good" Black mother is or isn't and a yearning to vocalize, cease, and/or limit black male endangerment. These schemas exist in tension across history, politics, religion, culture, and otherwise. They're misguided dog whistles for engaging black precarity intraracially, requiring rethinking. The general idea is that better Black mothers will make life more advantageous and/or safer for Black boys. I'll deal with Black mothers first and return to endangerment later.

The Black Church's obsession with Black women's and girls' bodies, sexual lives, wombs, and achievement of "proper" womanhood, which includes cisgender heterosexual marriage and motherhood, is forceful and in a class of its own, whether or not one is Christian and/or attends church.[19] Of course, not all Black women are mothers or othermothers or want to mother. And not all Black folks are raised with mothers as caregivers.[20] Yet, the presupposition that

Black cisgender girls one day marry and mother is persistent and persuasive, namely, as the black "nuclear" project, which requires a cisgender mother, is equated to black progress, freedom, and strength.[21] The belief is that strong black cisgender "nuclear" families equal strong communities and maybe one day a powerful diaspora. In tandem, becoming a Black wife and mother is pertinent to becoming a "real" woman.[22] Here, I mean to highlight the Black Church and cultural notion that only "real" women have uteri, breasts, vaginas, and the "natural" ability to birth children, as well as the idea that "real" Black women marry Black men and have babies. Thus, childless, unmarried, queer, and transgender women may not be seen as "real" by some.

Hence, I was called a "real" woman for the first time when I announced my pregnancy with my eldest son. The second time was when a male deacon at church asked if I had a C-section like his wife. When I said "No," he responded, "Oh, you're a 'real' woman!" To which another woman chimed in saying, "I had mine natural!" Corroborating birth stories about our vaginas, levels of "realness," and the efficacy of epidurals with a male deacon wasn't on my bingo cards. The rabbit hole for who is or isn't "real" is incessant and insatiable. Being a "real" woman is a virtue in the Black Church and black culture. More recently, social media serves as a site for embracing and mediating "real" womanhood among Black cisgender heterosexual women, as a response to transgender and non-Black women dating and marrying Black cisgender men. Simultaneously, online platforms have been widely used by Black cisgender heterosexual men and boys to articulate a desire for more traditional Black women and girls. To some, marriage and motherhood are "the" only and/or ultimate goals for punctilious passage from black girlhood to virtuous black womanhood.

These ideas aren't original. I discuss them at length in *Jezebel Unhinged: Loosing the Black Female Body in Religion and Culture* (2018). General views on Christian motherhood are shaped by beliefs about natural hierarchy between men and women and gender roles, which often interchange womanhood and motherhood because cisgender women and girls are expected to marry and populate the earth. As I write in *Jezebel Unhinged*,

> Aristotle's *Generation of Animals* (350 B.C.), which pioneered ideas about sex division and natural hierarchy, ... metaphysically constructs all females as deviations from the male "norm." While males realized their full potential because they had penises and could ejaculate, females were interpreted as imperfect, mutilated, and weak unrealized males. No penis and menstruation served as proof, confining women to a lower place in society based on "natural hierarchy." In *The Body and Society: Men, Women,*

and Sexual Renunciation in Early Christianity (1988), historian Peter Brown notes an appropriation of these ideas among second-century Christians in Rome. He argues that ideas about womanhood, couched in Christian and political beliefs about natural hierarchy and motherhood, shaped relationships between men and women and the Roman aristocracy and the enslaved. Brown posits that these ideas placed significant pressure on women and girls to populate the Roman Empire for fear of their world coming to an end due to a lack of (male) citizens. It was believed that girls as young as fourteen-years-old should move from puberty to child-bearing with "little interruption," becoming "bedfellows of men."[23]

Specifically, women's and girls' utility lies in service, pleasure, and parturition. This viewpoint can also be found in early colonial white America. However, neo/coloniality imagined motherhood as a sacred duty and vocation for white cisgender heterosexual women, on one hand, and Black cisgender girls, women, and mothers as unfit and unscrupulous jezebels, sapphires, mammies, welfare queens, baby mommas, and otherwise, on the other.

That is to say, the human and sexual trafficking, assault, rape, and forced breeding of African bondswomen and girls in North America reread them not as virtuous or dutiful but as bio-baby-factories for mass-producing commodified units of labor for populating and serving the slave economy.[24] To justify these conditions the bondswomen and girls were reinterpreted as inherently and categorically pathological and thus victim blamed for their treatment.[25] Those that failed to produce children were discarded and/or used for other sexual purposes. And though African bondswomen sometimes married, they and their children were properties of the state, which ignored sacred bonds, oaths, and marital unions in the same way it disregarded African tribal connections, autonomy, rituals, languages, communal structuring/s, kinships, spiritual beliefs, and more. In slavery, the black female body, married or unmarried, was reread as the site of gross national product, not nobility. The quest to define "real," "good," and virtuous womanhood emerges against that context.

The shift from African bondswoman to freed Black woman caused moral panic as the state and race tried to make sense of Black cisgender women's and girls' bodies, sex, and wombs in the new context. Freed Black cisgender women and girls had more choices in terms of what to do or not to do with their bodies and could aspire to respectability as wives and mothers (rather than slaves, work oxen, jezebels, and breeders) if they so desired.[26] Concurrently, freed men and women wanted Black cisgender women and girls to be more appropriately recognized so that they might receive better sociopolitical, sociocultural, and socioeconomic treatment. However, restoring black cisgender heterosexual girlhood, womanhood, and motherhood from the desecrations of slavery also led to more policing of bodies, identities, and sexualities, and therefore, to further misrecognition. For example, the Black Church necessarily countered colonial narratives on innate unscrupulousness, while often drawing on Victorian notions of femininity and virtue—nurture, purity, piety, submission, and domesticity. This led to a treacherous circular romp with racialized gendered stereotypes as well as unfair and unrealistic expectations of Black mothers.

Angst around proving that respectable Black women and mothers exist sometimes merged Victorian ideals with biblical figures, such as the "virtuous woman" of Proverbs 31 or Mary, the mother of Jesus, over and against stereotypes about "bad" Black girls, unmarried women, and/or mothers. Examples include tropes about illicit sex; aggressive, domineering, and castrating matriarchs who emasculate Black men and boys or who refuse to marry and/or have children altogether; "bad" mothers who neglect their children, husbands, and/or household duties; and so on. I've personally heard numerous sermons juxtaposing the virtuous woman in Proverbs and Mary, the mother of Jesus, against Jezebel, Bathsheba, and, of course, Mary Magdalene as a binary for cataloging Black women and girls.[27] A few years ago, I saw a Black Church flyer online advertising a sermon titled "Mary, the Mother of Jesus, not Mary Magdalene!" It was likely for Mother's Day or a special Women's Day service. The surfeit of religio-cultural production defining what Black women and girls should or shouldn't aspire to is cogent. Even if well-intentioned, countering white supremacist stereotypes with new ones in blackface isn't effective.

I refer to this tragic binary as black feminine-*ism* and black feminine theology, each of which is ardently positioned against black feminism.[28] The latter not only critiques sexism and patriarchy but supports women's right not to marry or have children—while still having sexually fulfilling and love-filled lives. Black feminine-*ism* is rooted in binary ideas about natural hierarchy, heteronormative patriarchy, hypermoralism, black gender ideology, toxic femininity, and the black "nuclear" project, which anticipates childbearing. It places emphasis on feminine utility and ideals, such as submission, respectability, conventional beauty, and sexual purity. Further, it undergirds a black feminine theology in the Black Church, invested in contrasting "good" and "bad" black girlhood, womanhood, and motherhood, and more, "proper" and "improper" ways of being and knowing. Black feminine theology counters "jezebelian/ho theology."[29] This reduces Black women and girls who have sex to either hos or wives.[30] And so-called hos, along with other tropes of "bad" womanhood and girlhood, especially as the biblical character Jezebel is seen as particularly scandalous and domineering, are blamed for reproducing pathology in black communities, families, and children.[31] Synchronously, wives (aka "real" women) are charged with helping to uplift the race through "proper" femininity, docility, child-rearing, resourcefulness, industriousness, and spirituality.[32] This is a heavy lift for Black women. It suggests they can fix or heal all that has been broken by racial dehumanization through their bodies and/or by contorting themselves to align with superficial gender ideologies and roles.

I don't care how sexy, appealing, necessary, or natural black popular culture and religion try to make them appear; black feminine-*ism* and black feminine theologies are prisons. They mean to problematize Black women and girls who fail to submit to Black men and boys and cisgender heteropatriarchal gender ideals and norms; limit expression; justify violence against them; and disempower them. Unconsciously or not, they fortify what Melissa Harris-Perry refers to as a "crooked room." As Black folks do in the Black Church, "Turn to your neighbor and say, 'they're not for our collective thriving, sis.' They won't make us better or save our children." In *Sister Citizen: Shame, Stereotypes, and Black Women in America* (2011), Harris-Perry argues that racial and gendered stereotypes were central to nation building as well as constructing a crooked room wherein Black women and girls must navigate against consistent systematic misrecognition, which denies full and equal participation in the state and the ability to act as citizens.[33] Building on bell hooks's oppositional theory of looking, Harris-Perry asserts looking—as a person of relative power and privilege defining a person or group of less power and privilege—is infused with power and thus is a political act. Therefore, proper recognition is a precondition for citizenship whereas misrecognition, the projection of stereotypical derogatory assumptions about character and identity, is the basis for dehumanization, violence, and denying equity, power, justice, resources, opportunities, and full and equal participation within the body politic.

Freeing Black Girls calls for an alternative and holds that the end game for Black girls, women, mothers, and othermothers must center autonomy, freedom, self-love, safety, power, self-definition, proper recognition of their complex humanity, black love, mutuality, equity, justice, opposition, survival, full and equal participation within the body politic, if they so choose, partnership, and more.[34] Additionally, it asserts that Black women and girls are emphatically not defective, second-class, or immanent nurturers. More, raising autonomous, productive, and empowered Black children in America is our collective responsibility across genders. Yet, good black mothering is, among many things, black feminist—because good mothering requires explicit rebellion against racist, heterosexist, heteropatriarchal, classist, and imperialist oppression. It has nothing to do with how one expresses their gender or sexuality, nor does it require a cape. That said, *Freeing Black Girls* emphasizes mothering not due to destiny or duty but because it was mothering my Black sons that inspired me to rethink the political role of specifically black mothering, which is the starting point for this book and my black feminism.

I began this project writing about mothering Black boys after the tragic shooting of Michael Brown in 2014. Focusing on Black boys felt urgent to me. I was sitting with sociopolitical fears around raising Black boys to men amid the multiple intersecting layers of endangerment they faced due to white supremacy, such as racism, militarized policing, violence, joblessness, poverty, school-to-prison pipelining, twenty-first-century public lynching by white vigilantes, and so on. I was also concerned with the religio-cultural effeminophobic, homophobic, transphobic panic around gender identity, representation, and sexuality, which was blaming Black mothers for raising troubled and/or "soft" boys and therefore leaning further into heteropatriarchal ideals.[35] More, I wanted to dispel the viewpoint that Black mothers can't successfully raise Black boys to men or are the cause for their demise. I longed to make it clear that being a "real man" doesn't have to be synonymous with patriarchy, birthing children, heterosexism, transphobia, or achieving "nuclear" status. As I was raising my sons to understand, black critical consciousness for collective freedom; lived commitments to race, sex, sexual, and gender equity; undivided political power; allied sexual subjectivity; and intracommunal love and healing were superior aspirations. I hoped to establish that surviving America necessitated building black feminist kinships rather than alienating Black mothers, women, and girls.

Additionally, as more Black boys lay slain in the streets and white and white-adjacent antiblack vigilantes became younger and more organized and ballsy, questions about mothering unfairly became louder: "Where are the mothers?!" I wanted to write something that resisted further burdening Black mothers for the social ills in society and instead focused on the radical possibilities of our work. And though I began the first book, initially titled *Parenting against the Patriarchy: Raising Non-toxic Sons in White Supremacist America*, with a spirit of immense and grossly naive hopefulness, it didn't last. The long game of normalizing fascism, ultranationalism, white Christian militia, and white supremacist governance, at the highest levels and ungraspable speeds, happened. More, a global pandemic happened. Each of these disproportionately killed Black folks. By the time I circled back around to finishing the book on Black boys, I was in a deep state of sadness and thinking a lot about death. Writing about my sons after 2020 made me weep. I was trying to explain and call forth what felt like an impossibility. The ancestors remind us that resisting oppression requires a kind of openness to violence and/or death. Notwithstanding, I refused to center death in my analyses on black life and leaned into survival for Lee and Seth. However, the project came to a standstill as I faced the fact that mothering Black boys with black feminist politics didn't happen in a vacuum.

How could I dream of their survival without first confronting mine? The narrative on black male endangerment expresses cultural fear around white oppression; "bad" mothering; absent fathers; cisgender heterosexual expression, emasculation, and castration; lynching; stereotypes about the black male monster and/or rapist; incarceration; law and order; preschool-to-prison pipelining; underemployment; and otherwise. However, it censors my experiences as a Black girl and woman, and as also endangered. As Black Church sex and gender politics and the Mother's Day sermon reveal, Black men and boys can be a danger intracommunally, too. That is, Black women and girls are threatened both by what bell hooks refers to as white supremacist capitalist heteropatriarchal masculinity and by aspirational black patriarchy.[36] I needed to explore who I hoped Lee and Seth would be, their experiences, and very real anxieties—as well as my exposure to racism, sexism, misogynoir, and heteropatriarchy. More, I had to look at and talk back to the Black boys and men I encountered while growing up. How could I center what Lee and Seth needed from me as their Black mother and not examine what I needed as a Black girl and woman, given the dangers and pleasures I experienced? Yes, Black boys are endangered, but what about Black girls?[37]

Freeing Black Girls resists the religio-cultural propensity to view Black cisgender heterosexual men and boys as endangered and needing power, capital, and protections while predominantly engaging Black women and girls in terms of problems, respectability, and/or whether or not they "properly" fit into the black "nuclear" project. It asks the following questions: What do Black girls need to powerfully thrive? What makes a "good" Black girl, woman, and/or mother in the current political context? How might we shift from sociopolitical, historical, cultural, and theological literacies that imagine Black girls, women, and mothers as second-class, demonic, insufficient, immoral, and/or inhumanely respectable and heroic in terms of proximity to patriarchy? How can we cultivate contexts for black love for all Black people rather than those in response to fear of black endangerment and dehumanization?[38] And how do we encourage autonomous Black girl revolutionaries, agitators, militants, and freedom fighters? This book energetically presents black feminist mothering against the patriarchy as my starting point.

To this end, *Freeing Black Girls* considers how we might parent in general, and mother specifically, Black girls to women so that their humanity, endangerment, delights, goals, and need for safety and sociopolitical power are centered over and against cisgender feminine ideals, respectability, or even imaginary black princess-damsels-in-distress tropes.[39] More, it explores what we can learn from Black girls, how these lessons might make us better, and what parents need to know. Most important, it calls forth a future where our contexts for how we arrive at certain places and/or decisions matter; where neither Black cisgender boys or girls nor nonbinary nor transgender nor genderqueer nor questioning children are misrecognized, invisible, hyperlegible, bound by scripts, or prey; where all Black children matter; where Black folks materialize emancipatory identities, goals, relations, communities, theologies, politics, and encounters; where Black cisgender, transgender, and nonbinary girls turned women have a chance to thrive without violence; where the black maternal is no longer synonymous with pathology and/or death but instead with warrior strength, political possibility, and power; and where Black folks aren't intracommunally endangered.[40]

After completing *Freeing Black Girls*, I turned back to what is now titled *Loving Black Boys: A Black Feminist Bible on Racism and Revolutionary Mothering*. The books are thematically linked using motherhood, and more specifically black feminist mothering, as a bridge. However, whereas *Freeing Black Girls* is about my journey from conventional black girlhood to revolutionary black feminist motherhood, *Loving Black Boys* is about the challenges of mothering, loving, and empowering Lee and Seth while collectively surviving white supremacist capitalist patriarchy; the black feminist politics and lessons I tried to teach them; and how I sought to help them realize a freer future. The books talk back to each other; take black precarity seriously; appreciate our need for healing and one another; and understand black feminist mothering as an imperfect and earnest ambition. While I'm no longer naive enough to think I can change the world (or maybe I am), I still project the possibilities of a black living hope that is irreducible to the immediacy and/or force of black suffering, recognizes the ancestors' delicate balance between terrorizing absurdity and the practice and anticipation of freedom, and dares to take old problems and engage them in new ways that may make a difference.

The Collective Endangerment of White Supremacist Capitalist Heteropatriarchy

If there was ever any doubt, the last ten years laid American toxicity bare and left the white supremacist capitalist patriarchy endangering us all completely naked. Undoing toxic literacies and encounters and imagining a different kind of future requires honestly facing the source of illness and working our way back. Aimé Césaire asserts, "A nation which colonizes . . . is already a sick civilization, a civilization which is morally diseased, which irresistibly, progressing from one consequence to another, one denial to another, calls for its Hitler, I mean its punishment."[41] Black people survive against an expanse of toxins. And by toxicity, I mean to name the social, political, institutional, structural, cultural, ideological, and interpersonal moral bankruptcy flowing through America's veins. I mean to pinpoint the stink of lethal settler and neocolonial domination and contamination that keeps Black people from living and experiencing joy without the threat of white gazing, regulation, disbandment, retribution, disciplining, dehumanization, or death. Some see this as manifest destiny.[42] Others more rightly call it white supremacist capitalist heteropatriarchal masculinity, the preeminent threat to black life and progress. And namely, as it not only holds us captive but also maintains and produces a host of other prisons.

The political battle for white Christian heteropatriarchal masculine dominance is presently on full display. Florida governor Ron DeSantis signed a bill into law prohibiting teaching general education courses "based on theories that systemic racism, sexism, oppression, or privilege are inherent in the institutions of the United States."[43] More, the culture war to silence words like *racism, misogyny, sexism, discrimination, antiblackness,* and *gay,* which serve to increase bigotry, violence, hate, heteropatriarchy, confusion, fear, and white power, is winning. From state to state we see emboldened white deputization; increased police brutality and racial profiling; the dismantling of the First Amendment; a flagrant and defiant merging between white Christianity and state; parents and politicians preaching hate while banning schoolbooks that lean toward equity; religious and sexual intolerance; normalization of racial and sexual violence; the collapse of civil rights and affirmative action; the co-opting of Black Lives Matter and "woke" ideology as treason; the razing of health care; the gutting of women's and abortion rights; unbridled gun violence with no hope for gun control; undisguised systemic sociopolitical disinvestments in predominantly black communities; climate change denial; housing and labor insecurity; vitalized antiblack alienation; a barefaced conservative court structure; a lack of safety and opportunity for Black folks; and more.

We're witnessing white supremacist capitalist heteropatriarchal power hysterically, violently, and legally protect itself and maintain power, wealth, and privilege with a renewed vengeance. Racial, gender, class, and sexual equity stand in opposition to that, producing competing pandemics for Black folks and keeping anxieties high between Black people and particularly Black cisgender heterosexual men and everyone else.[44] We're all screaming "danger!" because we're all one decision away from not being able to breathe, yet we're not pausing long enough to look at why this is and how our collective experiences both overlap and differ. Unresolved and unspoken slave beginnings and historical tensions around Black women's and girls' bodies, sexual encounters, and mothering provide a clue for interpreting and healing contemporary agitations passed from generation to generation, etched in our psyches and flesh. We need to discuss the patronymic, how it was an empty category for African bondsmen, and how, though slave mothers couldn't claim their children, their status as slaves, freed, or free foretold the child's status and identity. That the child inherited slavery or freedom from their mother, not the father, made some interpret the Black/African slave mother as a site of resentment and thus blameworthy for keeping the slave economy going and limiting Black men's possibilities for participating in patriarchy.

I discuss this more closely in *Loving Black Boys* but imagine the complexity of cisgender heterosexual masculinity being limited to providing, protecting, labor, land, legacy, leadership, wealth, inheritance, offspring, and otherwise, and having no inherent collective legal access to it, let alone a right to freedom and autonomy. One response to righting the empty patronymic was establishing "real" black manhood as a political priority, thus enabling certain performances of black masculinity within families, communities, and liberation efforts. That is, though North American slavery produced a ledger system that equated all Black/African slaves to animals and criminalization, the free black male body registered its own logic in race and patriarchy. Meaning that if Black captive mothers bequeathed bondage to their children and Black captive fathers were legally banished in name and body from all aspects of childbirth and paternity, then claiming patriarchy, even if aspirational, for Black fathers in freedom would be a priority for establishing black freedom and humanity. In the essay "Losing Manhood: Animality and Plasticity in the (Neo)Slave Narrative" (2016), Zakiyyah Iman Jackson writes, "Slavery is a technology for producing a *kind* of human," "the black body is an essential index for the calculation of degree of humanity and the measure of human progress."[45] Specifically, slavery created language, ideas, and laws to inscribe "Otherness" and false logics of second-classness on all Black folks.

However, as Ta-Nehisi Coates notes in *Between the World and Me* (2015), white men attempting to solidify their social status argued there were two classes of people in America, divided not by socioeconomics (the rich and the destitute) but by race: whites and Blacks, or really, white men (and eventually women) and Black men.[46] Regardless of class, many white men (and women) believed they were inherently superior to Black men. While divesting all Black folks of humanity and rereading the collective as nonessential, the complete erasure of Black women and girls leaves an opening for potential patriarchal aspirations. And though historians rightly argue African bondsmen were absolutely not seen as men, as the institution reimagined them as animals, mules, criminals, monsters, and breeders, the underlying ideology hierarchizing men in particular presents possibilities for free Black men and boys to engage patriarchy, even if within a supposed second class. Simultaneously, Black cisgender men and boys were seen as a different *kind* of male body—a lesser yet competitive male body—and therefore a threat, physically, sexually, and otherwise, to be hunted and tamed. The political and theological project of establishing "real" black manhood occurs against this backdrop.

Admittedly, it's easier to preach that there's something wrong with Black women, mothers, and girls and how they need to get it together to ensure better outcomes for Black children and communities in general and Black boys specifically than to do the difficult work of traveling through these traumatic lines of thought. hooks writes the following in *We Real Cool: Black Men and Masculinity* (2004), "It is not just society's investment in patriarchal masculinity that demands that Black boys be socialized away from feeling and action; they must also bear the weight of a psychohistory that represents Black males as castrated, ineffectual, irresponsible, and not real men. It is as if Black parents, cross-class, believe they can right the wrongs of history by imposing onto Black boys a more brutal indoctrination into patriarchal thinking."[47] As I assert in *Loving Black Boys*, Black folks are necessarily invested in Black cisgender heterosexual men and boys being free, autonomous, safe, and whole. Subverting black male–centered animality and monster narratives is mandatory. Yet, "real" black manhood, often synonymous with intraracial cisgender heteropatriarchal male dominance, enables intracommunal toxicities. In *New Black Man* (2015), Mark Anthony Neal asserts that social consciousnesses in Black men and boys often center a remixed version of black nationalism and/or Afrocentrism, which have histories of sexism, homophobia, misogynoir, and transantagonism.[48] We need to find another and more collectively emancipatory way forward.

A few years ago, I saw a social media post that included a picture of a lone Black boy sitting atop a soccer ball on a grass field intently looking ahead. The caption read: "'Toxic Masculinity' 43% of boys are raised by single mothers. 78% of teachers are female. So, close to 50% of boys have 100% feminine influence at home and 80% feminine influence at school. Toxic masculinity isn't the problem. The lack of masculinity is." Questionable math and statistics aside, and while it's true, society needs more men teachers, the establishment of "real" black manhood against femininity and black womanhood, and in this case Black mothers, underlines a primary tenet of heteropatriarchy: that women and girls are deficient and/or problems. More testosterone in the classroom or at home will not make "real" men. This in no way negates the importance of

Black fathers, husbands, brothers, uncles, or male partners, friends, mentors, leadership, teachers, or strength, however.[49] It's to say patriarchal masculinity is a product of white supremacist capitalist heteropatriarchy and therefore a colonizing prison that defines "realness" through hierarchies and oppressions rather than commitments to love of self and others and communal accountability. It's also to say, though I get the need to imagine a hypermasculine heteropatriarchal black cisgender ideal as a magical binary counter to white supremacy, what's broken and counterfeit can make one neither whole nor *real*.[50]

More, a pro-black consciousness rooted in heteropatriarchy, resentment, domination, and erasure is antiblackness camouflaged. And antiblackness from any angle is both illiberal and a danger. This includes the Black Church, black culture, and aspirational black patriarchy. None of this has enfranchised Black folks, stopped white supremacist capitalist heteropatriarchal violence, kept us safe, or healed the wounds we collectively face from previous and/or current human and sexual trafficking; sexual violence; biocapitalism; shame; broken kinships; theft of bodies, families, language, land, cultures, tribes, traditions, spiritualities, histories, and otherwise; forced surrogacy; sociopolitical regulation; and death-dealing uncertainty. None of it will recover what was lost. Ignoring these archives and tensions will impede progress and resistance efforts and cause Black folks to implode, however.

Undoing Toxicities and Dreaming Up the World We Want

I often wonder what led the pastor to preach that Mother's Day sermon outside of sexism. Were we scapegoats for hostilities toward his mother, othermother, or some other Black woman or girl? Was there something he needed or wanted from his mother or some other woman? Was he sublimating frustrations with white supremacist capitalist heteropatriarchy (or perchance his father) with Black mothers? Did he feel unsafe, unseen, misrecognized, disempowered, or misunderstood as a Black man in America? Was it the negative dividends of aspirational black patriarchy or maybe angst over promises of an "American Dream"? I can never claim to know. I find this 1984 dialogue for *Essence* magazine, titled "Revolutionary Hope: A Conversation between Audre Lorde and James Baldwin," particularly useful in thinking about the possible motivation for the pastor's theory/theology. Baldwin posits,

> One of the dangers of being a Black American is being schizophrenic, and I mean "schizophrenic" in the most literal sense. To be a Black American

is in some ways to be born with the desire to be white. It's a part of the price you pay for being born here, and it affects every Black person. We can go back to Vietnam, we can go back to Korea. We can go back for that matter to the First World War. We can go back to W. E. B. Du Bois—an honorable and beautiful man—who campaigned to persuade Black people to fight in the First World War, saying that if we fight in this war to save this country, our right to citizenship can never, never again be questioned—and who can blame him? He really meant it, and if I'd been there at that moment I would have said so too perhaps. Du Bois believed in the American dream. So did Martin. So did Malcolm. So do I. So do you. That's why we're sitting here.[51]

To which Lorde responds,

> I don't, honey. I'm sorry, I just can't let that go past. Deep, deep, deep down I know that dream was never mine. . . . I was Black. I was female. And I was out—out—by any construct wherever the power lay. So if I had to claw myself insane, if I lived I was going to have to do it alone. Nobody was dreaming about me. Nobody was even studying me except as something to wipe out. . . . Even worse than the nightmare is the blank. And Black women are the blank. I don't want to break all this down, then have to stop at the wall of male/female division. When we admit and deal with difference; when we deal with the deep bitterness; when we deal with the horror of even our different nightmares; when we turn them and look at them, it's like looking at death: hard but possible. If you look at it directly without embracing it, then there is much less that you can ever be made to fear.[52]

Black liberative and humanizing ethics begin not with America's dreams, definitions, limitations, oppressions, and toxicities but instead with the innate autonomous right to self-define and activate that meaning in the community and the world; to collectively imagine and create the communities of care we want; to insist on what feels like impossibility; and to talk back to and undo that which doesn't serve us.

Hope based on access to America's dream, which requires heteropatriarchy as a theoretical framework and, for some, deploying stereotypes as a methodology, causes dissonance at best. Put it another way: aspirational black heteropatriarchy, which needs both misogynoir and stereotypes about Black women, mothers, and girls to work, won't provide access to the dream because the dream, its politics, rules, and grammars on race, sex, gender, sexuality, and class were never meant for our survival. We need a motivation, theory, and method that seeks freedom and quality of life for all Black people. That said, the inspiration for *Freeing Black Girls* is knowing the dream isn't ours. Thus, the work ahead includes undoing its literacies and oppressions, rethinking what's good for us and how we might better survive, getting at what's really ailing us, reimagining the role of black mothering, and exploring "the blank" by foregrounding Black girls' everyday experiences.

The theoretical framework guiding this book is black feminism, and the methodology is "the personal is political." *Freeing Black Girls* notes that the personal, psychological, and emotional experiences of Black girls, women, mothers, and othermothers are inherently political. As the Combahee River Collective asserts, the most profound and radical politics come directly out of our own identities. Or, as Patricia Hill Collins posits, critical meaning, and thus the origins of feminist theory, emerges from our experiences. In *The Will to Change: Men, Masculinity, and Love* (2004), hooks argues that though feminists have done the work of critiquing patriarchy, they've been reluctant to speak about men and boys and specifically our deep connections as daughters, sisters, mothers, aunts, lovers, sex objects, and so on.[53] She asserts, however, our struggle to end sexist domination must begin where we live, and not solely with critiques but with explorations of our opaque connections as daughters, sisters, aunties, friends, nieces, and mothers. *Freeing Black Girls* begins at home.

Drawing from research, history, and my experiences as a Black girl, mother, wife, daughter, niece, sister, and black feminist, it represents *my* journey and struggle through black girlhood to motherhood. Concurrently, it serves as an offering to Black mothers, daughters, fathers, sons, and all Black children navigating a world filled with both incessant trauma and unrelenting possibility. This is not a claim on universalism or black gender essentialism. The personal narrative, which is political, recounts experiences while informing a universal story of living, surviving girlhood, and growing into mothering while Black in America. This collective history is indispensable for combating structural oppressions. In chorus, *Freeing Black Girls* recognizes my coming of age moves between socioeconomic struggle and privilege. It posits that white supremacist capitalist heteropatriarchy and aspirational black patriarchy ignore black mobility and means because misogynoir has no sex, race, sexuality, class, or gender. Regardless, it explores whether black identity and experiences with white supremacy, white nationalism, and black sexism differ due to class and whether progressive black feminist mothering is class based. The reader will have the last word. I only ask that you at least thumb through *Loving Black Boys* first, where it comes to the fore—as does my class positionality.

In full transparency, I struggled with critical honesty, imposter syndrome, and imagining radical possibilities in view of this. You can't discuss white supremacy, the slave trade, neocoloniality, or even aspirational black patriarchy without engaging in a critique of capitalism and imperialism, which for some of us feels implicating. The rise of Western capitalism required black occupation, ownership, dehumanization, and suffering. It hinges on a built-in underclass, sexual division of labor, and the world's resources being hoarded and controlled by few. However, black survivalist accumulation and white supremacist capitalist accumulation aren't the same. No one is poor or alienated from resources needed to survive because they are white. More, Black transgender, nonbinary, queer, and cisgender women, girls, mothers, and othermothers, whatever their limited participation in the capitalist structure, function at the bottom of this paradigm, with the poor, disabled, undocumented—*plus* beneath that. This makes for distinct experiences and inequities within the collective story.

A Spell Book for Black Freedom

While Black Church attendance is decreasing among younger generations who are increasingly more interested in black spiritual alternatives, religious pluralism, democratic practices, and justice-centered theologies, especially after 2020, most Black folks in North America are still Christians, and thus the Christian Bible remains an essential form of literacy.[54] In *Slave Religion: The "Invisible Institution" in the Antebellum South* (1978), Albert J. Raboteau asserts that many North American slaves who embraced Christianity were "Bible Christians" who used the Bible for literacy and to support and articulate their right to freedom.[55] It was a spell book for learning to read, naming, resisting, plotting, and a sacred object full of wise tales and sayings. Their interpretations of the text were irreducible and often oppositional to that of white missionaries, ministers, and slavers. In *African American Religion: A Very Short Introduction* (2014), Eddie S. Glaude Jr. posits that black religion in North America emerges in the encounter between faith and all its complexity, white supremacy, and imperial ambition.[56] This convergence shapes the slaves' reading of the Bible and the historic Black Church. More, it redeems the profaned Christianity of the slavers and constructs a site for self-recreation and communal advancement.[57]

Leaning into this, *Freeing Black Girls* reinterprets "bible" through a black feminist framework. Specifically, it deploys black feminist religious thought and black feminist religio-cultural criticism as lenses for reading phenomena and redeeming Black women and girls from profaned ideologies, theologies, and representations. Black feminist religious thought and religio-cultural criticism explore how religious meanings show up and operate in our cultural encounters. The primary task is to illumine religious practices, medias, and/or ideas important to Black people and especially Black women and girls; intervene on taken-for-granted ideas; and unwind Black women and girls from misogynoirist metanarratives.[58] *Freeing Black Girls* holds that such an offering is both oppositional and sacred. Explicitly, *Freeing Black Girls* is a sacred form of literacy and collection of stories meant to articulate and support black self-re-creation, communal advancement, and freedom. What makes it sacred is its unyielding commitment to black love, liberation, thriving, and sovereignty, and its belief that all black lives—whatever their gender, class, or sexual identity—matter.[59] Sadly, this is a distinctive shift away from conservative Christianity and some profiles in the contemporary Black Church.[60] However, this book is in no way a final authority. It's meant to shift, change, grow, push, and pull. As with sacred literature, it allows the reader to enter the world of the author to make sense of history, theory, and theology as well as their own narrative—and in their own way.

The structuring of this book entails a big letter, mini-letters, and a collection of stories (chapters). And though the book begins with a love letter to me, each chapter starts with a mini-letter to me and Black girls. However, the primary audience is inclusive. The chapters/stories, which aren't in strict chronological order, are thematic, theoretical, and personal.[61] Because of this, *Freeing Black Girls* makes use of "I," "we," and "us" in concert with the distant "they," "them," and "their." In addition, it proudly utilizes Black Language throughout the text, but especially in the letters. To this end, and though a "no-no" in academic writing, the reader has likely already pinpointed the perhaps alarming deployment of contractions, which aid the flow of storytelling, voice, and moving in between the personal, political, academic, and otherwise. In *Linguistic Justice: Black Language, Literacy, Identity and Pedagogy* (2020), April Baker-Bell argues that Black Language is the mother tongue, which comes out of North American slave experiences, and which imparts knowledge, reflects knowing, and socializes Black folks to understand the world and survive.[62] The academic tendency to suggest there's a standard way of writing or Standard English implies a racial linguistic hierarchy that is interconnected with the larger social ordering, which diminishes Black people, culture, life, and so on. This book doesn't just center Black people, stories, and language; it's meant to be both read and *felt*.

Chapter 1, "Black Girls Matter: Letter to My Fourteen-Year-Old Self," is a story of my genesis, rebirth, and retrieval, equipped with "ten commandments" I wish I'd known previously and for every Black girl going forward. Chapter 2, "'F*ck Y'all Feminism': Black Girls, *P-Valley*, Rape Culture, and Erotic Power," uses the television series *P-Valley* to explore the sexual vulnerabilities Black girls face regardless of class and how black- religion, patriarchy, and respectability work in tandem with and often reproduce white supremacist capitalist patriarchy, even as each intends to oppose it. Chapter 3, "'Break My Soul': Precarity and Resurrection in Evangelical Heteropatriarchal Antiblack America," examines my coming of age in Northern California against the threat of white evangelical, *nice* white liberal, and black sexist infernos, and how I found sacred and life-changing power in black feminism. Chapter 4, "Emancipating Proverbs 31: Liberating Rough, Nasty, and Aggressive Black Girls to Women," discusses the force of the "virtuous" woman and its emphasis on Black cisgender women's wombs, desirability, marriageability, male approval, submission, domesticity, and purity. Chapter 5, "Ordinary or Insurgent? From Toxic Femininity to Revolutionary Mothering," engages the US Supreme Court to explore the world we have and where it seems we're headed and turns to revolutionary black mothering and othermothering to dream up something different. The coda, "Toward Sanctuary (and *Loving Black Boys*): Black Feminist Mothering, an Alternative Literacy, Philosophy, and Practice," outlines foundational building blocks for realizing black communal refuge and points to *Loving Black Boys*.

The academic contribution of *Freeing Black Girls* is its exploration of black feminist girlhood, motherhood, and religion. My hope is that it challenges how we engage gender, Black women and girls, black femininity, black feminism, and black motherhood in the guild and beyond, while also changing lives. This is what makes this work valuable and, accordingly, scholarly. Given its interests in black, critical race, black cultural, and women and gender studies, and the black feminist study of religion, *Freeing Black Girls* is distinct. To my knowledge, there's no book-length work that does this kind of black feminist religio-cultural personal-is-political study on Black girls and motherhood. And that there are so few texts on Black girls in religion and black motherhood in general isn't happenstance. The black religious gaze emphasizes Black women. Some topics are difficult to engage out loud when centering Black girls, for example, sexual autonomy, subjectivity, and pleasure, which I explore in chapter 2. But more, some in the broader academe interpret scholarly works on black motherhood as lowbrow and/or unsophisticated. However, such readings are antiblack, sexist, and grounded in exclusionary practices in the production of knowledge, which have historically and systemically marginalized Black girls' and women's voices, experiences, and contributions. Simultaneously, they're informed by the denigration of Black girls, women, and motherhood during and after slavery. The reification of Black girls, women, and mothers into racial stereotypes remains forceful, even in academia.

Finally, *Freeing Black Girls* is an invitation, not a blueprint. The journey ahead is neither easy nor neatly defined. Black feminism in no way means flawless. Further, my black feminism ain't always radical. Yet, my passage to mothering through a black feminist lens is intentional. Notwithstanding, I don't claim to have all the answers or speak to all experiences. I'm calling forth what feels impossible: a future where Black folks abandon toxic literacies, are properly recognized, and build emancipatory communities where we safely express the full range of our being, identities, feelings, and emotions. More, I'm insisting that we center Black girls while doing this work.

Black Girls Matter

Letter to My Fourteen-Year-Old Self

Dear Black Girl:[1]

You were three years old when Stevie Wonder released his hit album *Songs in the Key of Life* in 1976. Whenever I think of that album, I think of Christmas, bright colorful lights, red wrapping paper, ninety-degree project heat set to counter the numbing New York cold, hot buttery macaroni and cheese, greasy pork ribs, salty greens, those curious fruitcakes Grandma used to love to make that only the elder family members were excited to eat, the perpetual side of White Castles cheeseburgers the family just had to have whenever visiting the city, and dancing. Lots of dancing. One on one. Solo. And in groups.

I think of dancing around the tan vinyl–encased furniture with Momma and Daddy, big sis, and our aunties, uncles, and cousins in Grandma's living room in her tiny apartment in the Bronx River Projects. Grandma loved to see us grandchildren dance, and especially do "the rock." Up and down we went, swaying left to right, on the beat and off, in unison, and opposition. Your absolute favorite song from that album was and continues to be "Isn't She Lovely."

Of course, you know Wonder is a musical prodigy. Literally, a natural wonder. In the future, you and the love of your life will spend decades gushing about the Stevie Wonder concert you attended at the Fox Theater in Atlanta, Georgia, when you first began dating as college students. Yes, you will attend college in your birth city and rise up in love.

Anyway, despite a few minor technical difficulties between you and your date mates, the night will be magical. You'll be dancing the whole time. And just wait until Wonder breaks out the harmonica and ushers the audience into the euphonic bliss that is "Isn't She Lovely." You'll be bursting with anticipation for him to take you to church. Hearing Wonder's love letter to his newborn daughter, Aisha, where he not only calls her by name but refers to her using words such as "lovely," "wonderful," "precious," "pretty," "angel's best," and the "product of love," will call forth so many memories and feelings. It'll take everything for you to keep your cool and not break out into a holy shout and ugly cry right there in the theater. Do you remember how powerful this song made you feel? I tear up now just thinking about how euphoric it was.

You especially loved Wonder's signature melodic instrumental break. You always felt as if the rhythms during that interlude were speaking that which words couldn't articulate. Knowing Wonder's canon of rapturous musical brilliance and radical critical consciousness and understanding now what it means to be a Black girl turned Black woman turned Black mother in America, I'm willing to bet you were right. He was speaking through melody, likely navigating visions of both the sanguine and the demonic to come for his baby girl. And there would indeed be both. However, not even Wonder's love and affirmation could protect Aisha from the hate toward Black cisgender, transgender, genderfluid, and queer women and girls in this world. And yet, his love mattered.

Though those days, Grandma, and her apartment are now long gone, I still dance my heart out to that song. In fact, while composing this book I made it a ritual to always start the researching, writing, and editing process by listening to it first. Without fail, tears moisturized my melanin-soaked cheeks as Wonder transported me to another rhapsodic realm. His love letter to Aisha was not just for her. It was for you, too. More, it was for all of us. And by "us" I mean Black people. Countering centuries of racial, gender, sex, sexual, and class-based stereotypes about so-called wretchedness, ugliness, animality, and immorality, Wonder called us *all* lovely, thus constructing a paramount narrative on black divinity, beauty, and preciousness. And, more, baptizing us in love. We were all born again.

It also matters that Wonder centered Aisha's voice by beginning the masterpiece with her cries and utterances, letting us know she's here, she has something

FIGURE 1.1. Me and Daddy in our mobile home on campus when he was a seminary student in Atlanta, Georgia. I was approximately one or two years old. Photo taken by a family member.

to say, we're to listen, and she's the center of his world. A "gift from above," to be exact. Over the years, I pondered if Aisha's cries might be symbolic for our own. By making her voice the starting and focal point, was Wonder centering our grievances, too? It's not lost on me that this was a Black man, a father, demanding that we see and hear the voice and lamentations of a Black girl, his daughter. They say daughters often have a way of tugging at their father's hearts. Whatever the case, we need to see Black men loving their daughters, Black girls, and women in a way that focuses on their powerful voice and needs. My God, you loved this song. It helped you dance through all kinds of pain and affirmed every fiber of your being.

While words alone can't set us free, Wonder reminded you of the glory and sanctity of *all* Black girls. You needed to know this so badly. Daddy made these messages clear to you in his own complex way since birth. But you couldn't hear him fully. And as you got older, he couldn't fully hear you, either. I think the weight he carries as a cisgender heterosexual Black man censors comprehension around what you've experienced. He doesn't seem to grasp the day-to-day hostilities Black girls generally face, or how they're just as debilitating as the burdens he carries. I wish he understood you better, especially right now. Still, he loves you deeply, and that'll carry you a long way, or at least as far as it can. And knowing what I know now, Momma knows and understands more than you think. She's simply not ready to face your trauma because it might remind her of her own.

Wonder will have to fill in the gaps and hold you tightly for now. I see you swaying back and forth while getting lost in that two-step frenzy. I still do the same dance, by the way. Do your dance, my love! Go ahead and get lost in the sweetness that is the boy genius. He's rightfully become your go-to mellifluent pastor, steadily calming your anxiety. You need him. You need this numinous escape. Notwithstanding, you synchronously need so much more. And this is why I'm writing to you. I hope you'll hear me better than you heard Wonder. I project what I'm about to say will help carry you through a great many trials. I can tell you that you'll survive, but my prayer for you is that you survive better. That said, there are some things I need you to know and to hold onto.

I need you to know that your cries matter, too.[2] I hear you and I see you. You're dancing through an internal and external battlefield. And when the music stops, you pause Wonder's message. You learned to criticize yourself long before you knew how to love—yourself or anyone. The church really has you believing Black girls are born sinners, inherently bad and lascivious. Tempters of men, like Bathsheba and Jezebel, they say. You're working so hard to be seen like that respectable Proverbs 31 "virtuous" woman the church is always implicitly and explicitly speaking about. However, the meeting ground between internal desire and curiosity and rape culture in the outside world has you thinking you're failing. And truth be told, the hindmost ironically makes you feel seen and pretty because it makes you feel something, or more, feel *like* something. You don't yet know feeling shouldn't be predatory, that beauty and worth are inherent, or that catcalling "pretty bombing" is a manipulative strategy for boys to get girls in bed only to discard them.[3] You don't understand any of this yet because no one is explaining it to you. No one is helping you navigate through these nuances. By the way, predators sense that you don't actually feel pretty, that you're unsure about your value and who you are. You hardly look in the mirror or even take pictures because you can't see anything good.

I need you to know that you're both unparalleled and beautiful. The church marked you with sin while beauty culture and the boys in elementary school had you hating your body by fifth grade. The family favors you for being born a chocolate girl because you look like Daddy and the boys don't seem to mind. However, though you personally escaped colorism thus far, it will circle back soon enough. Antidarkness is so tragic. But the fatphobia you've experienced will chase you for a lifetime. Remember trying on Momma's pants when you were twelve years old and not being able to fit them? You so badly wanted to look like her. Everyone stood in awe at Momma's beauty. You were no different. So, you put yourself on a diet that day and, sadly, several decades later, you've yet to get off. By sixth grade you were five feet four, 150 pounds, "developed," and thus the "big girl" in elementary school. And baby "big girls" are a playground for teasing as well as sexual assault and rape. You inherited hyperlegibility, violence, racism, sexism, classism, and misogynoir from slavery and learned early on that this world, including the black parts, can be cruel to Black girls. One day you'll read these essays by a woman named bell hooks, "'whose pussy is this?': a feminist comment" (1989) and "Eating the Other" (1992), and things will make better sense.

I need you to know that while all black lives matter, you don't owe anyone your body, sex, support, or silence. Remember when the older teenage boy from church pulled out his penis and asked you to touch it when you were five years old? Remember how confused you were and how you ran and hid? Fortunately, someone came in the room and relieved him of his babysitting duties. What about when your best homegirl, the deacon's daughter, got pregnant at thirteen years old and was disappeared down south? Remember spending the night at her house at eleven years old, building fortresses with blankets and playing hide-and-seek all night in her bedroom? You returned home the next day and told Momma that your bestie had a "fat stomach," having no idea she was with child or that that would be the last time you'd ever see her. What about when Mookie felt you up in fourth grade and got expelled because you told Daddy and he went up to the school, and everybody at school blamed you for "ruining" a Black boy's life?[4] And then there were all the grown-ass men in the community who put little boys like Mookie to shame. Black girls are prey to so damn much.

I need you to know that being a girl is your right.[5] You were forced to enter womanhood much too early. And the shame you felt after Mookie's expulsion kept you silent going forward. So, when you suffered sexual trauma the summer after sixth-grade graduation, you continued on as if nothing happened. You believed it occurred because you were "fast." Frankly, you lacked comprehension of your autonomy and language for consent. You didn't know how to refuse the latter, give it, or demand accountability. The church taught you that even thinking about this was a sign of sexual preplanning, which was a sin. It also taught you that slut-shaming and male dominance were divine rights. Remember all the church whispers about your pregnant bestie being "loose" and her mother not instilling morals in her? Remember the reigning query, "How could her *momma* not know?" Well, what about her daddy or older brothers for that matter? Somebody knew something. But absolutely nobody mentioned that a thirteen-year-old Black girl couldn't legally offer consent. And nobody discussed the father of the baby. You'll never stop thinking about and mourning the loss of your friend. You'll also learn that one thing this world hates more than Black girls is black teen pregnancy. On that, the right-wing politicians and the Black Church agree.

FIGURE 1.2. This was my kindergarten photo. My mother was traveling. Thus, my father allowed me to do my own hair and choose my own clothes. I chose one of my favorite "church outfits." Photo credit unknown.

Mess around and get pregnant out of wedlock and find yourself an outlier with the quickness.

I need you to know that the sexual trauma Black girls experience isn't their fault. Neither existing in a Black girl's body, nor physical development, nor the desire to be desired, nor sexual curiosity or expression is a solicitation for sexual assault or rape. You confuse these things because the church, culture, and community teach that they're the same. They aren't. Desire and the desire to be desired are human. However, there's a difference between being a sexual being and being sexualized. Racialized and gendered sexualization and dehumanization are terrorizing rites of passage for Black girls. This isn't to invoke black male rapist tropes. You have a lot of loving male friends and relatives. But some of the Black boys and men in your community have been fantasying and misrecognizing your and other Black girls' identities for a long time. This has repercussions. Remember all the Black girls in seventh grade with boyfriends who were in high school and/or who had graduated altogether? Remember how the older boys drove their thirteen-year-old "girlfriends" to middle school, and all the fly

FIGURE 1.3. I was about ten or eleven here. My sister, her friend, and I were returning to Syracuse after a day trip with family to Niagara Falls. Photo taken by a family member.

presents they'd receive? What about the pregnancies, pregnancy scares, secret abortions, and dangerous home remedies? Think about all the times an older boy angrily said, "So, you ain't gone give it up?" as if "giving it up" was somehow owed to them because they said you were cute, let you ride around in their car, or because they gave you some trinket from the mall. You feared they were going to shame you either way. Or worse, they might take "it." You were always navigating which wars to fight and how to stay whole and in community.

I need you to know that you deserve safety. Black girls are exposed to a spectrum of violences before they reach puberty and are taught not to talk about intracommunal traumas because they make Black people as a race, and Black men and boys specifically, look bad. Deborah Gray White posits that Black/African slave relationships on North American plantations were broadly egalitarian and supportive.[6] However, some slave men exerted sexual power and dominance over slave women within slave quarters. Slave owners and overseers didn't stop the abuses if they found them helpful, therefore legitimizing and supporting intracommunal sexual and physical abuse.[7] hooks argues that the homosocial war between enslaved and newly freed Black men and white men led to war with Black women because black manhood was often affirmed by subordinating Black women. She asserts that while Black men might not possess the political and economic power of white men, Black men and boys could outdo them on the sexual front and thus some embraced racist and sexist images and abused Black women and girls.[8] In this way, for a fair few, black male value was determined by the capacity to seduce and dominate Black women and girls, given lack of access to patriarchal sociopolitical or socioeconomic power.

I say all of that to point out this is a contemporary problem with historical roots. More, the lack of access to sociopolitical and/or socioeconomic patriarchal power does not and cannot cancel out participation in intracommunal and/or intraracial forms of patriarchal masculinity. The sexually domineering assaults you've already witnessed and experienced were symptoms of all of this. I also share this because you already care about racial matters. Your consciousness is budding. However, you will not even begin to comprehend racial rights fully until you realize that your right to bodily autonomy and sexual subjectivity is nonnegotiable and foundational, no matter gender or sexual identities. Any discussion about rights or safety is a charade without this baseline. Once you get this, you'll better understand freedom.

I need you to know that you deserve sociopolitical support. The precarity of Black girls is nonfiction. Yet some of us spend our lives fighting for Black men and boys who don't even see or love us or consider our pain. You're lucky to experience all the love that you do. Daddy has always tried to protect you. And you've tried to protect him, too. You were taught to "protect Black men" and that all Black men and boys are endangered. Remember when you threw a crying fit when Daddy got a driving ticket and had to sit in the back seat of the police car when you were five years old? You thought for sure the police were trying to take him away and harm him. They had to come get you and let you sit in the back seat with Daddy, so you'd stop crying. He wiped your tears and assured you that he was safe. I'm crying thinking about the irony of this now. The future hosts a "Black Lives Matter" movement precisely because the back seat of a police car is exactly what you imagined it was. Ain't nobody Black safe back there, not even a five-year-old Black girl.[9]

The point is, there can be no unified black social movement or loosely connected black political identity without radical love ethics, which demand justice, safety, and autonomy.[10] But what about the collective protection for Black women and girls? Who will cry for us? Just as racial oppression, disenfranchisement, segregation, and lynching denied the privileges of sociopolitical and socioeconomic patriarchal power to Black cisgender men, each, along with sexual violence and accusations of immorality, denied protections to Black women and girls. Regrettably, the intracommunal adultification and sexualization of Black girls cancels out the reality of racial misogyny.[11] It's a nonstarter for many. So, you silenced then mutilated this part of yourself and story. Daddy's love had to be enough. Yet, violence against Black women and girls is material, systemic, structural, and communal. The protections and love you receive from Daddy are personal.

You need a structural sociopolitical communal response to the violences you're experiencing, which doesn't erase or shame your human curiosities or desires. The church suppressed and scandalized sexual agency, pleasure, desire, and autonomy for Black women and girls to protect them. It failed to read the room, however, on how this caused isolation, abandonment, and physical and sexual danger intracommunally. I remember when you attempted to cancel your own sexuality and gender expression at thirteen years old. You thought being more masculine presenting or respectable would protect your image and reputation and decrease the currency of what was between your legs. It didn't. But while the Black Church claims to love respectable unambiguous expressions of black femininity, there were yet Black men and boys in your church and community who didn't seem to care one bit about your enigmatic play and thus completely ignored your mask. The advances and propositions didn't stop. And not that they happened every day. Still, they were often enough. And more, shouldn't have been at all.

I need you to know that you deserve consensual sex and pleasure and that neither ambiguity nor respectability is a cure for predation. You'll spend the next several years attempting to figure out the gender presentation you're most comfortable with. You'll later learn that you don't have to choose one or the other as you'll move effortlessly between a range of presentations. Notwithstanding, your quest for respectability, which you deploy as a source of resistance as well as a medium to purchase Christian notions of virtue, will be ongoing through college and after. Save your energy, love. You're fearfully and wonderfully made just as you are.[12] Desexualization, which historically attempted to produce a respectable womanhood, and in some instances aided in forms of invisibility, only causes more harm. As life continues, pressured desexualization will misrecognize your humanity, won't provide the respect or protections you're searching for, and will block your blessings. Please remember, the struggles for sexual and bodily autonomy, safety, and respect aren't unimportant, "a distraction," or "women's issues." They're central to the collective struggle for black freedom.

FIGURE 1.4. This picture of my sister and me was taken in the Bronx, New York, at my paternal grandmother's apartment in the Bronx River Projects. We loved listening and dancing to her record collection in the living room. This was the weekend of our big celebration for our cross-country move to California. I was fourteen years old. Photo taken by a family member.

I need you to know that you deserve love. You first need to find it in you. You needed something from those boys and men in your community that they couldn't give you because they didn't have the tools. You wanted them to love, respect, and protect Black girls in the same way you were taught to do for Black men and boys. Babygirl, most of them don't love themselves. But not to worry. You and love will meet. And this love will give you rest—and beautiful sons. It'll teach you the power of mutuality, autonomy, care, listening, understanding, safety, growth, honesty, healing, reconciliation, accountability, forgiveness, compassion, sharing, and giving—without expectation. It'll also teach you to live differently through pain. But most of all, it'll teach you that radical love is rudimentary to our rebirth and practices of hope. You need to know this because you're about to move across the country away from your family, friends, chosen kin, and culture, and it will be hellish. You'll long for love and to be valued and seen as a human being. I hate to say this, but it won't happen there.

Your new environment will introduce you to wealthy white liberalism, white supremacist capitalist patriarchy, a deep sense of antiblackness, and a shift in Hip-Hop music, which will have you singing along and calling Black women and girls all kinds of bitches and hos. More, the pimp/ho and gang culture will extend beyond your music.[13] It'll undergird a heightened misogynoir that sees and treats Black girls like trash and may even lead to violence.[14] Meaning that the warzone you've been navigating up until now will move from level 4 to level 10. You have at least experienced spaces of love and kinship in your current community. However, judging how you'll run up out of your future city after high school graduation, it will prove to be more and differently violent and terrorizing. In fact, you'll forget all the times Wonder called you lovely. You won't even experience "pretty bombing." These folks will straight up tell you to your face that they "don't like Black girls" and think we're collectively ugly. It'll take decades to undo the emotional and psychological harm. You'll also cry a lot. I'm truly sorry for this. On a more hopeful note, the misogynoir you experience will set the foundation for who you become and how you get free. Not because the antiblack/girl terrorism is or was necessary, but because your eventual will to live presses you toward revolutionary values and love—of self and others.

Finally, *I need you to know that you'll take part in making the world begin again.* In the words of June Jordan, children are the ways that the world begins again and again. "If you fasten upon the concept of your promise, you'll have trouble finding anything more awesome or extraordinarily exhilarating than the opportunity [to be nurtured into your] own freedom."[15] Black feminism will revive you. It'll teach you to unapologetically live and breathe radical justice, to courageously talk back, to dream out loud for Black girls, and to audaciously lessen the force of patriarchal terrorism. One is not born but becomes a patriarchal threat.[16] This in mind, you'll set out to nurture yourself, Black girls, and your Black sons against the predation of the patriarchy; to be better and different than the men and boys that you grew up with; and to imagine an alternative future, which Black girls—across genders and sexualities—so desperately need. I can't say if it will work or not. Time will let us know. What I can offer is this: the work you'll do to help create a better future together with others is divine, so call it forth anyhow. Wonder was right, my love. You are a lovely and precious gift to this world.

Love,
TL (The Future You)

2

"F*ck Y'all Feminism"

Black Girls, P-Valley, *Rape Culture, and Erotic Power*

Dear Black Girl: This is for us. And by "us" I mean all Black girls across every gender and sexual identity, expression, ability, and class. It says so many things I wish you, we, Black boys, and Black parents knew. Namely, your body is your own. You're not expendable. Your value is inherent in your entire being, including the sexual. However, while your sexuality makes you both feel and human, others use it to mark you as "fast" and/or prey. This is emphatically wrong. You're entitled to bodily autonomy, sexual subjectivity, safety, and wholeness—and by the hindmost I mean the capacity to embrace and articulate your entire person without shame, blame, or threat. Finally, you deserve a feminism that can hold all this together.

Love,
TL

I was late to the STARZ phenomenon that is *P-Valley*, created by Katori Hall.[1] My friends on social media had been raving about the show for months and how the writing and character development displayed the artistic integrity, racial accountability, class sensitivity, black southern vernacular, and sex and gender complexity we deserve. This was a welcome change from the imagistic hegemony we've been captive to since Tyler Perry (and his wigs) took over black television and cinema in the early 2000s. P-Valley, an adaptation of Hall's play Pussy Valley, is set in the fictional Chucalissa, Mississippi, and centers on The Pynk, a struggling strip club located on the Delta waterfront.[2] And as if holding up a mirror to history, The Pynk and its people intersect with the rippling and often converging effects of racist, sexist, heteropatriarchal, homophobic, transantagonist, misogynoirist, capitalist, and classist predation in the most mundane and obscene ways.[3]

P-Valley, a rich story about Black folks' survival mechanisms in the "cotton connect," despite dirty politicians, corrupt businesspeople, and villainous "Bible thumpers," delivers week after week.[4] Especially wonderful is how Hall extracts beauty from particularly ugly stories about racialized and gendered poverty, greed, exploitation, gentrification, mental illness, disease, disability, displacement, theft, corruption, political bullying, incarceration, domestic violence, state violence, theological misogynoir, sexual violence, requisite sex work, white supremacy, and more.[5] Unlike in other black productions, she refuses trauma porn, victim blaming, unchecked patriarchal violence, or making light of black struggles. Instead, Hall brilliantly produces complicated stories about love, pleasure, chosen kinships, spirit, community, gender and sexual fluidity, and intimacy, amid debilitating conditions. Of particular interest are the relationships between the veteran erotic dancer Mercedes, played by Brandee Evans; her mother, Patrice Woodbine, played by Harriet D. Foy; and Mercedes's thirteen-year-old daughter, Terricka, played by A'zaria Carter, and how their stories engage motherhood, girlhood, race, gender, socioeconomic class, sexual violence, religion-based sexual shame, and sexual subjectivity.

I define sexual subjectivity, which may include erotic power, pleasure, fantasy, desire, feeling, and more, as the powerful autonomy to experience and acknowledge the fullness of self. Additionally, drawing on Audre Lorde's "Uses of the Erotic: The Erotic as Power," I interpret erotic power as complex, messy, self-possessed, creative energy, and practice of the fullness of life and the depth of every part of our being. While there's overlapping here between sexual subjectivity and erotic power, and because we're talking about Black girls, I distinguish sexual subjectivity as the complete affirmation of self and self-possession. It's neither a signal nor an invitation.[6] It's a way of looking at Black girls as powerfully autonomous whole persons with inner lives, which require proper safeguarding. Here, I offer a brief synopsis of P-Valley, placing emphasis on Mercedes's narrative.

Mercedes got pregnant with Terricka at age fifteen by a well-to-do married man named Cortez, whom she told she was eighteen. Her mother, Patrice, a former prostitute and present-day hellfire-and-brimstone Christian evangelist, hustler, and pimptress turned newly elected mayor of Chucalissa, forced Mercedes to go through with the pregnancy for religious reasons and demanded that Cortez raise Terricka.[7] As he lay dying, his last wish was for his wife, Shelle, to assume custody of the baby due to Mercedes's occupation as an erotic dancer at The Pynk. In the present day, Mercedes wants to retire from The Pynk, purchase a dance studio, teach dance, and gain custody of Terricka in hopes that the studio will provide income and reflect more favorably in the eyes of Shelle and the custody judge. However, Mercedes can't retire from dancing or purchase the studio because she needs to get back the $20,000 she lent to her mother. Patrice originally requested the funds to help her pastor and their church qualify for a bank loan. However, when Mercedes asked for her money back to purchase her dance studio, she learned that Patrice reallocated the cash to outbid Mercedes on the dance studio in order to start her own church because her pastor didn't support women preaching. And though Patrice physically abused, neglected, sexually exploited, and otherwise unethically used Mercedes for financial purposes since she was a child; stole from her; pimped her out of her earnings; and countered her property bid and won, thus making Mercedes lose the opportunity to open her studio and gain custody of Terricka, Patrice sees Mercedes as a sinner and is ashamed of her.[8] Moreover, Patrice considers her daughter, who was forced to strip as a consequence of her mother's abuse and limited options, as not only a "bad" mother but an unmother because Mercedes gave custody of Terricka to Shelle.[9] As Mercedes declares, no judge was going to give a stripper custody of a baby. She notes the tragic loss of both her mother and her daughter throughout the series.

For example, in the episode "Belly" from season 1, Patrice and Mercedes are jailed after fighting over the stolen money and usurped property deal. Uncle Clifford, played by Nicco Annan, The Pynk's Black nonbinary owner and othermother to the dancers, visits the jail. When negotiating with an officer to see Mercedes, Uncle Clifford asserts, "That girl is like a daughter my ass can't never have." After promising Mercedes to help get her out of jail, despite The Pynk's financial woes, Patrice taunts, "Well, ain't that nice? A visit from your pimp." Mercedes replies, "That woman done done more for me in the last seven years than you done done in a whole lifetime." Patrice retorts, "So that thing been a better mother to you than me?" Mercedes responds, "Damn right! At least she ain't steal all my shit and make herself a goddamn church! You wanna talk about pimps? You need to be talking about your damn self. I was just three and already had a gas bill and Dillard's card." Patrice proclaims that she's forgiven by God because she became a Christian minister and demands Mercedes's forgiveness. Mercedes replies, "Go to hell!" For the duration of the series, Mercedes toils to be a better mother to Terricka, despite not having custody of her. In opposition, Patrice uses theological misogynoir and jezebelian theology to antagonize and shame each of them. Further, she deploys her religious platform to advocate for The Pynk's closure, thus further displacing and disenfranchising her daughter along with the entire workforce and "framily" (friends + family), predominantly made up of Black transgender, cisgender, genderqueer, gender-fluid, and non-binary women, several of whom are mothers, othermothers, and caretakers.[10]

This chapter places emphasis on the episode "Higher Ground," from season 1, and specifically the following scene and exchanges between Mercedes and her daughter, Terricka, who, though being raised by Shelle, is allowed to perform on Mercedes's dance squad, the Chucalissa Challengers. Unbeknownst to Mercedes, Terricka and the squad have been twerking on social media, advertising an invitation-only #badbitchparty. The following dialogue occurs when Mercedes catches them in the act.

> MERCEDES: Bless your thotty little hearts . . . y'all know what happens at parties like this?
>
> TAYLOR (fellow twerker and dancer on the squad): We should be free to express our sexual freedom without patriarchal consequence of rape, rumor . . .[11]
>
> MERCEDES: Taylor, *fuck y'all feminism!* [emphasis mine]. You don't want no stuff out there on the internet about y'all that look like this, point blank, period!
>
> TERRICKA: You do.
>
> MERCEDES: Well, Terricka, I gets paid for mine. You out here shaking y'all shit for free.

Later in the episode we see Terricka on Instagram at her backyard pool twerking and seductively squirting whip cream in her mouth with older boys. It's a precursor to the alcohol-laden "bad bitch party" held at Terricka and Shelle's mansion that night.

Mercedes shows up at the party and confronts Terricka: "You cute. You get it from your momma. But being bangin sometime more a burden than a blessing. Keep on. Some lil baller gon' pull on up, spit some whack ass game, and just 'cause your lil ass want to be liked, next thing you know, that nigga gon' have you bent over in the bathroom with your panties around your ankles and you deserve it. . . . The way you going, you gon' end up on *13 and Pregnant*. And what chu' gon' do then, huh?" *P-Valley* serves as a text for critically engaging Black girls' bodily autonomy and sexual subjectivity and as an entry point for rethinking black freedom and more emancipatory black intraracial relations, communities, and futures. It considers the politics of Black girls' survival and what's at stake, given history; misogynoirist mythologies, theologies, and religio-cultural sexual shame, which produces respectability politics while silencing both sexual subjectivity and sexual violence; and the potency of rape culture, including statutory rape.[12] Simultaneously, the show functions as an opening to explore Black girls' right to feeling, desire, fantasy, and consent as well as discuss my own traumatic rape at twelve years old and succeeding sexual assault.

Recasting bell hooks's idea that Black parents socialize boys to "bear the weight of a psychohistory that represents Black males as castrated, ineffectual, irresponsible, and not real men," thus indoctrinating them in patriarchy as a subversive form of power, this chapter argues the following: Black parents carry the weight of a history that re/presents Black women and girls not only as innately wanton, accessible, exchangeable, and expendable but also as vital to the foundations of American rape culture.[13] Specifically, the sexual stereotypes and sexual violence during and after North American slavery encourage an instillation of religion-based middle-class respectability politics in daughters (rather than sons) due to fear and shame-based panic around their sexual reputations, sexual images, and vulnerabilities to rape, assault, and unwed pregnancies, across socioeconomic class.[14] This isn't the kind of safeguarding Black girls need. This chapter unapologetically and unambiguously insists, one, Black girls are sexual subjects, and two, a more emancipatory black future begins with Black girls' full autonomy. Going forward, I explore the racing and gendering of shaming and victim blaming; the blemishes left by plantation sexual politics and rape culture, and how each informs aspirational black patriarchy, which plays out in black communities; and what I needed as a sexually curious and violated Black girl.

"Fast Ass": Nobody Deserves Rape, Slut-Shaming, or Victim Blaming

In *Hood Feminism: Notes from the Women That a Movement Forgot* (2020), Mikki Kendall writes about being labeled "fast," a form of victim blaming for early puberty and physical development that begins at a very young age for Black girls.[15] Being "fast" suggests Black girls, regardless of age, sexuality, and/or class, invite the attention of Black cisgender men and boys (inherently or through dress, makeup, conversation, or otherwise) and such attention, including sexual violence, is their fault. Kendall notes that projections about being "fast" serve as a deeply flawed response to rape culture. Simultaneously, she cautions that both unfair stereotypes about being "fast" and the intentional embrace of sexual empowerment may be seen as invitations for sexual violence in which there are rarely legal protections or recourse because marginalized women and girls are already seen as sexually available and disposable. This produces a dilemma for Black girls and parents. Paralleling fears of Black girls being re-encoded as "fast" and being subjected to rape ultimately limits possibilities for imagining and affirming their sexual subjectivity and empowerment.

For example, though Mercedes is sexually progressive (otherwise known as sex-positive), her initial sex talk with sexually curious Terricka merely involved telling her to keep her legs "closed" to boys. In my experience, having daughters interpreted as "fast," "loose," and/or "easy" limited sex talk with Momma to four words: just don't do it. It was nonexistent with Daddy, a Baptist pastor, until our father-daughter dance during my wedding reception. Daddy held me tight, smiled, and proudly exclaimed, "Tonight's your first night!" despite knowing full well that my college sweetheart/new husband and I had lived together four years prior to marrying. Daddy's denial reflected his intense opposition to our "shacking up." He let me know on numerous occasions that neither he nor God was pleased with it. It was immoral and a discredit to him, so much so that he never visited us until after we married, something my brother didn't experience. In each instance, there was a missed opportunity to affirm and empower the sexual subjectivity of a Black girl. While emphasis on Black women's and girls' chastity serves as an ill-considered protective mechanism from sexual violence as Kendall asserts, as evidenced in my case, it's not always about safety. Of equal import is shame and/or reputational ruin.[16]

Consequential to a sexually repressive puritanical culture that devalues and perverts black sexuality and subjectivity in general through racist mythology is sexual shame. Undoing it requires shedding light on the pornotropic gaze and resisting it. The problem isn't Black women and girls; it's the gaze. I write the following elsewhere:

In *Seeing a Color-Blind Future: The Paradox of Race* (1997), black feminist legal scholar Patricia J. Williams interprets the "pornographic seeing of race" as the nearsighted unblinking focused gaze that bounds fact, fiction, and fetishization and that splits identities between "who one is and who one has to be," making it so two chairs are always needed at the table: one for you and one for your blackness. . . . Pornotroping, then, is a critical interpretive category for critiquing the activity of "seeing." It calls attention to the deconstruction, analysis, and reencoding of subjects or phenomena in view of received knowledge, particularly that which reimagines Black [people] in general and Black women in particular, in mythical and homogenized ways. I define pornotroping as the categorical radiographic seeing of Black people in a culture of simultaneous anti- and phobic-blackness. Antiblackness draws attention to social, structural, institutional, and interpersonal opposition toward, hatred for, and/or marginalizing of Black diasporic people. Phobic-blackness denotes the concomitant obsession about, fear and loathing of, and fixation on Black diasporic people and culture. Pornotroping ... [highlights] ... how this way of "looking" fanatically and excessively pierces beneath the flesh attempting to see, read, and reread black inner workings in an effort to tear them apart, appropriate, and consume them.[17]

In essence, pornotroping reproduces and normalizes narratives on Black girls being "fast," which in reality is a merging of fear and fetishization. Such a gaze, held by both culture and religion, invites sexual shame, secrecy, dissemblance, and disempowerment.[18] More, it dispenses a range of consequences that impact Black women's and girls' lives.

For example, I saw a Facebook post that read, "Most predators pick the girls y'all call fast, hot, grown, and bad, to groom, exploit and rape because they know y'all ready to say she asked for it."[19] The post, accompanied by the crying emoji, may've been in response to a video of the rapper Sukihana being sexually assaulted on camera by rapper YK Osiris during a press meeting.[20] The video went viral the same day that the post was published. In the video, YK forcibly rubs, grabs, and kisses (twice) a resistant and distraught Sukihana, who yells "No!" and "Stop!" After running away from the scene and laughing, he exclaims, "She likes it." When called out by social media, YK apologized, stating he "understands the importance of consent" and "misread" the moment. He assumed Sukihana invited assault, which he initially saw as innocent play. Others sitting next to her in the video looked away, shocked, and unbothered. No one in the crowded room did anything to stop YK. And while some came to Sukihana's defense on social media after the fact, many others asserted that she asked for it, given her sexually charged rap lyrics.

Referring to Sukihana as "fast ass" and stating that "she led [YK] on," social media personality Tasha K posted the following on Instagram: "Over the last couple days people have been painting a picture like #sukihana is a victim & needs to be saved ... CAP!! You can't save someone who doesn't WANT TO BE SAVED.. you receive the same ENERGY you put out & that's EXACTLY what she has been getting!!"[21] The rapper Meek Mill, whose online bio reads "rapper, songwriter, *and activist*" (italics mine), tweeted the following before shutting down his page: "Don't do this to him please he a good kid. . . . Just slap him . . . we don't need our young bulls tore down for mistakes in this hyper sexual era. . . . I support suki . . . hold that s*** down on some street shit." He continued, "Y'all drawing a big line between men and women nowadays on social. . . . .it's getting bad in the black community! All this internet superficial shaming, judging gaslighting only hurt us people and it's alot of people who need strength especially young Black men."[22] In the aftermath, Sukihana expressed feeling hurt, isolated, and unable to stand up for herself, despite being violated. Few considered the fact that intracommunal sexual assault is a breach that requires accountability.

Similarly, and though Mercedes is a better mother than Patrice could ever be, when she confronts Terricka at the "bad bitch" party, she delves into victim blaming and borders on sexual shaming, even as she attempts to affirm Terricka's sexual subjectivity (for example, the "blessing" of her being "bangin"). Mercedes's words, "you deserve it," when discussing rape made me pause. Nobody deserves sexual assault or rape. This scene is beautiful and a mess all at once. On one hand, there's adequate concern that Terricka is hastily moving into adulthood before she's ready to deal with its consequences. On the other hand, Mercedes is communicating, albeit in a very harmful way, what's at stake for Terricka—namely, the casualness and sometimes seductive nature of male dominance and how that undergirds rape culture, especially for unassuming and/or sexually curious or expressive Black girls desirous of male attention. Mercedes was also that girl when she was Terricka's age. She knows that at thirteen, Terricka isn't old or mature enough to offer sexual consent or make the best sexual decisions for herself; neither was Mercedes when she got pregnant with Terricka by Cortez. Yet, Mercedes also understands how Black girls, even at thirteen, are sexual subjects with internal thoughts, questions, and feelings in their own bodies. However, they have a right to remain undefiled and untouched until they're legally, mentally, and fully empowered to consent to more. Full stop.

Still, Mercedes recognizes how simultaneously pornotropic, alluring, transactional, exploitative, and utilitarian male attention can be; how rape sometimes looks like pressured/unwillful/reluctant submission; how Black girls are blamed and slut-shamed either way; how quickly these events may occur, hence, the shift from "spit some whack ass game" to "next thing you know"; and how teenage pregnancy is a source of shame, shaming, and increased poverty for Black girls. Mercedes is a witness to how alienating and volatile sexual subjectivity can be when negotiating the "burden" of pornotropia and rape culture. Thus, she tells the twerking Chucalissa Challengers to mine their internet and otherwise reputations "point blank, period!" That is, while Mercedes is a master erotic dancer who uses her beauty, athleticism, desirability, and body to negotiate her survival needs, and though the "Mercedes Experience" is utterly mesmerizing, divine, empowered, and unapologetic, all of which is shot through with racial, gender, and class precarity, she struggles to find symmetry between self-possessed erotic power, racialized excitement, safely navigating rape culture, and steering as clear as possible of sexual shaming and victim blaming.[23] It's no easy task. She doesn't always come out on top.

By season 2, Mercedes is forced to move beyond The Pynk to dabble in sex work to make up for the money her mother stole. The arrangement she makes with Coach (aka Cedric Haynes), played by Sherman Augustus, and his wife, Farrah Haynes, played by Shamika Cotton, to dance privately and provide sexual favors for pay in their home doesn't turn out as planned when Coach realizes that Mercedes and Farrah share their own sexual connection, which neither centers nor includes him. Coach angrily calls Mercedes a "backwoods ho," kicks her out of their home, ends her sponsorship, and threatens not to pay her per their agreement.[24] Additionally, Terricka, now fourteen years old and pregnant by a fourteen-year-old boy she's in a relationship with, confides in Mercedes that she is with child, and Mercedes in turn offers the option of abortion. When Shelle finds out about the pregnancy, she blames Mercedes for teaching Terricka to open her "legs recklessly to boys." In an earlier scene during an argument between Shelle and Mercedes about how Shelle's drinking caused her to neglect Terricka, who's become Shelle's underage driver, Mercedes reminds Shelle that Terricka is a child. To which Shelle responds, "You sho' aint tell nobody you was a child when you were fifteen." Mercedes answers, "Not my fault my titties and hips came in early." Shelle hurls back, "Yo' titties and ass didn't lie to Cortez about you bein' eighteen." Shelle believes Mercedes deliberately lied about her age, slept with a married man who gave her money and impregnated her, and became a stripper *because* she was "fast." More, her status and struggles as an erotic dancer are consequences of the same.

Yet, as a girl, Mercedes learned from her mother, Patrice, how to interact with adult men, sexually and otherwise, for money. In one episode, when a younger Patrice and teenage Mercedes are short on funds after eating in a diner, Patrice tells Mercedes to do that "thing" she does while nodding toward an adult male onlooker, hoping he'll cover the bill. However, when Mercedes pulls out a wallet full of money from Cortez, Patrice notices a condom and violently beats her in the eatery. In another scene, Patrice admits to "hoing" and thieving to pay bills because Chucalissa "left her no choice." Though in love with Cortez, Mercedes dates him and becomes an erotic dancer for similar reasons. Instead of empathizing with her, Patrice shames Mercedes, while simultaneously exploiting her erotic labor.[25] The following exchange is from season 1, episode 1, "Perpetratin'," when Patrice visits The Pynk and sees Mercedes hypnotizing the crowd with her dancing and proceeds to shame and swindle her.

MERCEDES: Why you ain't tell me you was coming tonight, Ma? You know I don't like surprises.

PATRICE: They love you. Folks was willing to give up their rent and car note for you. I ain't know you made that kind of money.

MERCEDES (misreading Patrice's comment as a compliment): Well, tonight was a good night. What you think?

PATRICE (disapprovingly): I see how you manage your abundance.

MERCEDES (sarcastically): You always said I was blessed and highly favored. Thank you, Jesus.

PATRICE: Mercedes, where did I go wrong . . . why has God forsaken me? He must be so mad at me to have given me a ho for a daughter.

MERCEDES: Heifer, I ain't never been no ho.

PATRICE: Your body is a temple, Mercedes. Didn't I teach you that?

MERCEDES: You sure did. That's why when I was a youngun, you'd send me to bend my temple over in front of them niggas to get them to buy our breakfast at the Waffle House.

PATRICE: I ain't know the Lord then.

MERCEDES: Bitch, you barely know him now.

PATRICE: Stripping is blasphemous!

MERCEDES: No, Ma. It art. I transport mothafuckers. Dazzle them, something you wish you could do.

PATRICE: Oh, Mercedes this ain't gon' get you through the gates of heaven.

MERCEDES: Well, I heard hell hella lit, though.

PATRICE: With all this, church should have been getting double tithes and offering, with all the money I seen these heathens waste on you tonight.

MERCEDES: So, you think I'm a waste?

PATRICE: You're not a waste, Mercedes. But this is a waste of your time and talent.

Patrice drops to her knees and theatrically prays (and preys), "Oh, Lord! This all my fault. With everything I done done, I deserve this. Put her sins on me Lord, cause I can carry em. . . . I'll do everything in my power to save her . . . save this ho!" Mercedes, as if on cue and feeling the weight of her mother's shame, hands Patrice the bag of money she just earned from dancing at The Pynk. Patrice abruptly ends the prayer and walks off with Mercedes's profits.

Black women's and girls' sexual subjectivity, expression, and erotica (paid or unpaid) are generally viewed negatively, particularly as they've been interpreted as taboo, sinful, and dangerous. We see this explicitly expressed through Patrice's and Shelle's characters as well as in discourse about Cortez, the church, politics, and The Pynk. T. Denean Sharpley-Whiting writes about stripper culture in *Pimps Up, Ho's Down: Hip Hop's Hold on Young Black Women* (2008).[26] Sharpley-Whiting posits that the sex industry can be isolating, devaluing, and violent. That is, while it's freeing, counterculture, and powerful to express oneself sexually, stripper culture gives and takes sexual freedom as it frames Black women and girls as both hypersexual and easily accessible, and more, as they're susceptible to corporate notions of desirability, shaming, physical and sexual violence, disease, unwanted pregnancies, elected abortions, and otherwise. Sharpley-Whiting asserts that this kind of power is erratic as it's reduced to transactions on sex and beauty, which she posits are depreciating trade commodities. Another reading is that Mercedes participates in what Mireille Miller-Young calls "illicit eroticism"—an active confrontation with the taboo and "fraught history of black female sexuality . . . to pursue a prohibited terrain of labor and performance," in which stereotypes about hypersexuality are manipulated and re/presented to strategically "assert the value of their erotic capital" and gain the greatest advantage within the hierarchy of desire.[27] This framing is useful for engaging Sukihana as well. Each turns stereotypes about hypersexuality and "fastness" on their head.

Notwithstanding, sexual subjectivity, which may include illicit eroticism, occurs within a larger context that must be held in tension. As Sharpley-Whiting might note, both Mercedes and Sukihana remain in peril to exploitation, economic instability, and stigma.[28] For example, when Megan Thee Stallion, a rapper and self-proclaimed black feminist, was shot in her feet by fellow rapper Tory Lanez, Megan was viciously attacked online for "provoking" Lanez to shoot her. Underneath the claim was an adverse fixation on her sexual subjectivity, politics, and expression. In 2019, Megan had women and girls saying "no" to "pick me" politics and "yes" to "hot girl summer," an empowering anthem for sexual, emotional, and economic freedom from men and boys.[29] A major response to this turn of the tide was cisgender heterosexual male–centered misogynoirist vitriol. For Black girls, being "hot," carefree, and unbound by the patriarchy and/or respectability comes with a price, including a lack of empathy when shot by a former lover. This is what worried Mercedes about Terricka's twerk video. As Miller-Young writes, Black women (and girls) generally shoulder a burden of representing all Black women within a history and structure where they're already systemically racially and sexually denigrated as whores, commodified, and socioeconomically marginalized, regardless of industry or facts. That is, though Terricka and the Chucalissa Challengers were merely advertising a party through dancing, and though Sukihana and Megan (arguably the queen of twerking) rap and dance for a living as a form of entertainment, the greater race and gender narrative and context construct unfair conclusions that enable violent repercussions.

An additional consequence of pornotropia evidenced in Terricka's story is religious persecution. Any reading of Mercedes's and Patrice's relationship and the shaming and silencing of Black girls' sexual subjectivity that excludes the religious aspect is insufficient. And one need not be deeply religious or a weekly churchgoer to experience it. Theological misogynoir and jezebelian theology aren't simply personal opinions or random teasing. In a country that claims separation between church and state while concurrently being ruled by white supremacist Christocentric heteronormative patriarchal theological claims turned laws, theological misogynoir and jezebelian theology are powerful and impacting tyrannical ideologies that underscore the maintenance of racial and gendered tropes such as "fastness"—and more, how we ignore and justify its implications. For example, "fastness" prophesies futures (for instance, the threat of rape or burning in hell or some other general punishment) and is tied to communities, dictating who belongs and who's worthy of safety and protection. When I was younger, I was taught that God cared if I thought about, desired, or had sex or "shacked up"—or not. I was taught that there were rewards for abstaining in mind and body and punishment for giving in to "fleshly thoughts, dress, and desires." I was also told that I didn't get pregnant the first several years of marriage because God was punishing me for my sexual history. This never came to mind for my spouse.

The Black Church teaches Black women and girls to treat sexuality and sexual subjectivity with suspicion. We're called temptresses, told we have a "jezebel spirit," and blamed for leading "good" men and boys astray (for instance, Sukihana and YK and Megan and Tory). However, while it's easy to read Mercedes's and Patrice's critiques along the same lines, it's important to note how they differ. Each is fearful for her daughter. Notwithstanding, angst around the projection and consequences of racially charged religious and gender-based mythologies shouldn't be collapsed with parroting jezebelian theology and theological misogynoir. To be fair, fears of Black women and girls being seen as "loose" and/or "fast" are rooted in the quest for freedom, acknowledgment of personhood, and legal protections. Specifically, the construction of manhood and womanhood after North American slavery was central to arguments for black political rights. However, political discourses on black manhood and citizenship after slavery emphasized patriarchal rights while similar discussions on black womanhood focused on sexual boundaries and purity, particularly as stereotypical claims about Black women's and girls' promiscuity fueled racism, rape, and other violences as well as intraracial shame.

With this in mind, the Black Church and many Black people propagated the idea that heteropatriarchy, hypermoralism, erotophobia, and economic independence would aid in establishing political rights and counteract racial, gender, and sexual violence, namely, as they were left unprotected by the state. I write the following elsewhere:

> In "Demarginalizing the Intersection of Race and Sex: A Black Feminist Critique of Antidiscrimination Doctrine, Feminist Theory and Antiracist Politics" (1989), black feminist critical race theorist and law professor Kimberlé Crenshaw argues that Black women's race, sex, and class positionality require them to fend for themselves, particularly as they are left unprotected by both the state and the legal system. When examining how the courts frame and interpret the stories of Black women plaintiffs, Crenshaw asserts that Black women are protected only to the extent that their experiences coincide with either white women or Black men. That is, while discrimination against a white female is the standard sex discrimination claim, sex discrimination claims by Black women present a hybrid claim. These claims are unrepresentative of "pure" claims because race obscures the entire notion of purity.
>
> Historically, laws were put in place to protect white female sexuality/ chastity and white-owned property, not Black women. Crenshaw posits that the protection of white female sexuality was often the pretext for terrorizing the black community. However, "sexist expectations of chastity and racist assumptions of sexual promiscuity combined to create a distinct set of issues confronting Black women." When Black women are raped they are not raped as women but as Black women: "their femaleness [makes] them sexually vulnerable to racist domination, while their

blackness effectively [denies] them any protection." Some courts went as far as to instruct juries that Black women were not to be presumed chaste. Yet it was this way of racist and sexist "seeing" that enabled sexual violation in the first place.[30]

Sexual dissemblance, then, was and is a legal, political, social, cultural, and spiritual strategic defense. The spiritual realm becomes a particularly important source of self-re-creation and shelter for a people who can't depend on the law. Moreover, it's less complicated to place the onus on Black cisgender heterosexual women and girls to construct boundaries around their sexuality than to harshly rebuke racialized sexual mythologies and rape culture. Patrice's sexual shaming of Mercedes is not an exaggeration.[31] It is a product of both Black Church purity culture and white supremacist capitalist patriarchy and misogynoirist stereotyping, each of which makes it difficult for Black women to survive and mother.[32] Patrice is trying to establish "proper" womanhood for herself now that she's a Christian. Mercedes explodes these efforts. However, whereas Patrice deploys religious, respectability, and shame-based fear tactics to pimp adult Mercedes out of her money and to guilt her into leaving her occupation as a stripper, Mercedes expresses consequence-based panic for Terricka, rooted in her experiences and fears of rape, exploitation, teen pregnancy, and limited opportunities. Although there are slight similarities between them in terms of how they victim-blame their daughters and miss chances to sexually empower them, they aren't the same.

Mercedes isn't ashamed of Terricka, profiting from her, calling her a temptress or sinner, or striving for religious and gender-based sexual purity. There's a distinction between Mercedes's question "Y'all know what happens at parties like this?" and Patrice's statement "[God] must be so mad at me to have given me a ho for a daughter," where she concludes "stripping is blasphemous." Mercedes is trying to keep Terricka safe, not predestine her to hell. In fact, as they watch a mayoral candidate commercial of Patrice damning "the soul of Chucalissa," Terricka asks Mercedes if she's going to hell for having an abortion. Mercedes responds, "If you do, I'ma be right with you." Patrice, who has a general disdain for Black women's and girls' sexual expression and subjectivity, which she frames as diabolical and soul breaching, believes her future is in heaven. Nevertheless, distress around life after death or punishment for sexual "sin" on earth shouldn't be dismissed. It's real for those who believe it. The threat of burning in hell is an effective talk track against sexual subjectivity for Black girls. I spent many days and nights worrying about the possibility. However, emphasizing punishment, respectability, virginity, reputational risks, and/or rape over and against autonomy, pleasure, consent, and sexual subjectivity limits Black girls' agency, humanity, and opportunities for resistance, especially when Black cisgender heterosexual boys are being encouraged to explore (sexually and otherwise) and dominate.

Stereotyping, religious moralism, middle-class respectability, and aspirational black heteropatriarchy aren't providing the protective shields Black folks thought they would. Unlike Patrice and Mercedes, I was raised in an upper-middle-class religiously conservative loving home with both parents and still experienced fetishization and sexual violence. And like Mercedes and Terricka, I too was sexually curious and desirous of male attention. As with other Black girls, I didn't know how to articulate this outside of discourses on promiscuity and/or being "fast." I longed for a more humanizing and emancipatory explanation for my thoughts and feelings. It may have saved me a lot of pain and trauma. Black folks don't always know what to do with Black women's and girls' sexual subjectivities, expressions, and curiosities—other than demoniacal prognosis and estrangement. Yet, calling Black girls "fast" and shaming Black women for the same serves only to further oppress them. However, safeguarding Black girls' sexual subjectivity is as important as black freedom.

This isn't to say black freedom can be totalized in sexuality and sexual identity or that all Black girls need to follow in the footsteps of Mercedes, Sukihana, Megan, or Terricka. I'm saying sexual subjectivity, which is vital to humanity and personhood, shouldn't be alienating, a source of shame, or paradoxical to safety or morals. It should be affirmed in Black girls as a powerful fount of energy and "useful information," rather than treated as suspect.[33] More, I'm noting a range of powerful Black girl expressions and how we need a different way of talking about them. Theological misogynoir and jezebelian theologies render autonomous sexual subjectivity unthinkable for Black women and girls. This must be resisted and undone wherever possible.[34] Black girls need better ways of surviving and a black feminism willing to seriously engage all of this. This requires more balance between and a rereading of the fullness and articulation of self and the burdens of history.

Slavery and Its Relationship to Sexual Violence and Racist Misogyny

On April 21, 2018, my church hosted a #MeToo conference titled "Woke at The Wood," which included a panel discussion; a viewing of NO! The Rape Documentary (2004) by the director, writer, and activist Aishah Shahidah Simmons; and a keynote by me titled "#MeToo for 'The Wood.'" Not only was the heavily marketed conference predominantly empty, but some church members intentionally stayed away or were told to do the same while others deemed it a "women's conference" and therefore irrelevant to men and boys. Further, the Black Church in general had seemingly decided on silence in response to the hashtag and activism that followed. I preached:

> Given the centrality of Black women in the movement against sexual violence, Black women's stats as rape survivors, and Black women's pivotal place in the Black Church, you'd think this discussion would be front and center in the Black Church, and simultaneously, [that] the Black Church would be more vital to the current movement. It's not. I would submit that "The Wood" is either the first or one of the first to focus our attention here in this #MeToo moment. That said, we are about to keep it real honest up in here. So . . . if you're too holy to talk honestly about sex in the church, I suggest you find a string of pearls and clutch them right now—because we can't talk about sexual violence and not talk about sex. And we can't talk about sex in the Black Church and community without talking about the history of sexual shaming and how it's rooted in slavery. And we can't talk about sexual shaming and slavery and not talk about Black women's and girls' historical lack of consent. And we cannot talk about our historical lack of consent and not talk about toxic masculinity, the latter of which keeps rape culture alive.

I continued:

> We teach girls how not to get raped. Then blame and shame them when they do. And we have whole rituals and theologies on shaming girls and women: standing before the church [seeking forgiveness for sexual sin post pregnancy], handing out lap clothes to fully dressed women—as if they are emitting some sort of potent sexual power, etc. Men never have to stand and share their sexual sins. No lap clothes either.

I concluded:

> There are at least five reasons why the Black Church hasn't dealt with sexual violence: (1) Sex remains taboo in black communities due to . . . slavery; (2) the raping of women *and men* during slavery shamed Black folk into silence; (3) you can't talk about saying "no" without also talking about what it means to say "yes"—and most of us are uncomfortable with [that]; (4) dealing with sexual violence forces the church to deal with its own sexual wrongdoings—in both the biblical world and the [contemporary]

church world—among church folk; and, finally, (5) the Black Church often deploys stereotypes, which helps . . . keep rape culture alive . . . [through theologies] of sexual shaming . . . and . . . sexual silence.[35]

I'd come a long way since my youthful internalization of injurious theologies. The shift from traditional church girl ashamed of her own body and fullness of self to self-possessed black feminist scholar of religion was decades in the making. Notwithstanding, I ended the sermon and walked away from the podium feeling depleted, vowing to never extend my energies to the Black Church in this way again. The handful of Black women there who approached the altar for prayer when I asked if they'd experienced sexual violence or shame made me later rethink this, however. I knew we weren't alone, and the sermon was "not for nothing."

Still, the Black Church wasn't ready to engage the complex truths of black sexual lives and history. One member stated why they wouldn't attend, claiming that "talking about these things disempowers Black people and gives power to stereotypes." Yet, the fight for black political power and bodily autonomy includes a critique of white supremacist capitalist patriarchy, its relationship to racist misogyny, and honest discussion on sexual subjectivity and/or the lack thereof.[36] The black body is the locus from which black freedoms were taken. Therefore, bodily autonomy and sexual subjectivity must be the entry point for imagining and asserting black freedom. This discourse cannot exclude Black cisgender heterosexual men's and boys' shared histories in rape culture. Specifically, plantation rape culture, and its relations, stigmas, meanings, tropes, and influences, must be actively confronted and completely detached from how Black folks see and engage with one another. By not examining Black men's and boys' histories of lynching, castration, and emasculation as simultaneous histories of legalized sexual violence and misogynoir, and not critiquing patriarchy in black communities, which undergirds sex and gender dominance and thus rape culture, we miss an opportunity to explore more sufficient responses and resistances to history and to define our identities and futures.

Black sexual trafficking, which includes sexual violence and dehumanization, is vital to the story of Black folks in America as well as the story of how America came to be. In *Slavery at Sea: Terror, Sex, and Sickness in the Middle Passage* (2016), Sowande' M. Mustakeem argues that unchecked gender violence and sexual trafficking took shape in the Atlantic, the first dimension of the auction block system, with seamen, as an indulgence and a tool of fear, shame, and control.[37] Trafficking continued in North America as the slave trade produced a sociopolitical economy that required sexual exploitation, for example, breeding and/or rape, for its survival and success.[38] It's not happenstance that the North American auction block system, the second dimension of the auction block, provided a hippodrome for Black/African gender performance and sexual assault. Leslie Howard Owens, author of *The Species of Property: Slave Life and Culture in the Old South* (1976), posits:

> But before a buyer sealed his purchase of a slave, he usually wanted to examine him physically. He looked at his teeth, limbs, and back and felt and poked his muscles. Often buyers touched female slaves in the most familiar ways, and the auctioneer and members of the crowd told obscene jokes. An English observer at Richmond noted, "I beheld with my own eyes a man . . . go and examine a poor African girl . . . grasping her arms and placing his coarse hand on her bosom!" Many domestic slaves . . . broke into tears . . . as if for the first time the full weight of their bondage pressed down upon them. For more intimate exams, a small yard was set aside. Slaves carried back there . . . were "stripped and inspected more minutely."[39]

Slave women and men were each "examined" for future childbearing ability. Thus, slave men were also sexually assaulted. Owens writes that the slaves were sometimes forced to have sex in the presence of a master or overseer to ensure "production" prior to marriage.[40]

The economics of gross plantation product, driven by avarice and dehumanization, were also motivated by carnality and distortion. Distorting Black/African identity normalized exploitation. Ergo, sexual trafficking and violence against Black/African slaves weren't a narrative of exception, but rather procedural, legal, and routine. In *The American Slave, Texas Narratives* (1977), Jack and Rosa Maddox of Texas articulate a time when a "pretty mulatto girl" was brought home by their slaver, Judge Maddox. Jack recollects she was "bright," with long straight hair, and was introduced to the family as a "fine needle worker." However, soon after her arrival, Mrs. Maddox shaved the girl bald. Jack attests, "White men got plenty chillun by the nigger women. They didn't ask 'em. They jes' took 'em. Rosa'll tell you the same."[41] When Jack urges Rosa to speak more about the conditions of slave women, she replies, "A white man laid a nigger gal whenever he wanted her. Some them white men had a plumb cravin' for the other color. Leastways, they wanted to start themselves out on nigger women. But master was a good man and I never heard of him botherin' any nigger women. But they was some redheaded neighbors what had a whole crop of redheaded nigger slaves."[42] When asked about slave marriages, Jack and

Rosa said many slaves were "put together" and switched around, including a sixty-year-old woman and a twenty-four-year-old man.[43]

While Jack encourages Rosa to speak about women and sexual assault, he excludes how slave men and boys were also exposed to the sexual and gender politics governing slavery, which degendered and hypersexualized them and made rape culture de jure.[44] White supremacy and plantation politics, which required racial, gendered, and sexual sadism, were no respecters of persons.[45] Sex and gender distortion and assault were normative modes for engaging all Black folks. That said, we cannot disassociate the legalized sexual trafficking, devaluation, and dehumanization of Black folks during North American slavery from plantation sexual, gender, and class politics and white supremacist capitalist patriarchy.[46] Nor can we ignore the afterlife of slavery and the cult of race, sex, class, sexual, and gender jeopardy it created. While North American slavery has ended, the racial, gendered, sexual, and class scenes of the North American auction block system continue.[47] For example, mass-mediated repetitious images of dead Black folks murdered by the state should be read alongside the lynching postcards of old, meant to communicate the dominance of the white power structure and black gender and sexual animality and submission. The sexual component of slavery, lynching, and police violence alike shouldn't be negated. Each present landscapes against which Black people are sprawled out, exposed, assaulted, controlled, and touched, and often where the genitals have been struck, groped, damaged, and so on.

Toggle over to @ProtectOurBoys_ on the site formerly known as Twitter, which reported in 2022 on how the Milwaukee Police Department "molested 74 . . . Black men" over a period of time. They write, "Those are just the ones that came forward. No other Race/Ethnicity of men came forward."[48] Neither the quest for black freedom nor freedom from state violence in North America can be unwound from the black body, autonomy, and sexual subjectivity. Nevertheless, some of these violences are reproduced among Black folks. I refer to this elsewhere as residual black possessions—the ways in which Black people may maintain and reproduce certain harmful sex, gender, and sexual politics in black communities.[49] As bell hooks asserts, many Black folks have been indoctrinated to believe aspiring to patriarchy is a subversive form of power, thus teaching Black cisgender men and boys that domination—sex, gender, sexual, and otherwise—is their right as male subjects in the political economy. This reduces Black cisgender heterosexual women's and girls' value and needs to their utility to (a) the patriarchy and (b) Black cisgender men and boys. Yet, if the slave trade and imperial project depended for its success on state-sanctioned theft, dominance, dehumanization, and sexual violation, why would anyone hold that aspirational black patriarchy (a structure of intracommunal dominance within a society that believes that heteropatriarchal normativity is vital to the making of a strong America) is the linchpin of black freedom and making a strong Black collective of people in America?

Black cisgender men and boys are surviving patriarchy and the state with the rest of us. Black heteropatriarchal aspirations and respectability won't establish political rights, resist black emasculation, or stop state violence. To be clear, rape culture has no race or gender. Howbeit, racial and gender dominance are gateways to misrecognition, exploitation, and sexual assault. Rather than scapegoating and shaming Black women and girls, this is the conversation we need Black folks, communities, families, movements, and institutions, including the Black Church, to have. White supremacist capitalist patriarchy and imperial ambition distorted all of us and all our ways of being, seeing, and relating. No part of this is productive for Black folks. This way of looking hinders healing and building better kinships and survival mechanisms. My point here isn't about creating a gender line as Meek Mill suggests. It's about Black cisgender men and boys seeing themselves as cocreators and co-survivors in community; Black folks releasing structures of dominance as they are sources of harm; and seeing Black transgender, queer, questioning, nonbinary, bisexual, gender neutral, and cisgender women's and girls' right to safety and subjectivity—beyond and within black communities—as a priority. Suffering in shame and silence will no longer do.

Navigating Black Girlhood, Misogynoir, and Rape

I sat with Meek's tweets for days, reading them over and over again. His insistence on Black women's support for "young bulls [being] tore down for mistakes in this hyper sexual era" was familiar. The notion that Black women's and girls' resistance to the harms they experience intraracially destructs "the black community" because Black cisgender heterosexual boys "need strength" was essentially a cut and paste through history. It's the idea that Black men and boys need to be free to participate in patriarchal dominance and violence as a right, and the rest of us need to support their access to intraracial power as a win. We especially need not call any of this out and possibly ruin their livelihoods or, worse, doom them to an interface with the state. The quest for black freedom demands we #protectblackmen over anything and everything, including ourselves. In the 1984 dialogue with James Baldwin for *Essence* magazine, Audre Lorde shows us another way. Lorde asserts:

> We need to acknowledge those power differences between us and see where they lead us. An enormous amount of energy is being taken up with

either denying the power differences between Black men and women or fighting over power differences between Black men and women or killing each other off behind them. I'm talking about Black women's blood flowing in the streets—and how do we get a 14-year-old boy to know I am not the legitimate target of his fury? The boot is on both of our necks. Let's talk about getting it off. My blood will not wash out your horror.[50]

She continues, "We absorbed racism. . . . We must also examine the ways that we have absorbed sexism and heterosexism."[51] Lorde then invites Baldwin to consider what is particular about this for Black women and girls. She posits, "It's not Black women who are shedding Black men's blood on the street— yet. . . . We're saying, 'Listen, what's going on between us is related to what's going on between us and *other* people.'"[52] She asserts, "There are children growing up believing that it is legitimate to shed female blood, right? I have to break through it because those boys really think that the sign of their masculinity is impregnating a sixth grader. I have to break through it because of that little sixth-grade girl who believes that the only thing in life she has is what lies between her legs."[53] Lorde contends, "The true focus of revolutionary change is never merely the oppressive situations that we seek to escape, but that piece of the oppressor which is planted deep within each of us."[54]

Lorde wants Baldwin to grasp how toxic masculinity, sexism, heterosexism, and sexualization have made Black women and girls just as vulnerable to harm as racism makes Black men and boys. For example, toxic masculinity, sexism, heterosexism, and sexualization pornotropically see and treat Black women and girls like Patrice, Mercedes, and Terricka as prey while erasing antiblack capitalist disenfranchisement, poverty, patriarchy, misogynoir, and violence. Imagine if Patrice acknowledged fifteen-year-old Mercedes's simultaneous sexual subjectivity and exposures to sex work, rape culture, and teen pregnancy as opposed to exploiting her. Or, if she attended to how or why Mercedes may have been enchanted by a well-to-do Black man "spitting game." Imagine if there were sociopolitical-communal consequences for grown men who "date" teenage girls. I was raped at twelve years of age by a sixteen-year-old local boy just after my sixth-grade graduation.[55] I thought he was my friend and was being nice to me. Maybe he thought I was cute, I fancied. But like Mercedes said—one minute the boy was "spitting game" and the next I was compromised, confused, and afraid. I said "no," but he didn't stop. I lacked language for anything more. I froze. I remember telling someone I trusted immediately after, "I had sex" and that "I lost my virginity." It wasn't until two decades later that I gave myself permission to say the words "I was raped." I

FIGURE 2.1. Part of the pastoral anniversary in the Black Church included the "first family" marching down the aisle to the beat of the organist arm in arm with a partner of the opposite sex. Even my brother, who is no more than two or three years old, has a "partner" charged with rolling his stroller. My younger sister is in front of me, my eldest sister is behind me, and our parents are in the rear. A requisite accessory after a certain age was a Bible. Photo credit unknown.

wept uncontrollably for months. A few years later I learned that the same boy had terrorized the whole community. He raped several girls in the area and was eventually arrested and imprisoned.

Yet, rape neither dissolves nor explains sexuality, sexual subjectivity, and/ or sexual curiosity. By the time I turned thirteen, I had a "boyfriend" who was nineteen. Many of my friends had older "boyfriends." We thought it was cool. Like Mercedes and Terricka, we liked the attention and that they were grown enough to drive their own cars. This made us feel seen and womanish.[56] We didn't know we were prey. One late night I was riding around in the car with my "boyfriend" when he tried to force me to have sex. Though sexually curious and desirous of attention and companionship, I wasn't and didn't long to be sexually active, despite the rape the year prior. I resisted.[57] In response, he drove to the darkest and seediest part of town he could find and violently yelled, "Bitch, get the fuck out my car and walk yo' ass home!" He never even looked in my direction. He was livid. Physical or sexual violence was sure to come next. And though he failed to rape me that night, he intentionally exposed me to a host of other violences while walking home alone in the dark. As he sped away, he told me I was a "piece of ass" and that he "deserved" my body and my sex. I was to be conquered and consumed. My autonomy and rejection required punishment.

FIGURE 2.2. This photo is of our church youth group, who were also my friends. I'm on the far left in the two-tone jeans. We were on a church trip to Newark, New Jersey, to celebrate with another church. What I loved about these trips was the freedom the youth were given to explore the city and express ourselves through clothing as we desired. This was after my rape and during my androgynous stage. It's also when I began to "date" older boys. Photo taken by a friend.

I arrived home safely after walking about forty minutes. It was late. Momma was still awake and asked if I "had fun" while "out with my friends." By that time, I'd perfected acting normal in front of my parents, irrespective of the events of the night.[58] I smiled and said "yes." I didn't want her to think less of me or that I was a "fast ass." "This was my fault," I thought. I locked away the incident and never thought of my nineteen-year-old "boyfriend" again—until Facebook suggested that I add him as a "friend." He looked the same and was wearing a "Black Lives Matter" T-shirt. I examined his page, noticed that he had a lot of posts on police violence and black male power, and blocked him instantaneously. I bemoaned all the years spent slut-shaming and victim blaming myself for "leading him on," my choice in clothes, and wanting male attention. Most of all, I refused the facade of normalcy. Seeing his greasy face and raggedy rapey bucktoothed smile made me sick and pissed me off. I sat in anger and cussed him out loud.[59] A year after the nineteen-year-old tried to rape me, I was a part of a church youth group, and as my friends and I were sitting around talking, a male leader walked up and joked with us girls, "Make sure you're keeping your panties up and dresses down." In the same breath, he turned to the boys and jokingly asked, "Have you gotten some yet?" The pressure we girls felt to be "respectable" and "chaste" existed in opposition to how the boys were coerced to prove that they were on their way to becoming "real" (heterosexual-sexually dominating) men. Not getting "some" by a certain age was unquestionably a heterosexist fear.

We laughed and assured the leader that we were "good" girls—not because anything was funny but because we understood the significance of our virtue and performing it precisely. Being a Black girl means negotiating raptorial questions and smiling at predators so as not to out, embarrass, disrespect, or anger them, but to instead in some way make them feel affirmed—and their participation in rape culture, ordinary. History and experiences tell us that there're consequences if we don't. For example, being abandoned, raped, called "fast," or lied on—like my seventeen-year-old friend who'd previously been sexually active but was called a ho when she refused to engage with men and boys that were preying on her in the church. Some even claimed to have had sex with her when they hadn't. Once, when among us girls, she taught me a lesson I'd yet to learn and have yet to forget. She stated she liked sex, not the lies. "I'm sexual," she said, but when and how she wanted to be—with and without a partner.

The World We Deserve

I wish I felt comfortable telling Momma and Daddy about all that was going on inside and outside of my body. Or that I at least had the tools to both affirm my sexual subjectivity and recognize patterns of assault before they arrived. I didn't. Many Black girls don't. Momma and Daddy, and possibly unknowingly, consigned a state of bodily crisis to me. I thought the most important threat facing Black girls was sex before marriage or teenage pregnancy, and that my principal job as a Black girl was protecting my sexual image—and especially my vagina.[60] Like Mercedes, I was taught that my body was "God's temple" and that God, "the father," along with others in the community, stood in judgment of how sufficiently I "saved" it. While this may seem appealing and/or feel like protection and love, and though I have no doubt my parents loved me profoundly, verbosities on heteropatriarchal hypermoralism and shame, and silences around empowering sexual and gender politics, such as bodily autonomy, sexual agency, pleasure, mutuality, and resistance (for example, resisting rape culture, gender-based discrimination, and violence), sent conflicting messages and shaped me in harmful ways.

Because sex was something you "just [didn't] do," I lacked a model and criteria for ensuring my consent and safety as a young girl. More, I learned to ignore my needs and rewrite my rape as my sexual sin to absorb liability. Carrying the shame of my rape helped normalize rape culture and toxic masculinity and femininity, and later, led to post-traumatic stress syndrome in my marriage as

I experienced disassociation from my body at times and vivid nightmares for years. Some mornings I awoke crying and panicked while protecting my body with my hands. In all the beautiful times shared with Daddy, one on one, and in all the ways he taught me to assert my voice and demand respect in this world, I grieve that he never told me to claim my body as something more than God's "temple" or "vessel" to save for marriage, and, more, that he never shut down the heteropatriarchy and/or the mundane ways male dominance works out in our day-to-day lives. And while Momma and I often shared the deepest aspects of our souls, I lament never bonding over all the feelings and wonders awakened in me as a girl; my right to say "no" and/or "yes"; my complete authority over my body and self-actualization, articulation, and fullness; my entitlement to safety and pleasure; the perils of Black girls and predatory boys and/or grown men in the neighborhood and church; and how sexuality, sexual curiosities, and sexual experiences are human, and not inherently violent or bad. It pains me how much time was spent teaching my sisters and me not to look slutty and how sexual literacy for Black girls in general is either null or about sin, pregnancy, STDs, or marriage. There are other ways to love and protect Black girls.

The weight and absorption of white supremacist capitalist heteropatriarchal antiblackness and misogynoir are strangling us. Pornotropic ho/good girl binaries aren't subversive. They need interrogating and releasing. Too many Black girls have been ostracized out of homes, families, churches, communities, and otherwise for being desirous, sexually expressive, sexual, sex workers, pregnant before marriage, queer, transgender, teen mothers, sexually exploited, raped, misrecognized, and so on, leaving them especially vulnerable to overlapping misogynoirist oppressions. The demonization and regulation of Black women's and girls' bodies within a context where black bodies and sex are already seen as pathological, morally deficient, and nonnormative impacts our collective quest for freedom. We need safe space to be fully human; to claim and acknowledge the fullness of our being—what Lorde calls the "lifeforce"; and to claim the sexual inner lives of Black girls. Lorde posits that claiming the inner lifeforce allows us to gain a crucial weapon in resisting converging oppressions. For example, possessing my entire self as whole, good, complete, powerful, and fully human would've aided me in self-governance, defiance, and audaciously delineating between desire, feeling, love, sensuality, attraction, lust, lack, and game, at the same damn time.

This isn't about erasing historical and structural misogynoir and other dangers. It's about restoring agency to Black girls and women in a world that sees their entire humanity as taboo and forces them to navigate trite binaries. We spend so much time trying *to be* good that we miss that we *are* in fact inherently good. As Joan Morgan might say, claiming the fullness of our bodies and thus powerfully owning and affirming the complex messy space where all aspects of our humanity excitedly, consensually, and safely intersect is vital to and an act of freedom.[61] Black girls need to know that their creative energies are their own and blessed. Taylor and Mercedes were both right: Black girls "should be free to express [their] sexual freedom without patriarchal consequence of rape [or] rumor." Also, "fuck [a] feminism" that's not down with that.

3

"Break My Soul"

Precarity and Resurrection in Evangelical
Heteropatriarchal Antiblack America

Dear Black Girl: In 2022 when Beyoncé's "Break My Soul" was released she had most everybody dancing through pain to joy and different freedoms. I was especially desperate for a word of hope and rebirth. Pastor Bey preached resurrection in the face of global and personal uncertainty. I only wish I had such a homily in my earlier years. Between her and Wonder, I may have survived—better. Because being a Black girl here, where we're too often treated as though we're not enough, too much, too ugly, or just plain wrong, requires fighting y/our way through an array of fires to new dawning after dawning. Remember pastor Wonder called us "lovely," and the good minister Bey implored us to "seek," "see," "know," "think," and "be" the futures that we want. Don't let anything break your soul. You need it to push through to the other side of trauma and to create the happiness and foundation that you need.

Love,
TL

I stared out of the soot-covered windows in the kitchen and finally released, letting the water wash over me. I initially thought it was the dangerous drink of lingering smoke filling my tear ducts. I soon realized that it was the call-and-response between the precarity of the moment and the sermon I was listening to on my iPhone tucked away in my sports bra.[1] While I was writing this chapter, my younger son, Seth, home from college on summer break, mistakenly burned down our kitchen while cooking potatoes for lunch in the deep fryer. He was interning with a state senator and was in a phone meeting with her assistant when the fryer suddenly exploded, setting the tan oak cabinets, stainless steel microwave, and creamy white ceiling ablaze within minutes. Months later my spouse and I crossed paths with the senator and her assistant. "Tell the Lomaxes the story," the senator said. Apparently, Seth attempted to control the massive fire while remaining in the meeting with his supervisor. "I'm trying to stay on the call, but my kitchen is on fire," he calmly told her. I'm thankful the assistant told him to prioritize his safety at once. Nothing is more important than life. And fires require our full attention. After hanging up, Seth acted quickly, saving himself, our beloved miniature black-and-tan Dachshunds, and the rest of the house.

I was out of town handling business when I got the call. Juggling conversations between Seth and our security company, which alerted the fire department, I heard these words: "It's not too bad, Mom. We definitely need a new microwave." However, when I arrived home that evening, I discovered that we needed a whole new kitchen, and then some. All but the floors was either burned to a crisp or severely ruined. The fire devastated Seth. He slept on a hammock in the enclosed porch downstairs for the rest of the summer, punishing himself, despite our assuring him that, as my husband texted, we were "thankful for what didn't burn." While my initial feelings were a mix of sadness and anger, after confirming Seth's safety, I mostly wanted him to know that he and we were OK, that we loved him no less, that he did the most important thing by saving his life, and that his life would go on as planned. Thus, when Seth suggested dropping out of college to work at minimum wage "really hard" to "help pay for the damage," my spouse and I responded in unison, "Absolutely not." He was to go back to school with the new used car we previously promised him and everything else that he needed to have a successful year. Still, I appreciated Seth's sincere regret, emotional intelligence, and desire to offer reparations. It let us know the fire would motivate him to do well in school. Having his best college year ever was atonement enough.[2]

Having said that, I was breaking apart inside. The fire wreaked havoc on our entire home, filling it with smoke damage and forcing us to create a makeshift kitchen in the connecting dining room, thus upsetting my writing space. It generated a literal and emotional sense of fog and gloom. Seth is an empath like me, so I'm sure he sensed this. More, I'm self-diagnosed OCD as well as an introvert, thus my home is my refuge.[3] I prefer it over any five-star hotel, resort, or Airbnb, especially for writing. Writers are particular about our space. I always imagined that a clean, quiet, clutter-free, and beautiful writing area, equipped with natural lighting, a coffee stand, food, snacks, water, and a bathroom, was required for my inspiration to flow. In fact, over the years I developed an entire ritual for the writing process: Widen and fluff curtains for extensive natural lighting and aesthetic allure. Dust area. Vacuum. Straighten accessories, fixtures, books, or documents on the table. Water. Coffee. Write. Breakfast. Coffee. Write. Water. Lunch. Bathroom. Snack. Water. Coffee. Break. Write. Bathroom. Water. Dinner. Six-mile walk. Clarify ideas on walk. Coffee. Write. Water. Straighten. Clean. Bed. Declutter brain with trashy reality TV. Sleep. Awake. Repeat. Any changes to this routine could have a colossal negative result.

Yet there I was having to face a writing space that now existed among scorched debris, smoke-laced walls, and random stuff from the recently carbonized kitchen everywhere. It had only been twenty-four hours since the fire. Depression and anxiety were creeping in. A dear friend and colleague texted, "I . . . saw what happened to the kitchen and basically your life at the moment, damn. Keep writing and just try to ignore everything." It was just the perspective I needed. Determined to keep writing, I zeroed in on a fragment of beauty. A window. And turned my back to the rubbish, to face the sun shining through the opening on the opposite wall, and fixed my eyes on the landscape of greenery giving life outside. This portal would become my energy and lifeline for months to come. Rebuilding after fire damage is stressful, time-consuming, and costly. Not everyone bounces back. Recovery can be class-based. Some folks are completely undone, with their worlds forever emotionally and financially rocked, and never reset. It took the contractors over six months to deconstruct what was left of the old kitchen and build a new one. Good thing I didn't know that yet. I'm certain my downward spiral would've been difficult to recover from.

I'd reentered the charred area searching for the case of bottled water. The overwhelming loss and disruption brought me to a standstill. I pulled my iPhone from my sports bra, tapped the "notes" app, and typed, "best way through this fire," followed by the number one. This is how I organize my thoughts whenever facing an intricate problem or project. Sometimes the ideas and plan of action spill immediately and freely. At other times I can only muster a title. This was one of those days. Number one awaited assignment, but nothing came. Looking silently toward the smoggy windows facing the backyard, I put my iPhone back in my sports bra, drank my bottle of water, and tuned into the sermon randomly playing on YouTube. It was Beyoncé's first single, "Break My Soul," from her seventh studio album, *Renaissance*:

You won't break my soul, no, no
You won't break my soul
You won't break my soul
And I'm tellin' everybody (motivation, oh, yeah, yeah)
Everybody (oh, yeah, yeah)
Everybody (I done found me a new foundation, yeah)
Everybody (oh, yeah, yeah)
I'm takin' my new salvation (hey, yeah, yeah)
And I'ma build my own foundation, yeah (yeah, yeah, yeah, yeah,
    yeah, yeah)
Got motivation (motivation)
I done found me a new foundation, yeah (new foundation)
I'm takin' my new salvation (new salvation)
And I'ma build my own foundation, yeah (own foundation)

The 1990s house-style track, featuring Big Freedia's "Explode," literally "[took] me to the water" and resurrected my spirit while standing in the burnt toast-colored kitchen.[4] Amid feelings of defeat and material disaster, and against a global backdrop of uncertainty, isolation, injustice, lovelessness, and resignation, Beyoncé called us to seek freedom, safety, power, rebellion, joy, and inclusion, and more, to let go of that which is useless and reconstruct.[5] The defiant words "won't," "takin'," and "build" freed my exhale. I released fresh tears, rinsed my face, and thought, "How apropos."

Here I am standing in an unrecognizable kitchen burned by fire in the thick of writing a book on race, gender, religion, and black feminism in an America where Black women and girls must fight for dear life—from trial to trial—from every single angle while steadily endeavoring not to become broken or consumed by the scores of "fire" regularly telling us we're either not enough or too much, or worse, threatening to take us out. It's a wonder we persist. Pastor Bey drew not only on the beautiful resistance of black queer communities for inspiration in "Break My Soul" but also on Black/African enslaved and freed ancestors whose spiritual lives helped them fight to keep physical slavery from becoming mental slavery and whose historical paths remind us that there's hope in the practice of radical perseverance—the oppositional orientation toward the conviction that all isn't settled, despite the circumstances.[6]

This chapter is a journey of perseverance through fire, which traces my coming of age in Northern California and the combustible threat of white evangelical, white liberal, and black sexist infernos, and how I found an alternative foundation, life-giving portal, and sacred power at the well that is black feminism.[7] Notably, the chapter decenters theory and asks the reader to sit with the descriptive formation of indefatigable multilevel fury that Black girls may experience day-to-day; how we navigate between misogynoir, discrimination, and survival; and how this may impact us mentally, psychologically, and physically. That said, structural critiques of white supremacist capitalist heteropatriarchy, the religious right, white surveillance, aspirational black patriarchy, "Christian" democracy, and otherwise are secondary to *how* these structures played out in my life and/or how they may unfold in the lives of other Black girls.

I argue the following: First, three defining features of white supremacist capitalist empire, which steadily attempt to wreak havoc on our lives and break our souls, are antiblackness, heteropatriarchy, and misogynoir. Black folks have long histories of fighting against racism, but the last two mentioned, not so much. Yet, heteropatriarchy and misogynoir are forms of terrorism that cause damage and enable violence. Hence, the assertion of powerful black humanity becomes null when configured in light of each and thus at the expense of Black women and girls. Second, collective black power requires the recognition that Black girls are both powerful and sacred. This is not because we're perfect, superheroic, nonmortal, infrangible, or have some sort of special feminine essence.[8] Instead, it is because of all the ways we manage to survive while still loving ourselves and fighting in the interest of entire black communities.[9] Third, Black girls deserve sanctuary, which I interpret as both a philosophy and a practice. Inspired by Toni Cade Bambara and Toni Morrison, my usage of sanctuary notes places and spaces of revival and connection—absent of heteropatriarchy, misogynoir, and antiblackness—where we grow, rest, recharge, see, and value ourselves and one another as ends rather than means to ends, lay our oppressions bare, critically self-reflect, heal, dream new dreams, embrace difference, remove masks, rethink and interrogate who belongs in safe community with us, make mutuality and accountability nonnegotiable, and insist on nobody being prey.[10] Fourth, Black girls' precarity and resurrection necessitate unearthing and subverting everyday violence as well as building critical consciousness.[11]

The best way through a fire, particularly those set by heteropatriarchy, antiblackness, and misogynoir, is by prioritizing our humanity, safety, and identity; giving full attention to our vulnerabilities to danger; insisting on critical honesty about both the problem and the damage done; salvaging any good, courageously building anew, and refocusing on that which gives life; and letting anything that fails to support our humanity, sacredness, autonomy, dignity, and healing, and/or that which consistently requires our oppression, burn up in flames.

The "Promised Land" *Be* Full of Fires: Patriarchal Seductions and Toxic Christianity

I cried for months when Daddy told me that we were moving across the country from Syracuse, New York, to Mill Valley, California, just after my eighth-grade graduation in 1987.[12] Syracuse wasn't perfect but had been home since kindergarten. I especially appreciated that it was just a five-hour drive to the Bronx, New York, where my parents grew up and the majority of our family lived. I relished returning home to "the Cuse," as we affectionately called it back then, with a little bit of the "BX" with me. Extra-large bamboo earrings; 14 karat gold nameplates; sheepskin coats; suede Pumas; Coca-Cola sweatshirts; personalized hoodies, with my absolute favorite reading, "Bronx River Girl"; and other gifts from my aunties and uncles were put on full display in my bedroom after returning home from our visits. I was a certified B-girl.[13] For me, the Bronx represented Hip-Hop and black counterculture, survival, resistance, and creativity. It was where my parents let their hair down and didn't have to be "pastor and first lady," and where I first learned to press against conventional boundaries through music, art, dress, and more. I didn't care that the Bronx was dirty, dangerous, constantly on fire, and impoverished.[14] I didn't care that it maintained a hybridized melody between firecrackers and random gunshots in the air after midnight, that it lacked HVAC systems in the projects to block the grueling summer humidity, or that the elevators in my grandmothers' buildings hardly worked and smelled like a mix of the hot incinerator and stale vinegary pee. We were free and full of black joy when there. Life felt rich to me.

Perhaps because I was a kid not yet burdened by financial responsibilities. Or maybe because I was ignorant of the injuries of sociopolitical and socioeconomic deprivation in black and brown communities. Or perchance because I was responsible for neither keeping the family safe nor upward mobility. Or possibly because we had what mattered most: love, pride, home, and beloved community—that which lovingly embraced blood ties as well as othermothers and chosen kinships with those you lived near and/or were reared with. Maybe it was a little bit of all of these. Whatever the case, we were fortunate to find such communal wealth between the Bronx and Syracuse. Despite experiencing childhood sexual and other trauma, the connections were deep and sincere. In Syracuse, adults found community through neighborhoods, work, religious ties, familial bonds, schooling, social organizations, and other venues. Children hung together thick as thieves because they'd gone to elementary, middle, and high school together, as well as shared space in spiritual communities, youth groups, karate classes, public transportation, skating rinks, African dance troupes, after-school programs, concerts, sporting events, local parks, movies, malls, and more. Additionally, the Syracuse I knew was predominantly black working-class. I understood my place and identity there and never questioned my blackness or existence. It's one thing to *be* a Black girl in a predominantly black working-class community and wholly another to be read as "the" *Black* girl in a predominantly white wealthy antiblack environment. Syracuse was the former. Leaving was a departure from our home base, family, and friends as well as a decamping from Black people and ways of being, seeing, knowing, and relating.

Daddy, the grandson of South Carolina sharecroppers and eldest son to parents who migrated to the Bronx for a better life, was the first among his siblings to leave the city and one of the only persons in his family to pursue higher education. He was the "Don" of the family. At least that's how I understood him. Not criminal like the Corleones in *The Godfather*, yet smart, assertive, domineering, and calculating like Vito and Michael. Growing up, Daddy was my hero and a benevolent patriarch.[15] He was generous, good-willed, deeply loving, caring, and at times even feminist leaning, but also set the rules, had final say, and conveyed unspoken and spoken boundaries around sex (what people do), sexuality, and gender roles. For example, domesticity and childcare were often left to Momma, which meant they were delegated to me and my elder sister.[16] Women (and girls) being responsible for children and the household was "divine order," "natural hierarchy," and how black culture, society, and the church said it was supposed to be. While patriarchy is fundamentally about the structuring of power, race, sex, sexuality, and gender, it can also be intoxicating. It highlights sociopolitical, sociocultural, and socioeconomic self-interests for the preservation of power, dominance, and access. For socially and politically disenfranchised communities and people, however, it may be appropriated as a tool of resistance against superstructural forms of dehumanization, exploitation, and alienation.

In "Mama's Baby, Papa's Maybe: An American Grammar Book" (1987), Hortense Spillers posits that historically, Black men are the only American community of males to be legally disallowed to care for, raise, or provide the traditional paternal name for their children. This in mind, Black folks have a complicated relationship toward the "rule of the father," particularly as it feels like black freedom, justice, protection, and love.[17] Daddy held tightly to the role of the patriarchal father. Simultaneously, he instilled a powerful, industrious, fighting strength in me. One of our favorite pastimes was going to see the Syracuse University Orangemen play basketball. Me and Daddy bonded over our love for Pearl Washington. It was during these times that he explicitly taught me to claim my voice in the world, to demand respect, what to look for in a life partner while yet becoming an independent woman, that I was a "peach"—that which one must reach high to access—and our mantra, "We gonna do it . . . we gonna do it . . . we gonna do it." bell hooks argues that as long as society devalues the importance of male emotional nurturance and love, children will be denied healthy relationships.[18] Daddy's love and affirmation made me feel grounded and important.[19] Black girls need and want to feel that.

At the time of our move, Daddy was a Black Church pastor, finishing up his PhD at Syracuse University, and had just made history as a newly hired professor at a Southern Baptist seminary on the West Coast. Their "first black . . ." And though Daddy saw it as a kind of "promised land," a step up from the Bronx River Projects and our humble existence in Syracuse, coming of age in Northern California in the late 1980s and early 1990s was one of the most scarring periods of my life. If I ever needed Wonder's words, that I was "lovely," or Beyoncé's defiance, it was fall 1987. My arrival in Mill Valley was one-third Du Boisian, "How does it feel to be a problem?" One-third Fanonian, "Look, a negro!"[20] And one-third Shortian, "And, bitch, you just a bitch."[21] I'd never engaged with the weight of my Black girlness in this way. More, I'd never again have the luxury of not knowing what it means to obsessively think about how white people interpret race, sex, gender, sexuality, and class. Neither would I ever have the privilege of being ignorant about how white evangelical religion and politics help shape what we think about and how we experience each. Nor would I ever be naive enough to assume Black folks are immune to or above reappropriating a white supremacist gaze.

Despite Mill Valley being geographically stunning, I wholeheartedly hated it there. The race, class, and sex dynamics were plump, divided, and deceiving. Just outside of the city was a fenced-in black section of town affectionally called "The Jungle."[22] However, Mill Valley was predominantly rich and white. And by rich, I mean the average single-family home in the city costs over $2 million, and housing expenses are over 200 percent higher than the national average. Mill Valley was a long way from the Bronx River Projects, where many Black men had difficulty legally sustaining themselves and/or their families due to racism and the lack of jobs, resources, living wages, economic stability, and educational opportunities. Additionally, though some chose to abandon their families, leaving the heavy lifting to Black mothers, socioeconomic disinvestments and the welfare system forced many Black men and fathers out of the home when Daddy was growing up. That he debunked these structural violences and a host of racial stereotypes made us proud. He was determined to construct an alternative narrative for himself and us.

Yet, while this experience revised our zip code and opportunities, it also changed us, Daddy especially. His inner-city black cool was now dipped in the

FIGURE 3.1. This photo was taken in Mill Valley, California, on the seminary campus where we lived. I'm almost sixteen years old. I've just started driving. I wore black often during this time because I'd heard it made you look thinner. I was very sad and confused about my identity, value, and place in the world here. I was definitely in survival mode. Photo taken by a family member.

Birkenstocked valleys of Marin County. His black preaching style, like when he exhorted and sang while lying on his back, holding the old-school silver microphone upward as he fully embodied Lazarus of Bethany's rise from the dead, was no longer. His whoop, now a lecture. His mic, now a headset. His three-piece suits, sometimes leather and at other times a deep royal purple, now replaced with earthy casual wear. The Black Church, now a predominantly white seminary class and/or white/multiracial congregation. His conservative, though Black people–centered, theology, now colorless and rigid. His engagements on what was expected of us and social issues, such as sexuality, gender identity, respectability, and otherwise, now edictal and penal. To my mind, all of this pointed to a thing that I heard often after the cross-country move: The white people are watching. We lived in faculty housing on campus similar to an arrangement that Michel Foucault refers to as a panopticism, which allowed for surveillance, regulation, discipline, and control, as the buildings were set in a small courtyard with windows facing inward and outward.[23] My siblings and I often joked about people literally watching us from their windows. What was

FIGURE 3.2. This was my senior year of high school in California. It was taken of me and Daddy after church. My parents and younger siblings were living about an hour away from the seminary at this point. I'd stayed behind, living on the seminary campus alone while finishing up high school. I'd stopped attending church regularly and drove up for a surprise visit. Photo taken by a family member.

once handled in the home as a private matter between parent and child was now a matter of potential public scrutiny.

One day during my freshman year of high school, I decided to drink alcohol with friends. It wasn't my first time. But I'm pretty sure that I have the lowest tolerance in the history of humans. Of course, my teachers found out, and I was suspended for three days. Admittedly, this was on the heels of me taking my parents' brand-new Oldsmobile, driving it without permission or a license, and wrecking it along with three other cars in Syracuse a few months earlier. To this day, I can't explain why I did it outside of curiosity, joyriding, and wanting to look cool. On that occasion, Daddy shielded me from Momma's verbal and physical wrath after picking me up from police custody. The drinking incident was different. I might be inclined to think Daddy handled it more harshly because he and Momma were tired of my teenage shenanigans. Howbeit, while punishing me, Daddy declared, "You. Will. Not. Embarrass. Me. In. Front. Of. These. People." With every punctuation came a belt lash. And I felt Daddy's fear-induced rage with every single one. The belt leather burned my flesh, but it was Daddy's fury that crushed a tiny part of me. Perhaps, it broke a part of him, too. It was the first and last time that he ever hit me.

In a chapter titled "#ProtectBlackMen," in *Loving Black Boys*, I offer the following when writing about Toya Graham, the Baltimore mom who beat her son, Michael Singleton, near the Mondawmin Mall during the Freddie Gray protests in 2015:

> White supremacist capitalist patriarchy frustrates and contorts us. Graham hurled the weight of socioeconomic deprivation, over-policing, villainy, black single motherhood, and the pressure of the latter to produce respectable, obedient, successful Black sons who don't become thugs and/or criminals at Singleton in their exchange. Thus, in "protecting" him she was also attempting to protect her image because the world is cold-hearted to Black mothers who raise Black cisgender boys to "thugs" rather than men. Concurrently, it's unmerciful to those it deems as "thugs." After the incident, Graham and Singleton worked overtime to show he was a "good" kid and consequently she was a "good" mother.[24]

Citing Stacey Patton's essay "Why Are We Celebrating the Beating of a Black Child?" (2015), I continue, "From the plantation moms who whipped their kids so white masters and overseers wouldn't more harshly do the same, to the parents during Jim Crow who beat their children to keep them safe from the Klan and lynch mobs, these beatings are the acts of a people so . . . terrorized and enraged, that heaping pain upon their children actually seems like a sane and viable act of parental protection."[25] Undoubtedly, I deserved consequences for my joyriding. I willingly put myself and others in danger and placed undue emotional and financial stress on Momma and Daddy. I'm confident my underage drunkenness at school pricked their very last nerve. I'm also neither the first nor the last kid to make such decisions. I thought I was a "bad girl" for years. I wasn't. I was a Black girl who'd made dangerous, selfish, and injurious decisions.

It seemed Daddy struck me with the weight of centuries, of being the "first black," of needing to prove that he was a good Black man and father, and I was a respectable girl as a result, thus needing to cast the hell out of me. His lashes meant to reinstate order, particularly as we were to perform model black heteropatriarchal citizenry for the Southern Baptists and present an example for "the Blacks." The faculty courtyard served as a watchtower for the seminary administration and the larger Southern Baptist body. As bell hooks asserts, looking is a form of power. And in our case, it went one way, constructing an awareness of perpetual racialized, classed, and gendered observation. We conformed in response. I resented this. I wanted the man who had the potential and oratory gifts of Martin Luther King Jr., whooped while preaching like C. L. Franklin, and hooped like Pearl Washington as he played basketball with inner-city Black boys while still donning his church shoes and sheer silk dress socks, back. I wanted the man who met with Black pimps and gang members and helped them turn their lives around, back. I wanted the man who protected the job and dignity of an allegedly gay pianist in our church, despite the ire of the homophobic deacon board, back. I wanted my Black Church, my black culture, my black school, my black community, and my Black "framily," back. I wanted the complicated freedoms and virtues of Syracuse and the Bronx, back.[26] I wanted our lived solidarity with the black indigent and working class, back. I wanted our love for all black everything, back.

The conservative white evangelical theological gaze of the seminary was antithetical to this and thus a source of terrorism for me. Daddy's newfangled rigidity was felt even more deeply than his belt lashes. All of a sudden, what was black, what was black survival, what was black counterculture, and what was black joy, play, and typical teenage recalcitrance was measured for value, morality, and legalism under white, evangelical, and "first black" calculations. Without warning, being a Black girl seemed all wrong. And I couldn't bear to get it right. Christianity, which for me has good and bad parts, was no longer centered in black histories, traditions, and thrivings for the "not yet."[27] Rather, it was a political project for erecting rules, exclusion, borders, and empire. The 1980s were the Reagan years and the dawning of the fundamentalist takeover, in which the Southern Baptists served as major actors.[28] Collectively, the political and religious right produced policy directives that placed emphasis on the supremacy of Christianity, promises of "making America great again," and the eventual and hopeful legalization of conservative Christian governance. What's happening politically today, what some deem as a religio-political movement to right America's "unvirtuous" wrongs, are the consequences of what was brewing back in the late 1980s and thus evidence of the political and religious rights' success.[29] And though the Black Church has been vital in maintaining respectability, heteropatriarchy, and purity politics, white evangelical fundamentalism, and its use of culture, theological decrees, and state power to superintend people in general and Black and other minoritized folks in particular, is no trifling matter.

The policing I felt immediately after moving to the seminary and the regulations we're experiencing now derive from the same source and political theology and ideology, just a larger and more powerful platform. Today's primary aims include the "moral responsibility" to "restore America," thus doing away with *Roe v. Wade*; affirmative action; LGBTQ+ rights and "unnatural" relations and loyalties; critical race theory, radical protest and/or "woke" culture, Marxism, and feminism; diversity, equity, and inclusion programming; free speech;

and socioeconomic entitlements.[30] At the same time the political and religious right are forcibly inserting totalitarianism; law and order; Christian education; islamophobia; anti-immigration and border control; and patriotic "true" manhood, rule of the father, Christian heteropatriarchal order, and the cisgender heteropatriarchal Christian family as the center of American religious and political life.[31] Within this structure, it's believed that race, sex, and gender egalitarianism and rights; sex before marriage; pornography; "fatherlessness" and single motherhood; drug culture; transgender rights; and "sexual liberation" poison children, weaken the moral fabric of the country, and are weaponized against the "traditional" values of conservative Americans.[32] Specifically, conservative evangelical theology deploys the law to institutionalize who is or isn't human; who should be free, slaves, or imprisoned; who should live or die; who and what's legal or illegal; who and what gets to be read as "unvirtuous" or "virtuous"; who is and isn't deserving of legal protections; who gets to propagate their religion in peace or not; what is or isn't orthodox; who and what are to be policed by law and order or not; what forms of oppression and submission are acceptable, dutiful, and moral; what and whose labor should or shouldn't be counted; and which forms of xenophobia and genocide are manifest destiny. These aren't matters of opinion or haphazard absurdities. They're demonstrations of Christian fascism and thus matters of life and death.[33]

The ideological and political line from Reagan to the forty-fifth POTUS (henceforth, forty-five or forty-fifth)[34] was fixed in the MAGA slogan along with the work begun by Reagan and the fundamentalists over forty years ago. Responding to a *New York Times* article titled "Trump and Allies Forge Plans to Increase Presidential Power in 2025," by Jonathan Swan, Charlie Savage, and Maggie Haberman, Heather Cox Richardson posted the following on Facebook:

> The party appears to have fully embraced the antidemocratic ideology advanced by authoritarian leaders like Russia's president Vladimir Putin and Hungary's prime minister Viktor Orbán, who argue that the post–World War II era, in which democracy seemed to triumph, is over. They claim that the tenets of democracy—equality before the law, free speech, academic freedom, a market-based economy, immigration, and so on—weaken a nation by destroying a "traditional" society based in patriarchy and Christianity.
>
> Instead of democracy, they have called for "illiberal" or "Christian" democracy, which uses the government to enforce their beliefs in a Christian, patriarchal order. What that looks like has a clear blueprint

in the actions of Florida governor Ron DeSantis, who has gathered extraordinary power into his own hands in the state and used that power to mirror Orbán's destruction of democracy.

DeSantis has pushed through laws that ban abortion after six weeks, before most people know they're pregnant; banned classroom instruction on sexual orientation and gender identity (the "Don't Say Gay" law); prevented recognition of transgender individuals; made it easier to sentence someone to death; allowed people to carry guns without training or permits; banned colleges and businesses from conversations about race; exerted control over state universities; made it harder for his opponents to vote, and tried to punish Disney World for speaking out against the Don't Say Gay law. After rounding up migrants and sending them to other states, DeSantis recently has called for using "deadly force" on migrants crossing unlawfully.[35]

To be clear, "illiberal" and/or "Christian" democracy is underlined by white imperial ambition to seize power globally and is the profaned religion of the slavers in which radically progressive Black/African enslaved ancestors rejected.[36] It requires Black people, women, girls, immigrants, LGBTQ+ individuals, Muslims, and other minoritized populations to lose because it's centered in white supremacist capitalist heteropatriarchal power. More, it legalizes and penalizes our collective "Otherness" concurrently. This is a fire of mass proportions, and it impacts all of us.

On the heels of a deadly pandemic and summer of racial unrest, the religious right doubled down on their bigotry. In an article from 2020 titled "Seminary Presidents Reaffirm BFM, Declare CRT Incompatible," in the *Baptist Press*, George Schroeder writes,

> In recognition of the 20th anniversary of the adoption of the Baptist Faith and Message 2000, the Council of Seminary Presidents of the Southern Baptist Convention has reaffirmed "with eagerness" the BFM's status "as the doctrinal statement that unites and defines Southern Baptist cooperation and establishes the confessional unity of our Convention." In a statement adopted in the council's annual session, the seminary presidents assert that as "confessional institutions," the SBC's six seminaries stand "together in this classic statement of biblical truth." Additionally, the statement declares that while condemning "racism in any form," the seminaries agree that "affirmation of Critical Race Theory, Intersectionality and any version of Critical Theory is incompatible with the Baptist Faith & Message."[37]

In an article from 2023 titled "Southern Baptists Vote to Further Expand Restrictions on Women as Leaders," in the *New York Times*, Ruth Graham and Elizabeth Dias report: "Delegates to the Southern Baptist Convention's annual meeting in New Orleans approved an amendment to their constitution that their churches must have 'only men as any kind of pastor or elder as qualified by Scripture.' Until now, the fight was limited to pastoral leadership and was included in theological statements, not the group's official legal documents. The amendment must be passed again next year for it to go into effect."[38] Southern Baptist churches that failed to comply were ejected from the organization. Graham and Dias note that a fourteen-year-old girl wept when hearing the decision, stating, "It is not a sin to be a woman." One ejected pastor commented, "Some people want to take it back to the 1950s . . . when basically white men rule supreme, and the woman's place is in the home, and there is not a lot of diversity." He posited much of the recent rifts had to do with "splits over pandemic masks, vaccines, the #MeToo and Black Lives Matter movements, and who should be president."[39]

I propose that some of the people want to take things back much further than the 1950s. Evangelical heteropatriarchal sex and gender politics have historically held the position that women and girls are second class, that there's something inherently wrong with them and/or they're not fully equal to cisgender men and boys. The idea that only men are qualified by scripture to pastor or lead other men is held together by theological positions against sexual and gender equity, feminism, "woke" culture, and abortion rights. These convictions aren't separate from but rather bound up with antiblackness, capitalism, and misogynoir. This is an organization that emerged because of its support for North American slavery. Albert J. Raboteau posits that the Southern Baptist Convention asserted that Christianity should be taught to the Black/African slaves, the freed, and the free in a way that supported slavery, as abolition was against the gospel of Christ.[40] The Southern Baptists' history of racism, sexism, heteropatriarchy, and rape culture shouldn't be surprising—as each of these was essential to the institution of slavery. White women and girls weren't safe or equal within that institution, either.

In 2019 the *Houston Chronicle* reported 380 allegations of sexual violence and over 700 victims and survivors among the Southern Baptists since 1998 alone, and that registered sex offenders were often protected and/or moved to other churches.[41] One seminary president, who held that the "highest and noblest" roles for women are motherhood and grandmotherhood, encouraged a student to not report her rape, compelled her to forgive her rapist, and put her on a two-year probation for allowing her rapist into her room because it was against seminary rules.[42] Thus, when prominent Southern Baptist pastors called VPOTUS Kamala Harris a "jezebel," a racialized, sexualized, and gendered slur rooted in slavery and rape culture, it was on-brand. The insult meant to convey that Harris, a Black Indian woman, is not only out of place thrice (due to race, gender, and leadership) but also a salacious villain overstepping sociopolitical boundaries.[43] And historically, racial, gendered, sexual, and foreign villainy and out-of-placeness, which threatens the white heteropatriarchal social order, must be taken out.[44] This was a call for violence. It's unsurprising that the Southern Baptists are against intersectional, feminist, and critical race theories, necessary for calling this out.

These ideas aren't new. "Illiberal" and/or "Christian" democracy was fermenting when we moved to campus. The zoological ravaging of the soul and policing of an angry and disciplining god left me restless. I navigated guilt, feelings of unworthiness and second-classness, questions about virtue and if I'd ever experience good things or love, and fears of white people watching, judgment, and punishment. This led to a teenage life of secrecy and making sometimes unnecessarily dangerous decisions for joy and survival. It would've been helpful to talk more honestly with Momma and Daddy during this time, particularly on matters relating to sex, gender, sexual violence and exploitation, statutory rape, pregnancy, abortion, drinking, drugs, and otherwise. However, evangelicalism and Christian heteropatriarchal order, whether benevolent or totalitarian, aspirational or real, traffic in hypermoralist rules and performances and an endless chase after redemption. The pressures and politics of "being saved" for a Black girl trying to survive racism, misogynoir, classism, and projected ideas of religious, cultural, and social "Otherness" and wrongness produce schizophrenia, particularly as our being and experiences are perverted. A more emancipatory, equality-centered, and radically intersectional black feminist theology that affirmed my humanity, autonomy, sexual subjectivity, and right to safety could've made a world of difference. It would've let me know that I was OK, and that life would go on, at best.

Christian heteropatriarchal order, benevolent or totalitarian, exists on a continuum that was never meant for collective black survival or thriving. It took me decades to accept this. As a girl, I yearned to one day marry someone like Daddy, with a clear sense of Christian heteropatriarchal leadership and gender roles. And while I did marry someone who's in many ways like Daddy, and though benevolent patriarchs have or aspire to attributes that many find attractive (for example, protection, providing, influence, authority) and thus are especially easy to love, my spouse and I explicitly agree that heteropatriarchal constructions of dominion and submission, Christian or otherwise, emphatically won't do. We can't pick and choose the parts of Christian heteropatriarchy that we like without eventually cultivating the parts that we don't like or claim not to like. Some of the same Southern Baptist women and girls upset that they can no longer lead or preach in the church also stand against feminism, "woke" culture, LGBTQ+ people, and abortion. Similarly, some Black men who are supportive of these stances are against attacks on diversity and inclusion, Black Lives Matter, critical race theory, and affirmative action.

The complexity of benevolent heteropatriarchy is in how it can be concurrently beautifully empowering and acutely disempowering. That is, while vehemently resisting white supremacist heteropatriarchal extremes like DeSantis, or slavery, rape culture, the notion that women are banned by scripture from leading or preaching, and jezebelian theologies, those aligned with benevolent heteropatriarchy may engage in more passable forms of struggle, power, and dominion. For example, one of the things that Daddy loved to do was debate me. He encouraged me to argue my ideas with every emotion I could muster, including anger. However, I knew not to go too far. The times I did, which often had to do with sexuality and homophobia, led to Daddy not talking to me for periods of time. I knew to not even touch on drugs, premarital sex, teen pregnancy, or abortion. It's telling that I didn't feel safe discussing my rape and that my drinking was met with rage. While we always found our way back to each other, the silences were punishing, ungrounding, and subordinating, not empowering.

The truth is that Daddy wanted me to feel powerful, although within Christian heteropatriarchal order. Patricia Hill Collins argues that neither Black men nor women should be subordinated, as patriarchal dominance informs hegemonic black gender ideology and black sexuality in harmful ways and *disables opportunities for justice, mutuality, and more emancipatory relations.*[45] Ergo, heteropatriarchy, even if benevolent and/or Christian, cannot equate to or provide an opening for black freedom, justice, protection, or love because it requires Black cisgender, transgender, nonconforming, nonbinary, queer, immigrant, and otherwise women's and girls' oppression, second classness, misrecognition, harm, and/or abandonment. More, it's like a virus, spanning out into various forms of moralist policing and terrorizations across genders, which may also be internalized. Black women and girls are also gatekeepers of heteropatriarchy and toxic forms of femininity, particularly in our desire to be accepted as human, good, and respectable. Though living on the seminary campus demanded a more chaste racial, cultural, and gendered identity than I was willing to give, and while I resented the conservative evangelical gaze and theology that I was subjected to, I began echoing some of the talking points on heteropatriarchal order, heterosexism, and homophobia.

When one of my best friends was questioning her sexual identity, I specifically told her, "Being gay is a sin." Daddy had preached the trite "God said Adam and Eve, not Adam and Steve." "The" black "nuclear" family was the only way and goal—for everyone. After our talk, she twisted her image into this ultrafeminine version of herself to attract and date boys. She was so clearly miserable. Several years later, I called her and apologized for my ignorance, shaming, and harm. My words could've been a death sentence. I'd flung the load of hypermoralist evangelical heteropatriarchal claims and rules onto her while also struggling against them. Yet, heteropatriarchal evangelical theology had perverted both of us. As Lorde posits, "Nobody was dreaming about [either of us] . . . except as something to wipe out."[46] The shift toward conservative heteropatriarchal evangelicalism and misogynoir after our move impacted me emotionally, psychologically, and physically. Mill Valley was no promised land for this Black girl. Every day I lived was another day I refused to die.[47] I escaped after high school with many burns and bruises, sometimes deployed as weapons.[48] It took years to make sense of what happened there and all the ways I metabolized it.

Navigating the Firestorm between Nice White Racism and Unconcealed Black Sexism

Northern California was a flush of too much whiteness all at once, a foreign and unwanted cultural eclipse. My high school counterparts were predominantly neither Christian nor religious, however. But they read black girlhood just the same. The misogynoir between white supremacy and white evangelical or what Raboteau refers to as slave-owning Christianity is historical, corresponding, and ongoing. A homogeneous shuffle between each includes black wrongness, strangeness/"Otherness," second-classness, invisibility, hypervisibility, hypersexuality, and white patrolling/overseeing. I'll never forget the day I was called a monkey, an insult that was race based, gendered, and hypersexualized.[49] Or when I overheard the white girls on the school bus say, "Ewwwww . . . gross," after surveying me up and down and zeroing in on my unwaxed fourteen-year-old legs. Or when the white cheerleaders standing in a circle and apparently monitoring my weight and eating habits scoffed, "No wonder she's so fat," as I ate my favorite ice cream for lunch. Or when the career counselor refused to help me with college applications because "the Black students here don't go to college." Or when my dark-skinned South Asian English teacher stood over my desk, stared me down through the reading glasses sitting atop his nose with secondhand embarrassment, and made fun of my East Coast accent and use of the verb "to be."[50] He exclaimed, "Learn to speak *proper* English!" as the whole class laughed. Or when my predominantly white friends would look past me and announce, "White guys are to marry, Black guys are to fuck!"[51] Or that time we snuck into a black club in East Oakland and my white friends were mad because the Black boys preferred the pretty Black girls from Oakland over them, to which one person looked me square in the face and said, "We wish you were the only Black girl here, so they'd pay us attention," as I was a nonfactor. The black body is an "essential index" for the calculation and "false logics" of "Otherness" and regress.[52]

They never called me the N-word or waved a Confederate flag in my presence, yet they almost always made sure to remind me of my blackness and alleged place, while of course listening to rap music, smiling in my face, speaking in the black vernacular, and sexing Black boys. Today, when I think of colorblind feel-good nice hippy white racist misogynoirists, I think of many of them. And when I reflect on the casual tethering of racism, sexism, sexualization, class, and Black girls in America, I think of them. More, when I think of the white liberals Martin Luther King Jr. often discussed, I think of them. They'd say, "We love blacks, we have many black friends" while simultaneously setting fire to my life, telling me that I was both not enough and too much, and demanding my erasure.[53] Regardless of the niceties, they felt superior to me and other Black students. And despite dancing to our music and speaking our slang, they were unconcerned with the perpetual racial, gender, and class injustices and systemic cruelties Black folks endure, the ghettoizing of Black people, or the rub of their dehumanizing and discriminatory insults. Any good times we shared were often screwed by the underlying idea of black strangeness and deficiency.

As a teenage larger-bodied, dark-skinned, coarse-haired Black B-girl from the East Coast, I was at the same time never going to be pious enough for the Christian zealots, not white enough for the nice white liberals, and not the right kind of Black for the local Black boys from Marin City. When I first moved to Mill Valley, a beautiful deep chocolate brown–complexioned Black boy asked to see pictures of people from my old middle school on the East Coast because he wanted to see what "New Yorkers" looked like. I excitedly returned to school the next day with my yearbook to share my folks from back home. He opened it and shouted, "All these black bitches ugly as fuck!" The antiblack logic was that Black girls were unattractive and valueless unless biracial. Black girls that were "just black" were too ugly, too dark, too loud, too nappy, too mean—just overall grotesque and not right. It's interesting that he was constantly teased and rejected by the white girls for his dark color. Another Black boy once posited in front of his all-white friend group, "The only Black girls I mess with are the ones mixed with something. The others are to fuck." Everyone laughed in agreement. The irony was painful and vivid.

Concurrently, the gangsta and pimp/ho rap that influenced many of the male-female relationships in my high school, which made me both dance and feel diminished, constructed a related message: Black girls are hypersexual, problems, problemed, and disposable. The beauty and virtue naturally ascribed to the white girls bypassed us. So, though Daddy referred to me as a "peach," the boys at school regularly referred to us Black girls as "bitches" and "hos." This new level of antiblack misogynoirist hypermasculinist loathing also heightened possibilities for normalized violence between us. One day during a lunch period in my sophomore year, as I sat among a group of Black girls, some of whom were pregnant by or in sexual relations with grown men, I listened as they casually swapped stories about weekly sexual requirements and/or getting their "asses beat" by these men for minor infractions. By senior year, many had left school altogether. That same year, I lent a Black boy money because I thought we were friends. When I requested payback, he got in my face as if to hit me, threatened me, cussed me out, called me a bitch, and told me never to mention the money again. However, when my white friends approached him the next day, demanding that he return my funds, he buckled, apologized *to them*, and promised *them* he'd pay me back. Though his violent bravado recoiled in the face of white wealthy womanhood, and he didn't have the same fire and venom for them that he had for me, I never received my money back.

Perhaps this treatment of Black girls was the result of the dueling demonization of blackness and black masculinity, and being surrounded by white heteropatriarchal power, politics, and wealth for decades while also being rigorously locked out of their inner sanctum. Regardless, the Black boys were trying to establish their humanity by trampling on ours. Yet, none of us belonged. I wish they better understood how the perils of racial violence, poverty, demoralization, misogynoir, heteropatriarchy, police violence, and incarceration in Northern California in the 1980s and early 1990s targeted all of us. I wish they knew how to love us the right way. As Joan Morgan writes, many Black cisgender men and boys can't commit to loving us how we love them because "any man who doesn't truly love himself is incapable of loving us in the healthy way we need to be loved."[54] Heteropatriarchy, antiblackness, and misogynoir created a structure of knowing and relating that made otherwise disenfranchised Black cisgender men and boys feel seen and strong. Watching these same kids who were routinely animalized and criminalized by white and white-adjacent students, faculty, and administration turn on Black girls by stereotyping, objectifying, and at times being violent toward us, was satirical and dispiriting. We were all dispensable.

Black Feminism: A Whole New Kitchen

Navigating these synchronized firestorms alone wasn't living. I retrieved my black girlness from the grip of evangelicalism and antiblackness while attending my HBCU in Atlanta, Georgia, for undergraduate studies in 1991. I reclaimed the wonder of being and feeling "lovely," "precious," "pretty," "angel's best," and the "product of love" in the black mecca.[55] However, HBCUs can be steeped in hegemonic black sex, gender, and respectability politics and ideology. Thus, I was still consuming a diet of Christian heteropatriarchy. Black feminism found me years later in graduate school. The introduction wasn't intentional. I wasn't seeking it and didn't know I needed it. Yet, I was ready for it. At the time, I was in a school of theology.[56] There, I was learning about the radical politics of Jesus, who came to liberate the oppressed (Luke 4:18), under the tutelage of Black liberationist faculty, some of whom were feminists and womanists. It was there that I first heard God referred to as not only a woman but a Black woman.[57] I also learned that black liberation is holy work; that Black women and girls are sacred; that loving the black body and requiring its autonomy and full expression and feeling was nonnegotiable for black freedom; that queer, questioning, bisexual, transgender, cisgender, agender, and nonbinary folk are all God's good creation; and that anatomical authority was both a right and righteous.

This was the first time I felt my entire being affirmed. I realized, despite everything that had happened, all was not settled. There are radical possibilities in theories and practices of opposition. Simultaneously, I was in leadership at an open and affirming Black Church, which preached a black liberationist theology as well as a new mother.[58] Each cracked me open to black feminism in their own way. The church held progressive politics around racial justice, political resistance, and sexuality, and regularly called out white supremacy, racism, and homophobia, though still modeling aspirational black patriarchy. Notwithstanding, it introduced me to a practical theology of black freedom that was different from my Black Church experiences growing up, which were theologically conservative. Foremost, it stood in opposition to the white evangelicalism I encountered after moving to Mill Valley. Neither of my previous experiences had anything to say about metanarratives that call Black girls ugly, gross, wrong, strange, fat, not enough, or stupid, however. Centering a basic

FIGURE 3.3. This was my junior year of college at my HBCU. I loved this period of my life. Being surrounded by Black people and culture, after all I'd experienced in high school, "felt like heaven," I'd often say. I was safe, loved, affirmed, and confident. Photo credit unknown.

theology that intentionally claims that black is both good and beautiful goes a long way. Black girls need to hear how glorious, sacred, beautiful, powerful, and whole they are from the pulpit and other religious spaces. And as Lorde says, not because of "what lies between [their] legs."[59] We need black feminist and womanist liberationist theologies that center and encourage Black girls to live into their full range of possibilities.

Studying black liberationist and womanist theologies in graduate school and attending a black social justice–centered church created an opening for me to raise critical questions around sexism and misogynoir. In parallel, motherhood made me think more deeply about the world we inherit and consume and how differently I might raise children in it to avoid some of the traumas that I experienced, and to hopefully be better humans. I also wanted to be a good mother. I'd heard so many cultural, political, and religious messages on degenerate black mothering, including at the liberationist Black Church I was

FIGURE 3.4. I was approximately twenty-seven here, a new mother, and a graduate student at Candler School of Theology, Emory University. I was a baby black feminist, and my world had just completely opened up. Photo credit unknown.

attending,[60] I felt that I had something to prove. I even toyed with modeling my motherhood after the Proverbs 31 woman, whom even the blackest blackety black liberationist black churches seem to struggle with letting go of.[61] I also thought about Momma after we moved to the seminary campus and how she struggled to wrestle down "Cheri" from the Bronx, who wore furs and leather and was slick-mouthed and side-eyeing, to become an evangelical spouse and mother, now uncomfortable showing her bare knees, ankles, chest, and even arms, at times. I ultimately chose another path. I needed a route that talked back to my experiences as a Black girl turned woman turned mother, and that explicitly centered critiques of patriarchy, sexism, and misogynoir.

During my second year of graduate studies, I took a course titled "Gender and US Religion," where I learned from a feminist professor how gender is a social construct and about the Southern Baptists' support for slavery. Everything that I'd experienced after the move to Mill Valley began to make sense.

One night after class I called Daddy enraged and hurt. "How could you be a Southern Baptist," I demanded to know.[62] Daddy's response was simple: "They were hiring when we had you . . . when I graduated from seminary, I needed a job." Surely there were other reasons or options, I thought. Perhaps. Perhaps not. Daddy, a child of the Bronx River Projects, made this choice the same way Black folks choose positions in corporate America, academia, and elsewhere with employers and institutions that have histories and present realities in slavery, sex discrimination, rape culture, settler colonialism, and so on. Black impoverished, working-class, and middle-class people attempting to meet familial and survival needs are sometimes pressured to cooperate with historically and contemporarily bigoted institutions and ideologies, thus participating in maintaining an oppressive world. Daddy was trying to be the best man that he could be and support his family in the America that he was dealt and wanted something better for us than he had growing up.

However, while our move to Mill Valley was surely different and not entirely bad, living under surveillance on a majority white fundamentalist seminary campus that hired its "first black" in the late 1980s; that is connected to an organization that once championed slavery and Jim Crow segregation; that refuses to ordain women or allow them to lead or pastor; and that supports sexism, heteropatriarchy, homophobia, and transantagonism—while also navigating his and Momma's changes, and nice white racists and black sexism at school— almost broke my soul.[63] I got burned. Upward mobility came at a cost. And on some days, the expense could've been my life. Heteropatriarchal religious conservativism isn't for our collective advancement. We need another way. We need a whole new kitchen, or, in the words of Beyoncé, we need a new salvation and foundation. I interpret salvation as the power to redeem, honor, love, renew, and fully possess our entire selves, regardless. A new foundation for Black girls' survival must turn its back to the rubbish of America's ideals on race, sex, sexuality, class, and gender and insist on reclaiming and defining our autonomy, identities, needs, connections, value(s), worth, beauty, and otherwise for ourselves.

I turn to feminism, which I hold is a virtue. First, we need a feminism that can deal with religious practice, ideology, and theology that shape Black girls' lives. Second, feminism isn't biology. Third, it's not man-hating bra burning. This imagery is 9.9 parts caricature and .1 part truth. Historically, there was some symbolic bra burning. Notwithstanding, feminism—a politics, critical discourse, and movement that critiques and attempts to undo heteropatriarchy and sexism—is for everybody. In *Feminism Is for Everybody: Passionate Politics* (2000), hooks asserts that when the feminist movement began there were indeed feminists who were antimale.[64] Not because feminists innately loathed or wanted to be men. Rather, because most of them had had poor and violent experiences with toxic men in the past, whether fathers, brothers, lovers, partners, bosses, movement workers, or some other authority figure. Early feminists quickly realized that men weren't the problem; heteropatriarchy, sexism, and male domination (and men and women who espoused these ideas) were. That said, for those thinking feminism is a wholesale rejection of Black cisgender heterosexual men and boys, pause. Black manhood doesn't have to be patriarchal aspiring or adjacent to be whole. Black men and boys are so much more. Black feminism is to aspirational black patriarchy as black defiance is to white oppression.

Fourth, my feminism is unmistakably *black*.[65] It's viewing the world through the lenses of equity, mutuality, and justice and advocating for our collective freedom. It's wanting all of us to be better, accountable, respectful, caring, valued, loved, and safe. It's the quest for bodily, social, political, and economic autonomy and rights. It's demanding every single good, service, human entitlement, opportunity, privilege, dignity, luxury, and possibility desirable and necessary for quality of life for Black cisgender heterosexual boys and men, also for nonbinary and gender nonconforming folks as well as transgender, cisgender, agender, and genderqueer Black girls and women.[66] And though some see black feminism as threatening because, as the Combahee River Collective notes, "it calls into question some of the most basic assumptions about our existence" (for example, that sex should be a determinant of power in relationships), it's vital to our journey to healing, sanctuary, and reimagining salvation.[67]

Black feminism was the unconventional spell book for black freedom, new dawning, and the life-giving window that I needed for self-re-creation. It was the hope and rebirth, which freed me from the antiblack/antigirl world of ideas bequeathed to me. It articulated nondominating emancipatory possibilities for girlhood, womanhood, motherhood, and personhood and provided an alternative vision and expectation for relating; gave me a sense of power, pride, and responsibility; helped me to navigate through many fires; and taught me when to choose love, healing, accountability, and/or violence. Reading works by womanist theologians, particularly Kelly Brown Douglass, opened me up to black feminists like Audre Lorde, bell hooks, Angela Y. Davis, Toni Cade Bambara, Nikki Giovanni, Patricia Hill Collins, Beverly Guy-Sheftall, Michele Wallace, the Combahee River Collective, and many others who saved me from theological, cultural, social, political, and communal misogynoir. Not because these violences no longer exist but because I have a way of knowing and combating them. Black feminism forces us to see the humanity of Black girls and to produce counternarratives and histories to expose, undermine, and thwart structures of power, dominion, and oppression.

FIGURE 3.5. This was my first graduation from Candler. I was a proud black feminist who'd just been rejected from my PhD programs of choice. I was told that a project on "representations of the black female body in religion and popular culture" "didn't make sense" and wasn't "traditional" enough. I began an additional one-year master's program in theology at the school the following year to streamline my doctoral project. I was admitted to several PhD programs the following year. Photo taken by a family member.

Black girls deserve radically emancipatory relations and communities that love us (mutually, collectively, and wholly) back. We need to know it's OK to prioritize collective and individual safety; to deconstruct and reject harmful inheritances that burn us; to rebuild while calling forth the world we need; to face the parts of our communities that are salvageable and hold them accountable; and to let things and people that don't serve our collective freedom go up in smoke. Please be clear: this isn't a call to arson or to harm people. It's a summon to aggressive, subversive, countercultural healing and wholeness where we collectively refuse disposability; insist on black freedom and humanity for everyone; and, in the words of June Jordan, "love who loves [us] . . . as much as [we are] loved," are "hostile to hostility," and refuse to "be [any]body's fool."[68] It's this that makes Black girls and women sacred. Salvation reimagined necessitates saying "no" to anything that enhances our precarity. We honor ourselves by loving the fullness and potential of our complete being, we honor others by respecting their right to do the same, and we survive and thrive by honoring the differences within our collectivity and by unapologetically insisting on creating an emancipatory world house, which requires opposition toward heteropatriarchy, antiblackness, and misogynoir—in chorus.[69]

Finally, at the beginning of this chapter I posited that recovery from fire (literally my kitchen) can be class based. Black feminism is foundational to resisting heteropatriarchy, misogynoir, and antiblackness (symbolic fires), and building sanctuary. May it be class based as well? Maybe. Yet, the archives—from Sojourner Truth to unnamed Black/African slave women who refused to breed and/or birth children to the newly freed washerwomen to Ella Baker to Audre Lorde and on and on—say no.[70] Black feminism is vast and exists prior to and apart from literature, professionalization, and academic theorizing. To be sure, I got black feminist feeling, movement, and resistance from Momma as a girl (though this may not have been her intention and although she sometimes struggled away from this) before I had anything else.[71] Simultaneously, I understand how black feminism may disrupt love interests, partnerships, families, communal bonds, and otherwise, and thus economic interests. When I think about my Black pubescent and teenage girlfriends in Syracuse and some of the Black girls in high school in Mill Valley who "dated" older Black boys and grown men, as well as those that stay in, support, and promote patriarchal relationships, I recognize it may have been due to economic needs, although this isn't always the case. We certainly see this in the television series *P-Valley* with Mercedes.

Black feminism critiques the context that makes these needs and connections necessary while holding space for these Black women and girls. That is, it's antiexploitation and pro-Black women's and girls' survival at the same time. Yet, it holds the line that heteropatriarchy must be resisted, because navigating this world as a Black cisgender, transgender, nonconforming, nonbinary, queer, immigrant, poor, disabled, or otherwise girl, woman, mother, or othermother is fraught with antiblack misogynoirist dangers, whether against or within the heteropatriarchy. We protect ourselves through collective opposition and the black living hope of black feminist ancestors who impelled us to seek and be the futures that we want and need, despite the immediacy of the absurd and/or the unknown.

Emancipating Proverbs 31

Liberating Rough, Nasty, and Aggressive Black Girls to Women

Dear Black Girl: A price can't be put on your head because your value can be neither measured nor capitalized nor bartered nor prepackaged. Your fortitude, wisdom, industry, and capacity to love, partner, and "knuck" if others "buck" make you indispensable—not your vagina, womb, desirability, marriageability, or alleged feminine "essence."[1] You are whole, brilliant, intricate, and thoroughly whoever you make yourself to be. Don't waste your warrior strength on anyone or anything that doesn't match or affirm it. And be clearheaded and just in all your decision-making, including where you place your energy and give your love. Finally, shrink not in your embrace of your full self, preservation, business, and other Black women and girls. That is, be courageously aggressive, loud, and unyielding in y/our survival, autonomy, expression, joy, healing, combat, and refusal to be prey, second class, or typecast. Y/our freedom depends on it.

Love,
TL

I paused while listening intently to a widely circulating YouTube sermon by Bishop T. D. Jakes, "Real Men Pour In."[2] I'd previously written extensively on Jakes and tuned in to see if there were any changes in his messaging.[3] I could tell he was trying to do something different by emphasizing Black cisgender heterosexual men.[4] Notwithstanding, there weren't any theological shifts from what I could tell. Jakes was preaching black Christian heteropatriarchal order: aspirational black patriarchy and black feminine-*ism*, a lucrative trade in the Black Church and otherwise, often sublimated into declarations on biblical manhood and womanhood. While black religio-cultural definitions vary, biblical manhood among Black folks loosely refers to cisgender heterosexual male leadership, strength, protection, integrity, heads of households, providers, and devotion to the Christian church and God. Biblical womanhood, inspired by Proverbs 31:10–31, Ephesians 5:22–24, Mary, the mother of Jesus, and the Victorian ideal, is more definitive. Though remixed and canonized across a range of contexts, borders, ethnicities, and decades, in black contexts, it describes a cisgender heterosexual woman who is sexually chaste, delicate, nurturing, hardworking, desirable, submissive, domestic, devoted to her family and God, and a soft place for men to land.

In *Jezebel Unhinged* (2018), I refer to this as black feminine theology, an outgrowth of black feminine-*ism* and a counter to jezebelian theology. In addition to constructing the sermonic dyadic between biblical women (black feminine theology) and jezebels (jezebelian theology), black feminine theology preaches biblical manhood, which parallels aspirational black heteropatriarchy.[5] Jakes isn't one of the most famous, influential, and richest pastors in the world for nothing. He built his entire ministry on the theme of empowering allegedly troubled Black women, miraculously resurrected through feminine ideals and male power.[6] Jakes is a brilliant marketeer in this way. He knows how to retail the right mix of love, Bible, black feminine-*ism*, theological misogynoir, racial and gendered stereotypes, and woman-centered shame and trauma, with just enough—aspirational black heteropatriarchal messianic—tonic to keep his audience locked in and coming back for more.[7] The sermon was Jakes's Father's Day 2022 message wherein he chided (Black cisgender) women for bringing sin to the world and contemporarily acting like men (climbing the corporate ladder, thinking too highly of themselves), not shrinking enough to make (Black cisgender heterosexual) men feel "manly," and buying their own houses and cars.[8]

He posited, "real" women are "men with wombs."[9] They're ruled by and applauded for their femininity, which includes birthing and nurturing children and caring for and submitting to their husbands—rather than being "tough, rough, nasty, mean, aggressive, and possessive." "Tough" and "rough" women, he preached, may have careers and possessions but can't attract or keep their husbands and family.[10] "Real" women must "create a need that [Black cisgender heterosexual] men can pour into" to show them that they're necessary, thus allowing them to be "real" (Black) men. He expounded, "The conversation has become 'let's prove to the [Black cisgender heterosexual] men how dispensable they are.'"[11] "Real" (Black cisgender heterosexual) men are assets, set rules, have position, lack nothing, provide, control, fix things, and aren't "designed to receive from women."[12] They "die and bleed within and still stand" like Jesus did on the cross.[13] "Real" (Black cisgender) women wanting to be in relationship with "real" (Black) men yield to them as opposed to competing. Jakes's sermon making its rounds in social media wasn't shocking. The everydayness of black feminine and jezebelian theology is debilitating and dangerous, however. It's an agreeable form of ideological, spiritual, and cultural harassment, a kind of black heteropatriarchal Christian grooming, if you will.

Its entwinement with the evangelical fundamentalism of my youth now shaping American politics toward neofascist "Christian" democracy is especially concerning.[14] To be clear, Jakes isn't a fascist, nor does he support fascism or white supremacy. A quick Google search reveals a very humble yet authoritative Jakes with critiques of (white nationalist) power and its misuses, even as he wields his own.[15] Jakes posits that he's a servant, representative, and mouthpiece of God and Christianity, although sometimes appearing to stand in as God.[16] However, his hermeneutics and instituting of the prototypical black "nuclear" family as the kernel and rule of both Christianity and society, by way of black feminine and jezebelian theologies, align with the moral agenda of the religious and political right—namely, each advocates for a male/female binary, women's submission, and the rule of the traditional cisgender heteropatriarchal father. For the white religious and political right, these roles translate into evidence of national and economic strength and global power. That said, mass-mediated aspirational black capitalist heteropatriarchal conservative evangelical sex and gender theologies, which I refer to as black feminine and jezebelian theologies, toy with white supremacist capitalist heteropatriarchal ideals, offering a lifeline to friendly neofascism, whether intentional or not.[17]

To be sure, Black folks aren't causing fascism. I continue to hold that if enough harm was done to Black people and/or if America became a sundown country, we'd all be on one side.[18] That is, unless neofascism proffers rewards and protections against white militia for rich Christian heteropatriarchs across racial lines. By now, many of us have seen *The Handmaid's Tale*.[19] We can also take a look at history. Fascism begins with innocent and natural-looking structures of race, sex, and sexual and gender dominance; a slow removal of rights; and participation among oppressed classes that hope to access some of its privileges, for example, heteropatriarchal power and status. Say it with me: Christian heteropatriarchal and heterosexist sermons and theologies help normalize totalitarianism because heteropatriarchy and heterosexism are its fundamental building blocks. These kinds of sermons and theologies endanger us—because they erect borders around black identities, self-possession, kinships, and love; advocate for heteropatriarchal male domination and fewer rights for women and LGBTQ+ persons; collaborate with neofascist white "Christian" democracy; and thus threaten black communal advancement, sanctuary, collective resistance, freedom, and futures.

Yet, though Jakes is a noted prosperity capitalist who I project loves God, Black people, money, power, and empire equally, I maintain that he theologizes from a place of genuine concern, need, fear, and loss.[20] As I write elsewhere, "I can attest to the power of his message. Jakes comes across as electrifying, sincere, connected, reproving, and signifying—all at once. He has mastered how to let women know I see you, I care, the wait is over, it is your time, God is going to heal you, and you ain't shit, in chorus. The latter sentiment here does not mean the message is not heartfelt. Jakes very well means all the above."[21] I don't question Jakes's sense of call or attentiveness to Black folks, women, and personal empowerment. He centered and affirmed Black cisgender women and girls in his ministry when everyone else was doing the opposite. I take issue with his brand of compassionate Christian heteropatriarchal order and compelling sexism (black feminine theology), which I read as pretext. A conversation between James Baldwin and Nikki Giovanni, recorded in 1971, sheds light on what I think is the real bother behind Jakes's Father's Day sermon as well as his interest in empire.

In the dialogue Baldwin posits that Black men who can't protect and provide for their women and families due to state violence and disenfranchisement have nothing to offer them, thus leaving Black women to care for families and/or fend for their lives. In essence, there isn't a context for Black cisgender men to be ("real") men so they can't be, nor should they be expected to be. In relation to Baldwin's point about Black men not being able to provide, Giovanni replies, "I don't need the steak, I need you. I can get my own damn steak."[22] Though he is a Black gay man, Baldwin's assessment of manhood aligns with that of Jakes, as each reduces it to leadership, protection, and providing. Giovanni places emphasis on the relationships between Black men and women and the desire for partnership, love, comfort, and a place to experience vulnerability and emotional safety together—to feel one isn't facing the troubles and joys of this world alone. Jakes taps into both sides of this discussion. He knows that Black women are tired of holding down households without help, paying all the bills, playing the role of both parents, and carrying entire families on their backs. Thus, many would appreciate both the relationship and the steak. Concurrently, Jakes leans into Black men who are trying to make sense of the disjointedness between their precarity and the sociopolitical expectations of masculinity.

Though his commitments to Christian heteropatriarchy and capitalism are distinct from those of both Baldwin and Giovanni, Jakes's way of merging these yearnings is unparalleled. He values Black women getting their "own damn steak"; however, he'd prefer they do so within the fantasy of "real" manhood, specifically aspirational black patriarchy, not in black feminist partnership or completely independently of men. Women need to get their "own damn steak" while remaining clear about who's in charge and how to be "real" women. That is, get your steak but remain feminine and submissive. Don't think you're equal to or in competition with men just because you got your "own damn steak." Stuart Hall posits that fantasying highlights one part perceived reality, one part representation, and one part what's fantasized about and left unsaid.[23] The silent parts of Jakes's sermon note that he's trying to establish fixed boundaries around "real" black manhood and womanhood, an ongoing quest for patriarchal rights that he hopes will one day lead to political and economic rights, power, and recognition. Such boundaries function in response to the terror of disposability, disenfranchisement, and invisibility Black men face, which Jakes articulates in his sermon. However, instead of sitting with, assessing, and radically mobilizing against the anguish of state-sanctioned marginalization, abandon, and death Black men and boys experience, Jakes uses the church and his massive platform to hold up a sign toward Black women, bellowing, "I AM A [REAL] MAN."[24]

Yet, it's the state, not Black women, that oppresses, disposes of, de/mis/genders, and misrecognizes Black men. It's the state that claims Black men aren't men and attempts to disempower them. Demanding a subculture of black heteropatriarchal dominance where Black cisgender heterosexual women and girls shrink and/or create openings to ensure Black cisgender heterosexual men and boys feel powerful, authentic, human, and needed won't change the pain, disorientation, and dehumanization caused by America's violences. Further, accessing money, power, and empire won't dismantle tactics that disallow safeguarding Black folks from state violence. Black men's capability to provide for and protect themselves, let alone their loved ones, is wobbly. It would be helpful if Black men like Jakes spent as much time interrogating those layers as they do defining black womanhood and protesting Black women and girls. Exploring black manhood, identities, sexualities, challenges, statuses, and needs, beyond white supremacist capitalist patriarchal notions of dominance, power, empire, provision, protection, headship, and the phallus, may be a more emancipatory starting point.[25] The truth is, we need all kinds of black love, identities, kinships, families, leaderships, protections, provisions, and partnerships in our survival and sanctuary building.

The formation of mass-mediated visual language, in this case the fantasy of "real" Black cisgender heterosexual men and women, shapes not only situational or local knowledge and/or theology at Jakes's church and worldwide ministries but relations, conduct, power, and what's considered natural, providential, proper, and true—socially, interpersonally, culturally, politically, and institutionally. Specifically, "real" black manhood and womanhood are invested with power well beyond, prior to, and after Jakes. And as power and representation work, we're unequally impacted by its meanings.[26] A consequential property of the biblical manhood/womanhood paradigm in the Black Church is its reading of the Proverbs 31 woman, a technology of power that shapes expectations for "real," "good," and/or "proper" Black women and girls. Both Jakes's Father's Day sermon and the Mother's Day sermon outlined in the introduction to this book serve as scripts for Black cisgender heterosexual women and girls hoping to one day marry and experience successful unions with Black cisgender men. I too believed some version of this was destiny. Divergence brands us "bad" (and/or jezebelian) girls, women, and mothers, and dangers to Black men, children, communities, and progress, thus enabling punishment. With all that Black women and girls go through, I imagine nobody's begging for added discipline or alienation. Thus, some are trapped in the script. Some confirm it, consciously and unconsciously, in attempts to reject it. Others resist it completely. And some desire to sustain parts.

This chapter confronts the taken-for-granted legacy of the "real"/Proverbs 31 script in the Black Church and responds to the fascination with Black cisgender women's and girls' submission and wombs as well as the impulse to make our multilayered existence immaterial. It argues that the Proverbs 31 archetype, constructed in black feminine theology, for acceptable black Christian girlhood and womanhood needs emancipation. Synchronously, Black women and girls need liberation from its stronghold as well as its contemporary successor, "real" womanhood. The pressure for Black women and girls to be modest, respectable, stereotypically feminine, wives, mothers, and biological subdues creative energies, power, mutuality, critical consciousness, differences, self-possession, and autonomy. Additionally, it creates tensions between Black cisgender heterosexual women and Black transgender, nonbinary, gender nonconforming, queer, questioning, and bisexual women and girls. More, it sets up unrealistic expectations, makes common cause with heteropatriarchy and neofascist white "Christian" democracy, and limits freedoms. This chapter maintains that our power isn't in feminine fantasies, fixed roles, or decorum. It's in talking and fighting back—together. Furthermore, holding the Proverbs 31 archetype and all its articulations as essential for acceptable progression from black girlhood to womanhood is coincidingly participation in Black women's and girls' oppression.

bell hooks argues that the way to love is by letting go of patriarchal thinking. Or, as I've asserted previously, the way to love is by releasing the idolatrous embrace of Christian heteropatriarchal order as symbolic of black progress and power. This chapter is for those ministers in the Black Church who continue to preach black feminine and jezebelian theologies. It's for Black fathers who obsess over their Black cisgender daughters' virginity and purity (in opposition to how they treat their sons) and their Black queer, nonbinary, and gender nonconforming sons' presentation of masculinity, all while patting themselves on the back for being "girl dads." It's for Black mothers and othermothers who punish Black girls for not fitting into the Proverbs 31 script, despite knowing that it doesn't work. It's for Black parents, caretakers, family members, mentors, and influences that vilify Black girls and children for wanting to safely and autonomously self-define and chart their own humanizing path. Finally, it's for those Black women and girls holding up the countersign, "I Am Human and Powerful." I unequivocally invite you to be "rough," "nasty," "aggressive," and otherwise.

A word on "nasty." Many may recall when the forty-fifth POTUS used the term in 2016 to refer to Hillary Clinton during the third presidential debate, igniting a "nasty woman" (predominantly white) feminist movement for reproductive justice and women's rights against threats of misogyny and sex and gender oppression. During the debate, Clinton asserted that she'd tax the wealthy to improve Social Security, "assuming he can't figure out how to get out of it." To which forty-five responded, "Such a nasty woman." The insult was jezebelian. It noted disdain for having to compete with a woman for power and Clinton's lack of heteropatriarchal submission. It also implied a general sense of sexual immorality, uncleanliness, and pathology often ascribed to uncontrollable women because they're women. Jakes is no forty-five, yet his use of "nasty" means the same. This chapter uplifts the quiet part of "nasty"—a woman who talks back, refuses gender boxes, debunks power dynamics, and is serious about her and our freedom—as well as acknowledges how it may land on Black, minoritized, and/or poor women and girls differently. Going forward, I explore the dangers and values in mass-mediating aspirational black patriarchal ideology, I reread the virtuous woman through (1) black feminist critique, (2) womanist biblical criticism, and (3) Momma, and I explain why the goal *still* can't be Proverbs 31 for Black women and girls.

Heteropatriarchy Can Be a Death Sentence

Faux promises of the heteropatriarchy will have Black folks, including Jakes, betting against themselves every time. For example, he posits "real" men don't depend on or "receive" from women, yet, Jakes's entire ministry is built on the lives, backs, pains, support networks, and finances of women.[27] A colleague on Facebook wrote, "Men supported by women's dollars should shut all the way up." However, it's not just Jakes. His vast congregation of mostly Black women roared with applause during his Father's Day sermon, despite Jakes preaching it on the heels of the right-wing evangelical Supreme Court's vote to strike down the landmark *Roe v. Wade* decision, according to a leaked draft of the majority opinion.[28] It matters that he preached about Black women and girls diminishing themselves to make Black men and boys feel whole, as the state was literally reducing women's and girls' autonomy, political rights, resources, and participation in the body politic because that's the work black Christian heteropatriarchal order, aspirational black heteropatriarchy, and black feminine theologies on biblical manhood and womanhood intend to do. Black Christocentric "real" manhood struggles against women's and LGBTQ+ rights as much as it fights for heteropatriarchal power.

Maintaining power over one's body is a baseline for freedom. Black women in the Black Church, and Jakes's congregation specifically, should care about this. Aspirational black heteropatriarchy makes sexual and reproductive decisions for women. Or, as Jakes preaches, "real" men "set rules," "control," and aren't "designed to receive [orders] from women." In an article titled "Newest Misogyny/ies," Zillah Eisenstein argues, "The dismantling of Roe can be said to be a potential death sentence especially for Black women."[29] She writes:

> Racism and misogyny are at the helm of this right-wing dismantling of choice and access for people determining their lives in the US. The murder of abortion doctors and clinic health care workers and the bombing of abortion clinics is carried out by the people and forces who wish to destroy any promise of sexual, gender or racial equality. . . . The retraction of Roe is embedded and a spur to our present abortion chaos with its suffering. It is especially a catastrophe for Black women who die at four times the rate of white women while pregnant which makes this a full crisis for democracy. It is a tsunami for women's—trans, cis, non-binary, disabled, and undocumented—equality and liberation. . . . According to writer Michele Goodwin, a Black woman was 118 times more likely to die by carrying a pregnancy to term as by having an abortion. AND Black women are 2 to 3 times more likely to die than white women dur-

ing pregnancy. AND about 40 percent of the women who get abortions are Black. These egregious statistics will now worsen. Black women will be at greater risk of death and increased poverty.[30]

The dismantling of abortion rights, which Jakes supports, was never about a superior moral claim on protecting women, girls, or the sanctity of life.[31] America never had a problem with killing either a Black fetus or person or ignoring black parental rights.[32] Razing *Roe* was always about racism and men's right to control women and their bodies, and specifically, denying choice and sexual, gender, class, and racial equity, concomitantly.

It was a way for the Moral Majority, a prominent conservative Christian political organization founded in 1979 by Jerry Falwell, to mobilize Christians around fundamentalist ideas in opposition to feminism and the Equal Rights Amendment. However, prior to centering opposition to *Roe* in support of conservatism and "traditional family values" (read: white Christian heteropatriarchy, biblical manhood and womanhood, and Proverbs 31 women), evangelical and fundamentalist political activists, including Falwell, opposed desegregation, civil rights, and *Brown v. Board of Education*.[33] Falwell, who is credited with delivering two-thirds of the white evangelical vote to Reagan in 1980, founded a private, segregated school in the wake of desegregation orders, Liberty University, claiming that segregation was biblical. While he later distanced himself from these ideas as they became unpopular, the origins of both the Moral Majority and its opposition to abortion rights were racist. The Moral Majority formally dissolved in 1989; however, its influence and ideas remain alive and active among the religious right—namely, evangelical and megachurch leaders like Jakes and others who stand against abortion, religious freedom, and LGBTQ+ rights and are a crucial voting bloc giving shape to American politics. And while anti-religious pluralism is a defining feature of the religious right, it takes a backseat to ideas on women's and LGBTQ+ rights.

In an *Atlantic* article titled "T. D. Jakes on How White Evangelicals Lost Their Way" (2021), Emma Green asks Jakes about his thoughts on abortion and same-sex marriage. She asserts, "Just to be clear, I take it that theologically speaking, you might not disagree with, say, a conservative Southern Baptist pastor on abortion or same-sex marriage. But you're saying that there's a difference in emphasis." Jakes responds, "Yes, there's a great deal of difference—you're exactly right. There's a great deal of difference in emphasis. To raise the concern for the unborn above the born—to fight for the life in the womb and not in the prison or in the school systems—if life is valuable, then after the mother pushes out the baby, that life should still be that valuable."[34] He isn't wrong. The born matter, too. Jakes could hold a master class on weaving and serving radically empowering messages of love, value, and the right to life after birth with conservative dogma. However, he answered more directly in a CNN interview with Larry King in 2009 when King queried, "Do you agree with a woman's right to choose?" Jakes posits, "I support the right to life, you know. That's—that's my position on it." King retorts, "You're against abortion?" Jakes replies, "I'm against abortion, personally. I'm against abortion. And I think that one of the things that's important to me—for me, life begins at conception. My understanding of it makes me believe that life begins at conception."[35]

Returning to the 2021 *Atlantic* interview, Green posits that the forty-fifth POTUS "picked up support in 2020 from Latino communities and Black people, especially among men. I wonder if you saw that in your community."[36] Jakes asserts, "Black people as a whole tend to be conservative on certain issues." The "certain issues" he's speaking of are abortion and marriage equality for LGBTQ+ communities. More, "Black people" really means Black cisgender heteropatriarchal men, Jakes included. Still, he notes that he was "surprised" by the increased presidential support by Black men for the forty-fifth POTUS. And though it appears that he can't be counted in this number, Jakes mentored the forty-fifth POTUS's spiritual adviser, Paula White.[37] I'd argue that the mixed messaging (between black feminine-*ism*, black feminine theology, theological misogynoir, and aspirational black heteropatriarchy) that he and others in the Black Church preach may've also aided in the slight surge of support among Black men for the forty-fifth POTUS. Sermons on "real" men, which sell a tough-guy persona and performative heteropatriarchal power, appeal to the insecurities of men who feel shunned and that they don't measure up to what manhood is supposed to be. Jakes and the forty-fifth POTUS, and these images, resonate with certain men because they present a fantastic rescue from the misery of an oppressed masculinity. They stand up for "manly" men, problematize feminism and "feminized" men, and put women in their place.[38]

In *Black Theology and Black Power* (1969), James Cone contends that many black churches became particularly rigid during the rise of post–Civil War segregation and discrimination. New structures of white power, which placed emphasis on white notions of morality and obedience to the laws of white society as necessary for gaining both social acceptance and entrance into heaven, dampened the Black Church's radical quest for freedom.[39] Concurrently, and as I've argued elsewhere, the interest in white structures of power and acceptance includes heteropatriarchy and heterosexism. While the Black Church, Black people, and black culture are diverse, inelastic stances on women, gender identities and roles, sex, sin, sexuality, abortion, and so on pervade many corners.[40] Discussions in 2020 around black male support for the forty-fifth POTUS, which unfolded throughout social media, group chats, and otherwise, were revealing. Rappers like Kanye West and Ice Cube interpreted the forty-fifth POTUS and his blatant machismo, bigotry, and capitalism as a window of opportunity for Black cisgender men and inclusion in the heteropatriarchal "American Dream," previously denied.[41] Though Jakes appeared to stand against the forty-fifth POTUS, he, West, and Cube conveyed similar concerns around Black cisgender heterosexual men's place and role in America.

The race to be America's next black heteropatriarchal messiah and/or to build an aspirational black capitalist para-patriarchy encourages disadvantageous political affiliations, binaries, rules, and tropes, which sacrifice Black queer, transgender, agender, cisgender, and gender-fluid folks, women, and girls. The forty-fifth POTUS's Christian heteropatriarchal agenda and Jakes's Father's Day sermon each combat the contention that LGBTQ+ and women's rights have taken precedence over and against cisgender heterosexual men's rights. Historically, racial rights and Black cisgender heterosexual men's rights, along with these men's ability to protect and provide for their families, have been interchangeable. Hence, some presume Black women's right to choose and manage their own identities, bodies, connections, and roles and Black LGBTQ+ persons' right to love and marry freely interfere with Black cisgender heterosexual men's place in the "American Dream" as "real" men. Accordingly, equally important in establishing black Christocentric "real" manhood is for Black cisgender heterosexual men and boys to distinguish themselves from Black queer, gender nonconforming, nonbinary, and transgender men and boys.

I write elsewhere, "the talented tenth black messiah motif and black endangered male narrative," each central to the black "nuclear" political project, position black queer, transgender, questioning, nonconforming, and agender life as threatening to the priorities of aspirational black capitalist patriarchy and therefore black freedom. Thus, when thirty-eight-year-old Tony McDade, a Black transgender man, was killed by Florida police, and twenty-one-year-old Iyanna Dior, a Black transgender woman, was viciously beaten by a group of Black men in Minneapolis, days after the murder of George Floyd, few said their names or protested for them. Although the Black Church has historically been paramount to civil rights organizing, there's an archaeology of silence around violences against members of the LGBTQ+ community and an aquarium of verbosities for heterosexist bigotry.[42] Religio-cultural inventions on "real" manhood encourage sexism, misogynoir, transphobia, effemiphobia, and homophobia, enabling indifference. The Black Church, Black people, and black culture must explicitly stand against this. We can no longer claim to love or to fight for all people while negating structural and systemic violence and disengaging from justice work that ensures the humanity, rights, dignity, and safety of all Black people.

Several years ago, when Jakes appeared on *Oprah's Next Chapter*, he posited, "Same sex is condemned in the scriptures," though "everyone is accepted" in his church.[43]

> JAKES: Well, the perception in our society today is that if you don't say you're for same-sex marriage or if you say that homosexuality is a sin . . . that you're homophobic and you're against gay people. That's not true. I'm not called to give my opinion. I'm called as a pastor to give the scriptural position on it. It doesn't mean I have to agree with you to love you. I don't dislike anybody. I love everybody.

> OPRAH: But does it mean you perceive being gay as a sin? Do you . . . think that being gay is a sin?

> JAKES: I think that sex between two people of the same sex is condemned in the scriptures, and as long as it is condemned in the scriptures, I don't get to say what I think. I get to say what the Bible says. I'm not particularly political. I'm not particularly denominational. I'm not worried about any of that. I'm not anti-gay. I'm not anti-anything. . . . I don't want to even be known by what I'm against. I want to be known by what I'm for. I'm for people bettering themselves, no matter who they are, where they are.

Jakes confirmed his stance in a later interview with Marc Lamont Hill for Huff-Post Live in which he states, "LGBT . . . have to find a household of worship that reflects what your views are and what you believe like anybody else, and the church should have the right to have its own convictions and values. If you don't like those convictions and values, you totally disagree with it, don't try to change my house . . . to move into your own. . . . Find somebody who gets what you get about faith."[44] After the interview, Jakes clarified his commentary on Facebook:

> My comment on *HuffPo* TV drifted into issues of the Supreme Court ruling and changing the world through public policy verses [*sic*] personal witness.
>
> Further, I have come to respect that I can't force my beliefs on others by controlling public policy for tax payers and other U.S. citizens.
>
> Jesus never sought to change the world through public policy but rather through personal transformation.

All people didn't embrace him either. That's what I said and what I meant. . . . Nothing more and nothing less.

Just because a so-called Christian publication chooses to misconstrue my words using lazy journalistic tactics to further their own agenda and draw attention to their site does not make their statements an accurate depiction of what I said or meant.

Investigate.

Do not take everything you read online or hear repeated as truth. When asked about the "black church" and its role in ministering to gay people, I briefly mentioned (we were running out of time) the word "evolved and evolving" regarding my approach over the 39 years of my ministry to gay people who choose to come to our services.[45]

I simply meant that my method is evolving—not my message. I was SHOCKED to read that this was manipulated in a subsequent article to say I endorsed same sex marriage! My position on the subject has been steadfast and rooted in scripture.

For the record, I do not endorse same sex marriage

but I respect the rights that this country affords those that disagree with me.[46]

Except, the religious right and evangelical Christians do in fact force their beliefs on others through public policy and theological praxis. They shape policy and choose American presidents. "Christian" democracy, which includes Christocentric laws (for example, the dismantling of *Roe*) and personal transformation, is both a theological and a political project that demands a certain kind of biblical manhood and/or womanhood. Just as Jakes and others interpret the Bible to articulate a biblical cisgender heteropatriarchal manhood, they also weaponize the text to say what they think about women and sexuality. This is a source of power that may lead to policy, vilification, regulation, alienation, and violence.

And it's not just Christianity. While I was finalizing a draft of this chapter, O'Shae Sibley, a Black cisgender gay man, was stabbed to death by a group of boys at a Brooklyn gas station for dancing to Beyoncé's music. One of the boys said that he found Sibley's dancing offensive to his Muslim faith. It's imperative to reevaluate how beliefs around "real" manhood and womanhood leave us open to supporting contexts of injury and how our faith, when not rooted in justice, can lead to death. A liberating theology of "personal transformation" might begin with building sanctuaries centered in radically inclusive, mutually affirming love and safety, particularly for those seen as "Other."[47] Anything less supports the cult of death devouring Black LGBTQ+ kinfolk and women and girls. Jakes's Father's Day sermon isn't necessarily pro–cisgender hetero-sexual men, either. In addition to critiquing women and LGBTQ+ persons, it's also critical of those who aren't performing as "real" men (as assets who set rules, have position, lack nothing, provide, control, fix things, don't "receive from women," and "die and bleed within and still stand" like Jesus) although it appears to uplift them. One might read this as nuance or accountability. However, a close reading suggests that Jakes's play in biblical manhood and hypermasculine strength, which is transantagonistic, homophobic, biphobic, effemiphobic, and classist, creates a singular view of black masculinity while condemning those who fail to make the cut, placing them outside of or in the bottom tier of acceptable manhood.

What about cisgender heterosexual men who desire partnerships as op-posed to dominance? What of those who need jobs and/or economic help? What of those who enjoy bottoming and anal play with cisgender women? How about those that don't like to fight or "die and bleed" like Jesus, particularly in a state where black male death is rampant? Jakes's black feminine theology is synchro-nously theologizing toxic masculinity. And not in silos or sans interest. Imagistic "real" Black men can be incredibly attractive in a world where white suprema-cist capitalist patriarchy, antiblackness, and misogynoir (1) make life difficult for Black girls, women, mothers, and othermothers; (2) treat Black men and boys like monsters, kill them without cause, incarcerate them at high levels, and leave them with limited survival options; and (3) produce narratives that Black women and girls are unlovable. However, as these things go, Jakes's "real" woman requi-site for his "real" man, which eerily calls to mind the Shortian bitch/ho binary from my high school years, is a prison.[48] When Jakes refers to Black women as "rough, nasty, mean, aggressive" (bitch), reduces us to walking wombs (sexu-alization) that need to learn to submit to men, and problematizes our sexual identities and experiences (ho), he's telling us what he's for *and against*. The congruence between Jakes and Short is relevant, even if not exact.

Some might argue that they're opposing messages and messengers. Perhaps. Yet, each communiqué hierarchizes heteropatriarchal male power and needs over and against those of women and girls, totalizes our humanity in our sexual parts (while at least one denies access to reproductive rights and justice), mis-recognizes and re/presents us, and fantasizes about who we are and/or should be—*for men*. I do concur with Jakes on one thing, however. There's a need for Black cisgender heterosexual men and boys to safely express and work through their fears and challenges and to "pour in"—to the building and strengthen-ing of sanctuary.[49] Transformation isn't solely personal. It's also social and political. And for Black folks, the work of black freedom, which intersects with the Christian faith, as freedom and faith emerged together on North American plantations, must be radically inclusive. Transformation, then, should include working with and fighting for the rights of all Black people, including women, LGBTQ+ people, and men who define themselves beyond Jakes's definition of "real" men. We can't cut off, ignore, or actively work against the rights of others while claiming to love them. And if "real" manhood or womanhood requires the former, then it's necessary to undo those constructions.

Not "Men with Wombs": Freeing the Virtuous Woman

If you didn't hear or read Proverbs 31 aloud at any Women's Day celebration, funeral, Mother's Day service, tea, church fashion show, wedding, singles conference, women's conference, Bible study, or Sunday school, chances are you probably didn't grow up in a Black Church. Whatever "the" Black woman was not in the American cultural imagination, the Proverbs 31 woman was what a righteous Christian/biblical woman was supposed to be.[50]

> Who can find a virtuous woman? for her price is far above rubies. The heart of her husband doth safely trust in her, so that he shall have no need of spoil. She will do him good and not evil all the days of her life. She seeketh wool, and flax, and worketh willingly with her hands. She is like the merchants' ships; she bringeth her food from afar. She riseth also while it is yet night, and giveth meat to her household, and a portion to her maidens. She considereth a field, and buyeth it: with the fruit of her hands she planteth a vineyard. She girdeth her loins with strength, and strengtheneth her arms. She perceiveth that her merchandise is good: her candle goeth not out by night. She layeth her hands to the spindle, and her hands hold the distaff. She stretcheth out her hand to the poor; yea, she reacheth forth her hands to the needy. She is not afraid of the snow for her household: for all her household are clothed with scarlet. She maketh herself coverings of tapestry; her clothing is silk and purple. Her husband is known in the gates, when he sitteth among the elders of the land. She maketh fine linen, and selleth it; and delivereth girdles unto the merchant. Strength and honour are her clothing; and she shall rejoice in time to come. She openeth her mouth with wisdom; and in her tongue is the law of kindness. She looketh well to the ways of her household, and eateth not the bread of idleness. Her children arise up, and call her blessed; her husband also, and he praiseth her. Many daughters have done virtuously, but thou excellest them all. Favour is deceitful, and beauty is vain: but a woman that feareth

the Lord, she shall be praised. Give her of the fruit of her hands; and let her own works praise her in the gates.[51]

Jakes's preaching about the femininity of "real" women who have wombs and are fruitful, nurturing, and submissive and who care for their children, household, and husbands is a beckoning for the Proverbs 31 ideal.[52] Notably, as it counters harmful historical racial and gendered tropes, which denied womanhood and femininity, it concurrently dilates Black women's and girls' ability to be seen. However, such looking totalizes Black cisgender heterosexual women's and girls' virtue in heteropatriarchal desirability, domesticity, marriageability, their handling of the male ego and needs, and the capacity and willingness to bear children.

The Proverbs 31 ideal central to black feminine theology places women's roles, goals, identities, and bodies in perpetual service to men and especially husbands. Virtue is wedded to how she bears children *for him*; remains a virgin until marriage *for him*; develops a sexual life and appetite only *for him*; beautifies *for him*; runs a clean, orderly, and harmonious household *for him*; is reputable *for him*; keeps conversation agreeable *for him*; cooks *for him*; keeps quiet, soft, and feminine *for him*; labors *for him*; and, as Jakes preaches, creates a need *for him* to fill so that he can feel manly.[53] While feminine virtue allows for respectable legibility (Black women get to be recognized as "real" women), it's consequently a way for Black women and girls to superintend themselves and each other. First, the Black Church, black communal, and black cultural emphasis on "real" women, nature, and wombs excludes and condemns women who don't, won't, or can't have children; transgender women and men; and nonbinary, gender nonconforming, and queer people. Second, it accentuates transphobia and misogynoir between Black cisgender and transgender women. While the Black Church and cultural reading of the Proverbs 31 woman emphasizes wombs, marriage, and motherhood, a paralleling and overlapping discourse on biology, childbirth, and bleeding is worth noting.[54]

Some time ago, a Black transgender woman posted a video online saying that Black cisgender women "don't own" and therefore "can't gatekeep" womanhood, periods, and childbirth because Black intersex people and transgender men also share these experiences. The comedian Jess Hilarious, who's been mistaken for transgender, replied, "Who the fuck is going to stand up for us . . . real women, biological women, women who were born with all the parts that you guys wish that you were . . . how are you projecting your anger on real women? Because we *are* the gatekeepers . . . for periods. We the only ones who fuckin' bleed, honey. We the only ones that can give birth. We make y'all people . . . y'all come from us. You can't be us. You will never . . . be that."[55] Jess concludes that Black transgender women are "mentally insane." Though she rightly notes the precarity she feels as a Black cisgender woman targeted by white supremacist capitalist heteropatriarchal racism and sexism as well as misogynoir from both Black cisgender men who misgender her and Black transgender women who derogatorily refer to Black cisgender women as "fish," "tuna," "bonus holes," and "birthing channels," her representation of "real" women, or as Jakes says, "men with wombs," is also transphobic and denigrating.[56] The insults by both Black transgender and cisgender women have long histories and can lead to death.[57]

Third, the "real"/Proverbs 31 ideal demands sexual purity.[58] This perverts, suppresses, and attempts to regulate Black women's and girls' sexual subjectivity across genders, identities, and sexualities. We see this in the policing, demonizing of, and violences against Black transgender women, nonbinary and gender nonconforming folks, lesbians, sex workers and erotic performers, and cisgender hot girl/holy girl binaries. Hot girl/holy girl binaries, akin to the ho/lady binate, slut-shame unmarried sexually expressive and sexually active Black cisgender women and girls, limiting sex and pleasure to marriage with cisgender men rather than viewing sexual subjectivity and erotic power as a source of creative energy, self-actualization, feeling one's body, useful information, satisfaction, and self-possession. The politicized fury from the Moral Majority, religious right, and even Jakes has to do with women's right to sexual pleasure and bodily autonomy essential to feminism. Jezebelian theology (the opposite of feminine theology) harmfully notes this as "nasty." In 2018, I guest edited a special issue of the journal *Black Theology*, which the reader may find helpful, titled "Black Bodies in Ecstasy: Black Women, the Black Church, and the Politics of Pleasure."[59] There are biblical texts that support rather than debase Black women's erotic agency.

"How Sarah Got Her Groove Back, or Notes toward a Black Feminist Theology of Pleasure," by Brittney Cooper, and "'I Am Dark and Lovely': Let the Shulammite Woman Speak," by Keri Day, are insightful. Day asserts, "A part of the Hebrew Bible and the Christian Bible, Song of Songs introduces the reader to a woman who is 'Black and lovely,' who initiates sexual encounters, who roams the streets looking for her lover, who speaks openly about her sexual desires, and who does not refer to herself as married in this quest for sexual freedom and communion."[60] Fourth, the "real"/Proverbs 31 ideal notes a fetish for femininity, which translates into attitudes and theologies about softness, submission, labor, and Black women's and girls' mouths. In her anthology *The Black Woman* (first published in 1970), Toni Cade Bambara writes the following about the 1960s social movement: "When a few toughminded, no-messin' around politico sisters began pushing for the right to participate in policy making, the right to help compose position papers for the emerging organization, the group leader would drop his voice into that mellow register specially reserved for . . . the incontinent . . . and say something about the need to be feminine and supportive and blah, blah, blah."[61] Nine years later, in her book *Black Macho and the Myth of the Superwoman* (1979), Michele Wallace argues that black political movements of the 1960s propagated a vicious view of Black women as emasculating, aggressive, and unnaturally independent.[62]

These representations, which are also present in the Black Church, enabled black male movement leaders and others to ignore black feminist challenges to their political agendas and to suppress Black women's ideas and ambitions for political leadership, thus limiting the scope and success of the movement. Simultaneously, Black women's legitimate frustrations with their unequal circumstances were seen as irrational, pathological, controlling, distracting, and out of the "natural" order. In an effort to avoid tropes of angry, domineering, and unfeminine womanhood, many Black women were discouraged from demanding equal consideration for their sociopolitical and socioeconomic needs within black political discourse and movements.[63] Similarly, when Jakes preaches about women not being feminine enough because they're tough, rough, nasty, mean, and aggressive, he's telling them to be quiet and to submit to oppression, and thus critiquing their disruption of the social order. Cisgender women's independence, for example, talking back; sexual freedom and decision-making; economic and career successes, which enable audacious self-assertion and authority over men; ability to pay for what they need (their "own damn steak," house, car, etc.) without the help of men; and alleged diminishing household, emotional, and sexual labor—for the benefit of men—are signs of black heteropatriarchal regress.

It's to say, Black women aren't playing their position in the backdrop or as the underclass within the black underclass in the public sphere. They aren't setting the dutiful euphonious atmosphere at home that some men would like and/or see as their right, as such an oasis is both owed to Black men, given the harshness of the world, and Black women's tax within the heteropatriarchal structure.[64] One might suggest that Jakes is preaching to his wife, Serita, and/or the women in his organizations. Regardless, there's an archive on demanding Black women and girls to create conflict-free spaces for Black cisgender heterosexual men, to maintain respectability, and to be quiet and charitable with their words, despite their needs. Turn on any reality television show with Black folks and watch the most decorated Black cisgender heterosexual woman shrink when chided for not being feminine or submissive enough, for being too career focused and/or masculine, for not having children, or for having too many "bodies."[65] She's admonished for not doing enough in the home to make her man (or future man or the men in her life) comfortable and happy.[66] And she's criticized for having "too much mouth." As often preached to women in the Black Church, "You'll get more with honey than vinegar."[67] Black women and girls are told that this sweetness, along with their wombs, sex, submission, and domesticity, is the power of "femininity": a woman's strength. And, as Jakes says, vital to "divine order."

This calls to mind toxic forms of femininity produced by black feminine-*ism*, for example, a "pick me," a cisgender heterosexual woman who seeks black male approval by expressing ideas that align with aspirational black heteropatriarchy and/or the script on "real"/Proverbs 31 womanhood, although detrimental. A "pick me" might attempt to gain attention and alliance through slut-shaming and victim-blaming; expressing antiwomen or LGBTQ+ politics or being against choice and/or pro–heteropatriarchal male dominance; or name-calling like referring to women as too aggressive, angry, domineering, or otherwise. A "pick me" might be the first standing and loudest "Amen!" during Jakes's Father's Day sermon. Perhaps this is a kind of survival, a way to avoid further damnation or being seen as unreasonable, problemed, or less of a woman. Whatever the case, whether "pick me," biblical womanhood, or the "real"/Proverbs 31 ideal, the script is largely the same and has taken on a life of its own, requiring critical interrogation and liberation.

I turn to a womanist biblical scholar who offers a critical analysis for undoing the religio-cultural heteropatriarchal reading of Proverbs 31. In "Commentary on Proverbs 31:10–31" (2015), Wil Gafney first positions the text and the author. She asserts that the collection of proverbial sayings, specifically chapters 30 and 31, are from non-Israelite sources, an unnamed mother of the unknown King Lemuel. Proverbs 31 opens with this:

> The words of king Lemuel, the prophecy that his mother taught him. What, my son? and what, the son of my womb? and what, the son of my vows? Give not thy strength unto women, nor thy ways to that which destroyeth kings. It is not for kings, O Lemuel, it is not for kings to drink wine; nor for princes strong drink: Lest they drink, and forget the law, and pervert the judgment of any of the afflicted. Give strong drink unto him that is ready to perish, and wine unto those that be of heavy hearts. Let him drink, and forget his poverty, and remember his misery no more. Open thy mouth for the dumb in the cause of all such as are appointed to destruction. Open thy mouth, judge righteously, and plead the cause of the poor and needy.[68]

Gafney writes, "The description of [the] woman the Queen Mother seeks as a royal match for her son may reflect how she sees herself. At one level the text is a royal woman's articulation of the characteristics she wants in a daughter-in-law. At other levels the text is part of the often patriarchal, always androcentric scriptures. . . . A close reading demonstrates that the woman being described is much more than a housewife on steroids."[69] In *Daughters of Miriam: Women Prophets in Ancient Israel* (2008), Gafney reads King Lemuel's mother as a prophet and oracle shaper through whom wisdom is sought and given. In this way, the Queen Mother is in the company of Nahum, Habakkuk, Isaiah, and others.[70] She first advises her son (verses 1–9), "Do not waste warrior strength (*chayil*) on king-destroying women" but instead "Find a woman whose strength matches his own" and "Be moderate in consumption so that his decrees on behalf of the oppressed will be clearheaded and just."[71] In other words, find an equal partner and don't drink too much to ensure wise and socially just decision-making. The text that follows (verses 10–31) offers instructions for choosing a wife.

It's unclear if the Queen Mother is married.[72] What she advises will make a fine partner-wife is unambiguous, however. The Queen Mother describes a suitable partner as "a warrior who brings home the spoils of war"[73] "resulting from a military campaign,"[74] a "hunter who can take her own prey,"[75] and someone who is ready and equipped for combat and thus "prepared to go to war at a moment's notice."[76] She is entrepreneurial, industrious, generous, wise, caring, considerate, attentive, and a craftsperson.[77] Above all, she is God-fearing. What she's not is an archetypal religio-cultural heteropatriarchal domestic queen, "pick me," what we've been taught about biblical womanhood, or Jakes's "real" woman. Gafney asserts, "The text does not present itself as descriptive of real women apart from the prospective mate. Yet this text is revered by many Jewish and Christian readers as presenting a wifely ideal. It is recited or chanted by many men or families to wives and mothers on Shabbat (Friday evening). It is the subject of Women's Day sermons, marriage retreats, and women's devotional literature."[78]

The woman's warrior strength, power, fight, intelligence, and hustle are commonly redacted. Gafney posits:

> Translations that erase this woman's physical strength and power create a construction of stereotypical "femininity" that is not present in the text. When the same word occurs in v 3 referring to the man, translators broadly agree[,] translating it nearly unanimously as: *Do not give your strength to women*. . . . As a general rule, Biblical Hebrew adjectives do not change meaning when applied to people (or animals or objects) of different genders. I translate v 3 as: *Do not give your warrior's strength to women* . . . and v 10 as: *Who can find a woman of warrior strength*, to demonstrate that

the Queen Mother is seeking a woman for her son who will match him strength for strength.[79]

With this reading in mind, it seems virtue for the Proverbs 31 woman lies in her warrior strength, industry, and partnership. The Queen Mother presents a woman who refuses to be prey, is an aggressor, and whose children call her blessed and Lord praises her because she protects her household and ensures the survival of herself and her family through hunting, combat, care, love, successful trading outside of the home, shrewd business practices, purchasing land, and independence, all while caring for the destitute—and dressing to the nines when she so chooses.[80] It's the entirety of her being that makes her priceless. Evangelical Christians who place emphasis on biblical inerrancy should appreciate this. However, something tells me that socially and culturally constructed heteropatriarchal feminine ideals eclipse any biblical and otherwise meaning pointing to women's warrior strength, socioeconomic independence, landowning, combat, and partnership.[81] The preference for submissive, chaste, and soft women in need of saving who make men feel manly is far greater.

It's also not lost on me that I've never heard the Queen Mother's charge to her son, to find an equal partner and not to drink too much to ensure wise and socially just decision-making, emphasized in my experience. Perhaps I missed all of the sermons, conferences, films, songs, workbooks, and special days that made being a desirable, woman-approved man and husband/in the making a priority in the Black Church. It would be fascinating to see a mass production of religio-cultural products and theologies on Black cisgender heterosexual men's and boys' trustworthiness, desirability, marriageability, partnership, wholesomeness, reproduction, nurturing, childcare, domesticity, and generosity, and how they might create loving, noncompetitive, and conflict-free homes, institutions, communities, and otherwise. This is the Father's Day and Mother's Day sermon Black folks need.

When Jakes's Father's Day sermon was released, an article titled "Pastor T. D. Jakes Says Families Are Lost Because 'We Are Raising Up Women to Be Men'" caught my attention. Optimus Fine @sunnydaejones tweeted in response:

> TD Jakes and all the other Black mega pastors spent 20 years telling Black women to know their worth, get educated, and wait in our prayer closets for our husbands. Now in 2022, we changing the rules because men don't measure up to what y'all were telling US to do. . . . Cause how quickly we forget the woman's conferences. The sermon series. The books. The lock ins. Y'all told us the only men we needed was God and our husband. But now the man who is not God OR a husband also needs to feel

important. So here we are. . . . Did men close their bibles cause they don't feel needed? Did the Word change? What happened to "equally yoked"? What happened to Proverbs 31? What had happened was . . . men now have to rise to the bar they set for women. So now we don't live by those scriptures no more. . . . If the conference tickets not selling like they used to, just say that. But where in the Bible does it say a woman needs to create a need for a man so he wont punk out and run away from his commitment? What scripture say that. . . . How bout this? BLACK WOMEN NO MORE TITHING TO THESE CHURCHES OR BUYING THESE PASTORS BOOKS OR SUPPORTING THESE FEMININITY COACHES AND DROP SHIPPING BUSINESSES. Since our success is losing families.[82]

However, neither the heterosexist cultural reading nor the womanist reading of Proverbs 31 is a good look for cisgender men. The critical reader is left to wonder what the man and/or husband is doing all day. One might suggest that the woman or potential wife "level up." His labor, hustle, strength, and energy aren't matching hers. Going back to Nikki Giovanni, Toni Cade Bambara, and Michele Wallace, Black women and girls deserve equity and mutuality—in their partnerships, households, and labor and in terms of their sociopolitical and socioeconomic needs. Black Christian heteropatriarchal order won't do, and having a penis clearly ain't enough. If Black women and girls must "create a need" for Black men to feel like "real" men, then manhood and/or "realness" may not be reducible to biology. Wholeness and identities, for whatever gender or sexuality, thrive beyond scripts and in relation.

Momma the Warrior: Worth Far More Than Feminine Ideals

Writing this chapter had me thinking quite a lot about how Momma fit or didn't fit and/or resisted the "real"/Proverbs 31 ideal. She presented a site of tension for me as well as an opening to consider alternatives for womanhood and mothering. Momma was born into a context that had recently survived the Great Migration, the Great Depression, and World War II. She was raised in the Bronx River Projects in New York City and was just six years old when *Brown v. Board of Education* was decided; seven when Emmett Till was murdered; a teenager when President John F. Kennedy was assassinated and when Addie May Collins, Carol Denise McNair, Cynthia Wesley, and Carole Rosamond Robertson were murdered at 16th Street Baptist Church in Birmingham, Alabama; came of age when President Lyndon Johnson signed the Voting Rights Act into law;

and entered adulthood when Martin Luther King Jr. was assassinated, President Richard Nixon was inaugurated, legal segregation was outlawed, the Vietnam War finally ended, and *Roe* was decided. As racism and new labor technology eliminated semiskilled and unskilled jobs, black unemployment in the Bronx and other northern urban inner cities increased, exacerbating abject poverty, substandard living conditions, and redlining, locking many Black folks out of the modes of production necessary for survival and quality of life.

Race, sex, gender, and class made Momma especially vulnerable to violence, exploitation, trauma, and a range of other sociopolitical and socioeconomic disinvestments in the overcrowded projects that she grew up in. In addition to racial deprivation there was intracommunal domestic abuse, assault, alcoholism, mental illness, and abandonment. As my grandfather repeated a sequence of deserting and returning to the family, my grandmother, a former singer and pianist turned stuck-at-home mother of seven, did the best she could in their tiny public housing apartment. When my uncle, the eldest sibling, left for the Vietnam War, eventually returning to America but leaving the family—emotionally and physically—for good, Momma, the second in line, was forced to become an adult before her time, as she became the caretaker and much more for her younger siblings. To say her early years were no crystal stair is an understatement. Both white supremacist capitalist patriarchy and aspirational black patriarchy failed her. Momma was forced to fend for herself and care for others while just a girl. Her need and will to survive as a Black girl—too soon turned woman—in the underbelly of a deserted American inner city necessarily made Momma a fighter. Besides surviving the intersecting outcomes of misogynoir, the Bronx, which was a kind of war in the middle to late twentieth century, helping my grandmother protect and preserve her household, and ensuring the survival of her younger siblings, Momma stayed ready for combat when it came to her dignity or me and my siblings.

She honored herself foremost by refusing to take shit from anyone. Momma had to be tough, rough, and aggressive to live. Though I never saw her in a physical fight, I'm sure she'd win. When I was kicked out of Girl Scouts in second grade for refusing to allow the troop leader to continue mispronouncing my name, it was Momma that rebuked her on my behalf. And even though she didn't explicitly share this with me back then, Momma understood that Black girls are born into combat zones that fire all kinds of lethal meanings at their bodies. She resisted this the best way she knew how. I call her blessed and a "good" woman and mother not because of her softness, childbearing, domesticity, marriageability, or purity. This world makes it difficult for Black women and girls to access social interpretations of the hindmost, anyway. And

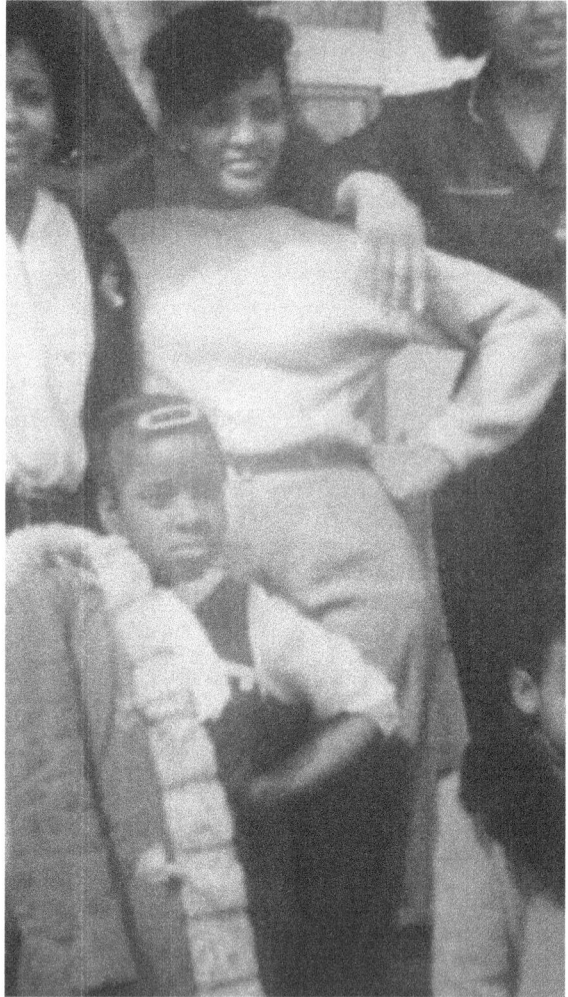

FIGURE 4.1. This is one of my favorite pictures of me and Momma. We had no idea we were posing alike. This was taken in Syracuse, New York. I'm approximately seven or eight years old. Photo taken by a family member.

unbeknownst to Momma, I certainly didn't have a chance at it. More, Momma wasn't all that domestic when I was growing up, so her strength wasn't crafts, trading, or cleaning. But that's her story to tell. Nor was it entrepreneurship, industry, or landowning. This aspect of the Proverbs 31 woman is class specific and doesn't consider what it means to be a Black girl raised in the projects in twentieth-century America.

Nevertheless, Momma is blessed because through her determination, resistance, survival, and love of self and us, she created new worlds. Momma saw our lives as having sacred meaning and potential and insisted that the future yield to her prayers. She spoke Jeremiah 29:11 over me almost daily and likely

FIGURE 4.2. Me and Momma at my wedding. She called this her "dream wedding." Photo taken by a family member.

still does. It was her prophetic wisdom to speak vision, purpose, and grace over my life when I needed it most and to offer warrior strength protections and affirmations when I needed to feel them most that guided me into womanhood. Black girls need somebody who will claim the future for them.

I couldn't have outlived my teen years without her. Momma taught me to be futuristic and to pray, fight, persist—and dress. And though she was no feminist, I wouldn't be a black feminist without her example. Momma laid the foundation in her own way. She was never one to shrink or hold her tongue, and she never attempted to silence mine. I still recall her response in the parent-teacher meeting held for me in middle school. She came dressed head to toe, first of all. My friends raved about how pretty she was and how she looked like Clair Huxtable. But second, upon hearing what the meeting was about, Momma cocked her pretty head, squinted her gorgeous yet fiery eyes, and said, "I know you didn't call me up here for this . . . because my daughter is proud?! What's she supposed to do? Walk around with her head down?!" And with that Momma ended the parent-teacher meeting, put the misogynoirist teachers in their place, and sent me back to class with my self-esteem intact and emboldened. Black girls need mommas who will ride for them.

Though my homelife was structured in benevolent heteropatriarchy, Momma is in no way docile. Her faith leads her to respect some version of submission, and she trusts Daddy to lead the family. However, she never existed in service to him. They always served and honored each other. Momma resisted and stood up for herself, including to Daddy, when she saw fit. And she never feigned harmony or sweetness for him or us. Momma said what needed saying, how she felt like saying it. She instilled talking back in me—as a political practice and an assertion of power, equity, authority, interrogation, oppositionality, and challenge to hierarchy through knowledge, opinion, disagreement, pedagogy, and storytelling—long before I ever read bell hooks or any other black feminist. Not only did Momma not spare anyone her tongue, but she also shared her personal stories with me from a critical lens that was raw, honest, fearless, and ofttimes disrespectable, countering other performances of respectability. It was as if she was revealing a struggle between two versions of herself: her inner "Bronx River Girl" who survived and the "real"/Proverbs 31 ideal that evangelical Christianity said that she should be.

Perhaps these subversive moments hoped to push me toward the radical politics and possibilities of black feminism that she couldn't access at the time. I'm not sure. What I know is that Momma's unfiltered personal/political narratives about her life and struggles as a Black girl empowered my voice, defiance, and agency as a Black girl. Sharing the ugly and complicated with me and how she fought through it let me know that I would be OK, that life is to be lived, and sometimes things are messy. Biblical and Proverbs 31 womanhood don't allow for that. At any rate, I'm thankful that she and Daddy inserted a fighting spirit in me in their own complex ways. I wish I could've shared more with Momma and that she knew the power and salvation of her honest talk back then. Momma curated an imperfect vision of freedom for me. I say imperfect because Momma both resisted and accommodated patriarchy. The Combahee River Collective argues that Black women are forced to choose their battles. Many decide against creating ruptures at home and/or with the Black men in their life for the sake of self-care, love, capacity, economic needs, and social acceptance. Also, heteropatriarchal and Proverbs 31 aspirations allow for legibility and rewards. Notwithstanding, Momma's dissidence taught me what I needed to know: Black girls must know how to fight, survive, resist, talk back, and call upon new futures.

Proverbs 31 *Still* Won't Cut It

Even with Gafney's radical reading of the Proverbs 31 warrior woman, the formula still won't work for me. She asserts, the figure is a form of orthodoxy produced only in terms of a prospective mate and is thus grounded in heteropatriarchy and nonviable ideas of service. In the end, the text is still about men choosing a wife. Even the warrior woman's value is located in her womb, male approval, and domesticity. Cheryl Kirk-Duggan argues, the Proverbs 31 woman is overcaring, unrealistic, and unhealthily overvigilant.[83] Black women and girls aren't mere objects waiting to be found, picked, chosen, or placed into a puzzle to make aspirational black patriarchy sound.[84] Though some may desire exactly that, we also make choices, beyond and with/in our bodies, relationships, and otherwise. Let's let King Lemuel have the woman his mother fantasied for him, if he so chooses, or let's give her back to the Queen Mother's imagination. And let's let Jakes and others work through what they're working through. "Real" manhood is in a crisis, and it's not because of Black women and girls, nor is it ours to fix.

We need other ways to engage womanhood outside of childbirth, periods, sexuality, biology, and traditional forms of femininity so that Black women and girls, collectively, can cooperatively and unapologetically develop social justice discourses and strategies to combat that which impacts all of us, namely, violence, sociopolitical and socioeconomic disenfranchisement, sexism, misogynoir, transphobia, heteropatriarchy, homophobia, and the lack of reproductive justice and other women's rights. The strength of Black women and girls is in how we create more just, powerful, and loving experiences, encounters and communities, how we embrace our full humanity and that of others, and how we bust up fantasies of what's "real." Anything that fails to affirm our sacredness, autonomy, and self-possession can go. We don't need it. Withal, I wish to preserve Gafney's notion of women's and girls' warrior strength, combat, prophetic voice, intelligence, industry, hustle, spirituality, shrewd entrepreneurship and business practices, and right to equity and land, as well as their capacities to hunt, love, and dress themselves fiercely. And I invite Black women and girls to be rough, nasty, aggressive, loud, creative, critically conscious, self-defining, and powerfully feminist in their politics and survival—because that's what living here requires. On the same note, I honor care, pleasure, and gentle living. On top of lacking language on mutuality, autonomy, safety, and sovereignty, Proverbs 31 leaves no room for self-care and play. We never see the warrior woman cared for, honored, pleased, amused, luxuriating, or resting. Black women and girls need idle time, a good "kee-kee" (gossipy laughter), gratification, tender and attentive bonds, revolutionary refreshment, to feel beautiful, and to freely take up space without expectation, damnation, or consequence. And as with our survival mechanisms, we demand to define what this looks and feels like for ourselves.

5

Ordinary or Insurgent?

From Toxic Femininity to Revolutionary Mothering

Dear Black Girl: I know the world says your vertex is love, marriage, and a baby carriage. I need you to know that you're called to something more. Foremost, loving and mothering can be magical if you want it, with the right partner, and in a context of freedom. Next, please pay limitations dust (no mind). Your crown isn't in the patriarchy but rather how you choose to participate in emancipatory worldmaking for Black folks. These are repressive times. As the world insists on your labor and ingenuity, it exploits and blocks your power to will new realities, foundations, and spheres. Yet, your mother, grandmothers, othermothers, and the ancestors collaborated with the future for you to birth a revolution. Will you be ordinary or insurgent? While the former is conventional and seemingly less risky, the latter gratifies as it makes black love powerful, makes the world begin again, and nurtures yourself and others into y/our/their own freedom.[1] Neither will be easy.

Love,
TL

I stood in the shower long enough for all ten fingertips to wrinkle and the skin to blister and peel. It must've been an hour. I have a ritual of showering before bed because my overactive mind is known to ransack my sleep. The kiss and music of water soothe me. As I stood in the tranquility of the cascade, I was aggrieved by the recent news. Seven days before the most contested presidential election of our lives—forty-one days after Supreme Court Associate Justice Ruth Bader Ginsburg's death, and four years and seven months since President Obama nominated Merrick Garland for associate justice of the Supreme Court, to which Senate majority leader Mitch McConnell considered null and void because it was an election year—Amy Coney Barrett was confirmed and sworn in by political force, solidifying a 6–3 conservative majority Supreme Court of the United States for the next several decades.

Barrett, the former clerk and mentee of Associate Justice Antonin Scalia, an "originalist" like her mentor who held that judges should interpret the Constitution as the authors intended when originally written, spent most of her professional career in academia until the forty-fifth POTUS nominated her to the Seventh Circuit Court of Appeals in 2017 over and against other qualified candidates.[2] Effortlessly sashaying between white heteropatriarchy and evangelical Christian nationalism, power, piety, mediocrity, and entitlement, on one hand, while demanding hard work, hypermorality, and law and order from everyone else, on the other, Barrett represents a dangerous yet familiar kind of white traditional womanhood essential to repressive worldmaking. The kind that vexes the souls of Black women taught to work three times as hard to get half as much in hopes of surviving America, being seen as valuable, and participating equally, fully, and justly within the body politic. Stephanie Mencimer writes in *Mother Jones*:

> She had never been a judge, never worked in the government as a prosecutor, defense lawyer, solicitor general, or attorney general, or served as counsel to any legislative body—the usual professional channels that Supreme Court nominees tend to hail from. A graduate of Notre Dame law school, Barrett has almost no experience practicing law whatsoever—a hole in her resume so glaring that during her 7th Circuit confirmation hearing in 2017, Democratic members of the Senate Judiciary Committee were dismayed that she couldn't recall more than three cases she'd worked on during her brief two years in private practice.[3]

It bears noting that President Obama nominated Myra Selby—a Black woman and experienced commercial mediator and arbitrator with "a broad-based practice [focusing] in the areas of corporate internal investigations, appellate practice, compliance counseling, complex litigation, risk management, strategic and other legal advice"—to the Seventh Circuit Court of Appeals in early 2016. However, Selby's nomination was blocked by McConnell for reasons similar to his reasons for blocking Garland, which we know today had more to do with conservative court-packing than timing.

Selby not only aligned more closely with Ginsburg, who spent her life fighting for the rights of the likes of Barrett, but also was a participant in "several landmark decisions involving state property taxes, insurance and tort law reform"; the author of "more than 100 majority opinions receiving national recognition"; a visionary leader in increasing "the Court's accessibility to the public by expanding education and outreach activities"; the first woman and first Black American to serve as an associate justice on the Indiana Supreme Court; and the former chair of the Indiana Supreme Court Commission on Race and Gender Fairness.[4] That Ginsburg walked so that Barrett could run, while the white Christian supremacist capitalist heteropatriarchal power structure blocked Selby, was enough for a restless night. The time is never right to center a Black woman or girl. More, Black women and girls are regularly blocked from autonomy, equity, resources, and opportunities at all levels regardless of qualifications and experience, therefore hindering futures. Further, Black women and girls must be extraordinarily prodigious just to be recognized as second-rate. But most of all, women like Barrett will credit grit, destiny, superiority, grace, and good luck for their successes rather than racism, misogynoir, and heteropatriarchy while reproducing and maintaining a world that relishes in and survives off of terrorizing Black girls, women, mothers, and othermothers—yet needing our creativity and labor.

Barrett's unwavering stanning for Scalia, written opinions while in the Seventh Circuit Court of Appeals, posturing as America's neo-Victorian–Proverbs-31-"true"-woman-working-mom ideal, and breakneck nomination and confirmation by the forty-fifth POTUS just before the 2020 election inflamed my nerves. First, a conservative SCOTUS where originalists and Clarence Thomas hold the majority and seniority should concern us all, especially Black women and girls. Second, Scalia was no friend to social justice and/or imagining a more emancipatory world house for Black folks, women, and LGBTQ+ individuals and/or collectives. Third, here's what we learn by looking at Barrett's opinions: that she's against women's rights to choose; that she's for gun ownership, despite a person's criminal history; that she's fine with certain people losing their right to vote but not their right to legally own a gun; that she believes "the n-word is an egregious racial epithet" but does not enable a "hostile or abusive working environment"; that she thinks rape "boil[s] down to . . . 'he said/she said'"; that she's for immigration officials denying green cards to legal immigrants who use public benefits such as food stamps, Medicaid, and/or housing vouchers; that she's opposed to LGBTQ+ marriage; and that she's a conservative evangelical Christian with illiberal sex and gender views.[5]

Barrett's allegiances to Christian heteropatriarchal order leave women and girls across genders and sexualities and Black folks in general more vulnerable to varying structures of violence. Especially endangered are poor Black immigrant queer and/or transgender mothers and parents escaping violent contexts while also needing assistance. I'm reminded of my childhood summers in the Bronx River Projects and how so many Black and brown mothers fit this description. Undoubtedly, Barrett wasn't handpicked for the most prestigious credential in American law for either experience or abolitionist white feminism.[6] With our very democracy (despite however fragile), right to have elections, right to protest, women's rights, *Roe v. Wade*, affirmative action rights, immigration rights, LGBTQ+ rights, right to accessible and affordable health care, science, religious freedom, climate change, need for gun control, and right to be alive and joyous while living as Black people all on the line, Barrett is decisively not someone I'd call for help.[7] Not unless building a "Christian" democracy where women and nonwhites lack political power and bodily and sexual autonomy; or where evangelical Christian nationalism is the totalitarian governing and educational structure; or where far-right heteropatriarchal extremist misogynists are charged from the highest level of the state to "stand back and stand by" in counterprotests against radical freedom struggles for black lives, hence normalizing the long history of deputizing white citizens as a legal line of defense against nonwhite folks.[8] If these were my ambitions, Barrett would absolutely be my person.

Fourth, the display of white traditional femininity and innocence gives colonial vibes reminiscent of how white Christian slavers historically positioned themselves as philanthropic manifestations of the good while waving missus, overseer, law enforcement, and legislative wands that enabled the theft, kidnapping, destruction, captivity, terrorism, defilement, breeding, mutilation, broken kinships, disenfranchisement, and genocide of Black/African diasporic people trafficked to American shores. We know how antiblackness and misogynoir function together in illiberal law-and-order white supremacist capitalist heteropatriarchal transphobic conservative evangelical contexts. We also know where Black women and girls land in white supremacist oppressive regimes and states of massive destruction set on denying humanity, freedom, rights, agency, safety, and choice while concurrently using our bodies, labor, and male dominance and violence as normative modes of engagement.[9] We suffer most, tragically, from all angles, and often with a literal or figurative whip in one hand and a Bible and the law in the other.[10] Fifth, the role of white traditional womanhood and mothering in empire cannot be underestimated. The repetitious trotting out of Barrett's children—Vivian, Emma, Tess, Liam, Juliette, Benjamin, and John Peter (two of whom, Vivian and John Peter, often serving as visual bookends, were adopted from Haiti)—during the confirmation hearings was political.

I stood in the shower completely disjointed from time, staring into the steam, thinking about the world Barrett bequeathed, would likely maintain, and possibly envisioned. One thing's for sure: we inherited the same world but experience and hunger for something different. The impetus for this book was to talk back to the world that I inherited and imagine the one that I needed—from black girlhood to black motherhood. Nothing brought this more into focus than Barrett's ascension to the SCOTUS and what her motherhood and power means to white nationalist evangelical America, Black folks in general and Black women and girls in particular, and my location as a Black girl turned Black woman turned Black revolutionary mother to Black sons in an antiblack world. In this chapter I argue that all mothering is a political act. It's a collaboration with the future for children who will in some way rebegin the world, or at least the contexts around them. Such a coopetition may be repressive or revolutionary. Whether repressive, revolutionary, or a bit of each, this work is as much deliberate as it may be unconscious. If the family is a primary institution for political education, mothers have an opportunity to help remake the world in reverse or toward the future.[11] And sometimes we move backward or forward knowingly. No one person can maintain or stop white supremacist capitalist patriarchy, heterosexism, antiblackness, neofascism, homophobia, transantagonism, or misogynoir. And no individual can change the world. However, collectively we can participate in nurturing neofascist white supremacist capitalist heteropatriarchy or more emancipatory worldmaking.

I exited the shower, put on my favorite cotton pajamas, snuggled into my sleeping spouse, whose arms seem to await me even in his deepest slumber still after almost thirty years, and stared out the large moonlit window lining the bedroom wall. The massage of the steamy hot water didn't make me sleepy. I wondered: "Where're we headed?" "Who will love, center, protect, see, care for, value, and ensure the rights, power, and thriving of Black girls?" Black girls deserve worldmaking that tends to their humanity, futures, safety, joys, self-possession, dignity, traumas, choice, sexual subjectivity, voice, health/care, and emotional well-being. Anything less is a petition for their oppression and/or death. Going forward, I explore worldmaking through the lenses of "true" and "real" womanhood, toxic femininity, and how I came into black motherhood doing my best mimeograph of the Proverbs 31 ideal only to free myself to black feminist insurgency.

Worldmaking in Reverse (Part I): "True" (White) Women and White Feminine Futures

As I lay awake studying the moonlight, I was reminded of a tweet by Jamilah Lemieux after the "unite the right" white supremacist rally in Charlottesville, Virginia, on August 11, 2017, where members of the neo-Confederates, KKK, neo-Nazis, alt-right, neofascists, and other far-right white supremacist militias marched through the University of Virginia campus terrorizing onlookers with chants, fire, and violence. Lemieux wrote, "White women, don't think the Charlottesville photos let you off the hook for even a second. A lot of those men went home to cuddles and pie."[12] Of course, Heather D. Heyer, whose friends describe her as "a passionate advocate for the disenfranchised who was often moved to tears by the world's injustices," lost her life during the rally.[13] On that account, "not all white women" and/or mothers are included in Lemieux's critique—just enough to construct the socio-political-cultural-historical framing for "Karen" and her predecessor's "missus" and "Miss Ann," with each playing a seminal role in maintaining American bigotry and inciting black oppression and death.[14] In this world of "very fine people on both sides," weaponized white motherhood is a source of terrorism.[15] Namely, white traditional women and mothers have historically mechanized the law against Black folks specifically, as the law as originally written meant to do, and are thus nurturers of white/European empire and supremacy and "true" femininity and womanhood, which polices while requiring state protection and black genocide.[16]

"True" womanhood draws on nineteenth-century middle- and upper-class ideology on the cult of true womanhood, used to define "proper" Protestant femininity in terms of the private sphere, domesticity, piety, purity, and submission, similar to the Victorian and Proverbs 31 ideals and also paralleling T. D. Jakes's "real" woman. Historical, religious, social, and cultural sources on "true" womanhood, such as magazines, speeches, politics, and sermons, advised women how to act, dress, speak, please men, mother, maintain their homes, and otherwise. However, dissimilar to Jakes's "real" woman, "true" and Victorian womanhood excluded Black women from its definitions of femininity. In the essay "Women and Capitalism: Dialectics of Oppression and Liberation," Angela Y. Davis asserts that white colonial women were charged with chastity, childbearing, sex with their husbands, and governing the private sphere. Conversely, Black/African slave women, who were interpreted as neither women nor feminine, were unprotected and unfree commodities to be bought, sold, bred, raped, and worked (domestically, externally, and otherwise).[17] Thus, the yearning for postbellum Black women and girls to access "proper," respectable, Proverbs 31, and Christocentric "real" womanhood ideals.[18] Davis holds that whereas white women oversaw and maintained the protective covering of the domestic sphere, white men were exalted as conquerors and workers in the public sphere. As such, white men and women have interpreted themselves as the supreme standard of mortals.

To this end, humanity is deemed inherent in "true" (white) womanhood and manhood whereas it's a sociopolitical and cultural pursuit in "real" (black) womanhood and manhood. Therefore, I use "true" manhood to refer to white traditional manhood. I also apply "true" (white) manhood and womanhood to distinguish between them and "real" (black) manhood. Additionally, I deploy "traditional" and "reactionary" to underline adjacency to and/or support of heteropatriarchy. Ergo, "traditional" and "reactionary" may highlight the social role of "true" white womanhood and manhood as well as "real" black womanhood and manhood in contemporary worldmaking in North America. Also, though "true" women were historically fantasied as middle- and upper-class Protestant domestic queens of the private sphere, World War II restructured both the homelife and the labor market, requiring many "true" women to work wartime jobs outside of the home. Once the war ended, many "true" women retreated to their homes. However, many others continued to work in both the public and private sphere. My usage notes this nuance, particularly as the 1980s Christian fundamentalist takeover re/presented interests in the "true" woman childbearing domestic goddess, despite many white women working both outside of the home and in the home, also known as the second shift. Further, I use "true" womanhood to discuss those who contemporarily deploy white traditional and/or reactionary toxic femininity, which is political, to enforce white supremacist capitalist heteropatriarchal household politics within the public sphere.

Such politics prioritize white cisgender heteropatriarchal needs and wants over and against everyone else's, engaging in social, political, cultural, and economic forms of black oppression, death, and worldmaking. We don't have to look far for this. A defining feature of white supremacist capitalist heteropatriarchy is its subjection and leverage of and support from white women. For example, white traditional mothers are at the forefront of changing American politics. Over 55 percent of white women who vote voted for the forty-fifth POTUS in 2020 for a second term.[19] Of the white evangelical voters who voted, between 76 and 81 percent voted for the forty-fifth POTUS.[20] White women also had prominent roles in the January 6 "Stop the Steal" insurrection. They help fund and organize extremist groups and militias. They mass mediate conservative messaging through news outlets, websites, and social media.[21] And groups like Moms for Liberty are dismantling public education through book banning and burning and making curricula on race, sex, gender, sexuality, diversity, and otherwise illegal. Much of this is unsurprising. White traditional women supported slavery and Jim Crow, even if it meant supporting their own oppression. For some, second-best citizenry is better than no place at all—because if white heteropatriarchal men aren't in a dominant social position, white women aren't either.

There's a misguided belief that white people will lose power and privilege if Black folks achieve equity. This makes the trope of the black boogeyman/woman/person extremely productive. Problematizing Black people as social dangers necessitates the deputization of white citizenry across genders and sexualities, which historically originated to keep Black folks in line, to protect whiteness as property and power, and to safeguard white wealth.[22] The merging of militarized police, a white nationalist government, and white people who function as the police, whether or not it's their paid job, works similarly: to offer protections from those perceived as threatening. Particularly vulnerable to the imagined big black monster trope are white women, white womanhood, and white femininity: thus, white women's personal use of the police to endanger Black people doing normal and lawful things like swimming, barbequing, walking, bird watching, sitting, and breathing. These aren't isolated events. We must consider them within the history of racism. This collective view makes Barrett significant. She's a white conservative Christian mother with deep affiliations in the People of Praise, whose "2010 directory shows Barrett served as a 'handmaid,' a key female adviser to another female member."[23] She's also the highest representation of the law with important and corresponding views on sex, gender, sexuality, immigration, rape, race, and otherwise. While freedom of religion is proposed as a basic right in America, charismatic conservative Christian dogma is hardly a personal matter. It's juridical.

One can only wonder what this means for her Black daughter, Vivian, and Black son, John Peter. I won't pretend to know the inner workings of their homelife and relationships. My wish for Vivian and John Peter is that they're happy and whole. However, Barrett's description of Vivian during her Senate Judiciary Committee opening statement is telling. Some saw a loving and devoted mom describing her children. Others noted an exemplary postracial traditionalist Christian motherhood. I was immediately reminded of the backhanded gaslighting compliments that nice white Christians often reserve for Black folks, particularly Black girls; how normalized misogynoir-ist language constructs taken-for-granted literacies that hurt us and distort our humanity; and how these harmful ideologies participate in worldmaking. Barrett posited:

> Emma is a sophomore in college who just might follow her parents into a career in the law. . . . Next is Vivian, who came to us from Haiti. When Vivian arrived, she was so weak that we were told she might never talk or walk normally. But now she deadlifts as much as the male athletes at our gym, and I assure you that she has no trouble talking. . . . Tess is 16, and while she shares her parents' love for the liberal arts, she also has a math gene that seems to have skipped her parents' generation. . . . John Peter joined us shortly after the devastating earthquake in Haiti, and Jesse, who brought him home, still describes the shock on JP's face when he got off the plane in wintertime Chicago. . . . Once that shock wore off, JP assumed the happy-go-lucky attitude that is still his signature trait. . . . Liam is smart, strong, and kind, and to our delight, he still loves watch-ing movies with Mom and Dad. . . . Ten-year-old Juliet is already pursu-ing her goal of becoming an author by writing multiple essays and short stories, one of which she recently submitted for publication. And our youngest, Benjamin, is at home with friends. Benjamin has Down syn-drome and he is the unanimous favorite of the family.[24]

While Vivian and John Peter are illustrated in reductive bodies and smiles, their siblings get to be brilliant, and their parents, saviors. Holding history and Barrett's originalism, legal opinions, and statement on her children in tension, I was left with more questions than answers.

What else has Barrett said about Vivian's speech, walk, body, or strength? Does she tell Vivian that she talks too much while proudly allowing Emma and Tess to ramble on? How does Barrett know that Vivian can deadlift as much as the male athletes in her gym? Does she scuttle Vivian out to compete against them?[25] Does Barrett refer to Vivian as threatening when she's angry? Does Viv-ian get to be angry? Does Barrett project white Western ideas of "true" woman-hood and beauty onto Vivian? Does Vivian know about rape culture? Is Vivian told to fend for herself or to ignore pain and/or illness because she's strong? Is her strength used to differentiate her femininity against stereotypical ideas of "true" women's softness and delicacy? Does Vivian get to be the center of attention? What are her intellectual strengths and goals? Does Barrett tell Viv-ian how smart she is? Is Vivian being tutored to become a handmaid, too? Has she seen *The Handmaid's Tale*? How does she experience her mother as both a handmaid and representative of the law? Does the family affirm the fullness of Vivian's being? Who does Vivian turn to if she has sex or needs birth control? Is the sexual part of her being cut off?

And do the Black Barrett children see Haiti as a "shithole country"?[26] What do they think of immigrants who need assistance? Do they know that black is beautiful? What if they're called the N-word while out in the world? Are they told to brush it off because words are neither hostile nor abusive? Do they know about North American slavery, black resistance mechanisms and histories, or the Haitian Revolution? What if they're queer? How do the Barretts engage blackness with or in front of Vivian and John Peter? What do Vivian and John Peter know about white history and, specifically, the history of white supremacist capitalist heteropatriarchy, which includes both white women and Christianity? Are they allowed to process antiblack racial and gendered dehumanization, violence, and other trauma? Are they forced to smile through pain like the man formerly known as Andre played by Lakeith Stanfield in Jordan Peele's film *Get Out* (2017)? Do they have thoughts on their mother's originalism? Do they know her political beliefs and legal opinions originate in sources and people that would've excluded them as humans? Did they support their mother's SCOTUS votes against affirmative action and *Roe v. Wade*? Are they against science, efforts to address global warming, and black freedom? What kind of world do they believe their mother is making for them and people who look like them?

Senate majority leader McConnell referred to Barrett as "a woman of unparalleled ability and temperament."[27] Given that her ability is mostly unknown, it seems that her conservative Christian values, "true" femininity, and allegiance to the right are what really matters. The last thing that conservative Christians and the political right want is a defiant "nasty" and "aggressive" woman on the Supreme Court who speaks her mind, says what she and other women need, and demands equity. This sounds a lot like Associate Justice Ketanji Onyika Brown, nominated to the SCOTUS by President Joe Biden on February 25, 2022, and confirmed on April 7, 2022, as the first Black woman Supreme Court justice by the U.S. Senate, with a vote of 53 to 47. As an undergraduate at Harvard University, Brown participated in the Black Students Association, led protests against racism and for the hiring of Black faculty, and produced a senior thesis titled "The Hand of Oppression: Plea Bargaining Processes and the Coercion of Criminal Defendants." As a public defender after attending Harvard Law School, Brown shortened and erased unfair prison terms for crack cocaine offenses.[28] During her time on the United States District Court for the District of Columbia, she reminded forty-five that "presidents are not kings."[29]

Barrett, the perfect blend of public power, private domesticity, maternal "virtue," loyalty, and felicitous juridical opinions and ambition, serves as a site for new age "true" womanly duties and the significant place of white womanhood in making America great again. And just as blackness is propped up in culture to serve as an "Other" to whiteness, Vivian takes up similar space in Barrett's speech. Similarly, Barrett's ability, temperament, and "true" womanhood stand in opposition to Black girls, women, mothers, and othermothers. Imagine, if you will, a Black liberal judge and mother of seven with Barrett's lack of experience being paraded around the Rose Garden as the hallmark of "ability and temperament." Now, visualize the collective with a present husband and father. Michelle Obama and all the times she was referred to as a slut and a whore provide a history lesson here. Though asserting herself as "mom-in-chief," FLOTUS Obama wasn't applauded for her maternal politics and virtue. America wasn't willing to see a Black woman as the symbol of womanhood and motherhood or to center her Black girls as the nation's children. Black girls, women, and mothers, married or not, have never been emblematic of moral order, aptness, or character in America.

If the past provides intel on the future like Octavia Butler says, such op/positioning and worldmaking could be nightmarish for even Vivian.[30] Some might say that world is already here, that the world Barrett is maintaining and may be envisioning is already operative. A world perhaps where white Christian nationalist politicians demolish what's left of democracy and build a governing structure based on a "superior" race and religion. A world perchance where white evangelical Christianity and the law justify and/or ignore the rape of Black women and girls.[31] A world possibly where marginalization, discrimination, intimidation, and violence are normalized and/or privatized forms of engagement with Black folks, women, LGBTQ+ individuals, and those deemed disposable, "Other," "unvirtuous," and/or weak.[32] Or maybe a world where white supremacist capitalist patriarchy is understood as the decisive divine mission of manifest destiny. Or perhaps a world led by a conservative and morally corrupt court structure, a police state, an assembly of local white vigilantes, and troops of frenzied "Christian soldiers" that enable and defend the murder of innocent Black people.[33] Or perchance a world where white women perform irreproachability while paying tariffs on undeserved successes and for the maintenance of social place by doing the bidding of the heteropatriarchy. Or percase a world where the rest of us fight to live or die—where such a fight for collective black humanity is seen as obscene, irrational, and criminal.[34]

I awoke the next morning from the restless slumber feeling an oncoming anxiety attack and lay glued to the bed, staring at the blank white ceiling. I was overstimulated by previous scenes and future possibilities of terror. Namely, the reality of Black folks in America and beyond, specifically Black women and girls, my Black sons, as well as what was happening at the southern border. Black people of the diaspora have our own relationship with the border. I wondered if the latest violences with Border Patrol might be a precursor for Black folks. Thinking the worst, my mind bounced between present-day anti-immigration practices and North American slavery—particularly, the slave trade's commitments to trafficking, violent sexual politics, and genocide; the commodification and sale of Black people; the tyrannizing of children ripped from their tortured parents' arms; shameless cages; dead children; dead adults; gutted families; motherless children and childless mothers. The different horrors have much symmetry. I traveled over a century in my head, landing on the 2020 year in review, where the public lynching of George Floyd and the home invasion and senseless murder of Breonna Taylor set the nation on fire; where the global pandemic snatched hundreds of thousands of lives; where presidential executive orders put forth barefaced lies about the nonexistence of structural and systemic racism and sexism; where newly minted Supreme Court justice Barrett failed to educate herself in any way about the oppressions of others, even as a veteran college educator and adoptive mother to Black children; where a president viciously hostile to women, feminist politics, and equal rights could still maintain a colossal base of white women; where the forced sterilization of Black mothers continues; where impoverished and unmarried Black mothers are ceaselessly pathologized; where illegal underground abortions are in our foreseeable future; and where possibilities for neofascism linger stronger than ever.

I queried silently: What is this world? What kind of ordinary everyday terror was Barrett selected to help create? How will her lack of experience be used against her or us or both? Will Barrett risk it all for the heteropatriarchy and feign innocence and ignorance while legislating more black pain? How will she use white power, girlhood, womanhood, and motherhood against the disinherited? What would Scalia do? What would the originalists want? What kind of dismay was the conservative court gearing up for? What would Barrett's inner religious circle say in private when they thought nobody was listening? How might they influence her decision-making? Do they have a say in her mothering? Maybe one day Vivian and John Peter will tell us how they survived being a Black girl and Black boy here. Maybe their stories will overlap. Maybe they'll be completely different.[35]

Worldmaking in Reverse (Part 2): "Real" (Black) Women and Black "Nuclear" Futures

I finally arose from bed, headed to the bathroom, and was halted by my image in the mirror. Was I always this girl, woman, and mother? No. Though not a powerful lawmaker like Barrett, and though toxic black femininity doesn't reproduce and maintain white supremacist capitalist heteropatriarchal dominion in the same way "true" womanhood and femininity do, it, like aspirational black patriarchy, does its own violent works, offering sustenance to and alignment with a retrograde world. My initial dance with motherhood negatively shifted and shaped other people's experiences around me at best. As a child, I didn't plan on or long for motherhood. I didn't play "house" or mommy to dolls. I understood the religio-cultural political scripts on "good" and "bad" black mothering growing up and didn't see myself represented on either side. Watching Clair Huxtable played by Felicia Rashad on *The Cosby Show* was the first time I ever considered motherhood as a possibility for myself, mostly because I saw Momma as the Bronx version of Huxtable's intelligence, beauty, and sass. Nevertheless, once I became a mother, I charged full speed ahead toward traditionalism: black feminine-*ism* personified.

"You're a 'real' woman now!" These words were offered by my peers and elders at church upon learning about my pregnancy with my elder son, Lee. Men did that weird James Evans from *Good Times* laugh as they fist-bumped my husband. Women encircled me with joyful hugs, well-wishes, smiles, tears, and advice on everything from breastfeeding to sleeping with a pregnancy pillow to weight gain to pregnancy sex to finally gaining entrée into bona fide womanhood. I'd crossed over into a new sororal order. Undoubtedly, Black folks partner, have sex, love, marry, procreate, and celebrate childbirth because each of these brings pleasure and joy and because connections and kinships are pivotal to living and community building. Convergently, my pregnancy "counted" and was celebrated because I was an expectant cisgender heterosexual upper-middle-class legally married Black woman. Black women who take this route are often seen as more valuable. Those who don't aspire to or realize this narrative may be interpreted as incomplete.

Dissimilar to recent tensions between Black transgender and cisgender women, which emphasize biology, blood, and childbirth, being a "real" woman in my Black Church context over twenty years ago wasn't innate or about my birth, cisgender identity, survival, or passage to adulthood or about my future child. "Real" womanhood on this occasion more closely related to Jakes's sermon. It was about the fact that I'd entered the next level up in a special club of black respectability. As a church elder said, I "did it right." For some, establishing a middle-class black "nuclear" family is agitational enough in neocolonial America because these kinds of families were never supposed to exist. Additionally, I was having what had been identified as a boy child—who'd be proudly named after his father and maternal grandfather. It was as if I was birthing a nation—a fresh bloodline to eventually lead the family, or maybe the race. A "real" Black man in-training to one day solve the war on black life, perhaps. Whatever the case, having a baby boy meant graduation into a new black world with honors—an authentication of my humanity, marred with both romantic delight and pragmatic anxiety. Questions abound. Specifically, what kind of mother would I be to this future Black boy? Would I raise him the "right" way? But if I'm "real" now, what was I before? And what if I mess things up or something tragic happens—am I no longer "real"?

I was twenty-six years old when I got pregnant with my elder son. Was the fetus in Momma that grew into me immaterial when she prayed over her womb? Was I not substantial when she gave birth to me? How about when I first cried out? Or when the doctor first placed me in Momma's arms? Was she not a historical fact until she married Daddy and gave birth to me? Did it matter that I was a girl? What about when Daddy used to hold me while watching the rain fall? Was I authentic then? Is there a special level in the great chain of being designated beneath Aristotle's "unrealized males" for Black baby girls? How was I not "real" all these years? As Jakes reminds us, the energetic drive to establish "real" black womanhood and motherhood remains potent. The enslaved woman or girl, forced into breeding, and thus symbolic of the market, transactions, expendability, unscrupulousness, and unmotherhood (rather than maternal virtue, respectability, and "true" womanhood), still haunts us.[36] We so badly want to be "real" to counter all the ways our personhood was distorted. As I argue elsewhere, politicians, from Thomas Jefferson to Ronald Reagan, and backward and onward, obsessed over defining Black women's and girls' so-called sexual depravity, which Reagan held (like Freud before him) led to pathology in children. The science of misogynoir serves as the basis for centuries of epistemological and ideological assault and moral and political panic.[37]

The discourse on oversexed, irresponsible, morally loose bad Black mothers carried over into black communities, specifically shaming and demonizing young, unmarried, and/or impoverished Black mothers for their reproductive experiences and histories.[38] And just as white/European empire required an "Other" to substantiate the mythology of white supremacy and "true" womanhood, Black young, destitute, and/or unmarried mothers are "Othered" to ground black respectability and differentiate between "real"/"good" and "bad" Black mommas, women, and girls. To look at it another way: while originalists valued slave women's and girls' motherhood and offspring only inasmuch as they could sell or work them to death, and while Black/African slave populations may have valued Black mothers and othermothers for pertinent roles played in their communities, contemporary communities may decrease this value, especially if the Black mother is teenage, poverty-stricken, and/or unmarried. An unmarried Black woman consenting to conceiving and mothering children today, regardless of socioeconomic class, may be villainized as depraved, and undeserving of respect, care, and support.[39] The ghosts of Daniel Patrick Moynihan, E. Franklin Frazier, and others, who put forth that matriarchal homes were too unnaturally independent, immoral, and emasculating, are still with us.[40]

Jakes proselytizes in his "family values" message that these women destroy their chances at finding a husband and torpedo their children's lives and futures. This critique is also linked to the disparagement of Black lesbian women and cisgender, transgender, intersexed, and gender nonconforming people who love, marry, and/or mother but don't adhere to the heteropatriarchy. The refusal to participate in and uphold the black "nuclear" project leaves some Black women and girls across gender identities and sexualities blameworthy for maintaining moral crookedness and the social ills of society. To be sure, choosing heterosexual love, marriage, and motherhood is emphatically not the issue. Making this women's most important achievement and means of currency, progress, and credibility is a problem. And weaponizing cisgender heterosexual marriage and childbearing against other ways of making families, loving, partnering, and parenting is an issue. We don't teach boys that their ultimate goal is to marry and nurture children. Boys are taught to attain power, not domesticity.

Notwithstanding, after giving birth to Lee, I personally didn't want to carry the burden of mothering a Black boy or loving a Black man the "wrong" way. When baby Lee was born, my spouse and I both worked in corporate America, making well over six figures, thanks to the technological boom, corporate mergers, and rising stock shares. This allowed me to eventually stay at home, which I decided to do after briefly returning to my wage-earning job once my maternity leave ended.[41] Assuming I should "pay" for staying at home, and in an effort to maintain value and perform "real" womanhood "properly," I attempted to enforce a more rigid idea of gender identity, gender roles, and parenting in our home—and to anybody who asked for my advice. My politics were isolating and judgmental. Though cleaning duties were shared, I thought childcare and meals should be solely my work. Additionally, after caring for baby Lee all day and preparing meals in the evening, I would get all dolled up just before my partner came home, just like on television, and have dinner waiting on the table. And like all the sexist memes suggest, I was sure to fix my spouse's plate first. I took extraordinary pride in making black America great again, modeling traditional black feminine virtue, domestic goddessing, doing my best Proverbs 31 rendition, serving my man, and uplifting the race.

This lasted all of a week. My spouse passionately, firmly, and lovingly resisted. His parents shared tasks and took the lead on things they loved and/or were better at, despite gender. And, perhaps most significant, his mother went back to school, earned a graduate degree, and pursued a career and job across the country—as a wife and mother of four and with the support of his father—when my husband was in eighth grade. One day at dinner he turned to me and said, "If you love doing *all* of this, fine, I guess . . . but don't do it for me. I don't expect this from you . . . and you know I didn't marry you for your cooking." We laughed. I'm a terrible cook and likely because I hate it and all other things domestic. Then I cried. Because while I should've been relieved, my limited vision of respectable and successful black married motherhood had just burst apart. "This is the *right* way," I thought. Yet, the entangling of my identity, womanhood, and motherhood with heteropatriarchy, Christianity, and socially constructed notions of femininity was strangling all of us. I was using the same paradigm of "proper" womanhood foisted onto other Black mothers in history and inflicting it on everyone in our household, including baby Lee, and beyond. It wasn't just about the cooking, childcare, and dress-up. It was about the classist hierarchy of aspirational black maternal and moral virtue and the supermothering heteropatriarchal Proverbs 31 Christian drag beneath it all that I was performing and weaponizing, the compassionate heteropatriarchal paradigm that I was designing for my partner, and the politics that I was soon to instill in and model for Lee.

My spouse was also letting me know that I wasn't to curb who he was and wanted to be: someone who loved cooking, nurturing, and caring for me and baby Lee, and partnering in our home.[42] Someone who didn't want to be restricted by racial and gendered fantasies of what's "real." Someone who wanted to express and enjoy his whole being and raise a free and whole Black boy rather than construct additional prisons. Someone who rejects the binary notion that emotional and household care is women's work and providing material needs is men's work. bell hooks posits that patriarchal men are disinterested in being caretakers.[43] However, in *New Black Man* (2015), Mark Anthony Neal writes that present and partnering fathers in all day-to-day activities, including the division of household labor, are significant, despite gender restrictions, because collaboration in the home offers images and expectations of mutual respect and cooperation. As long as masculinity identifies nurture and care as feminine and unmanly, men's socialization will work against them rather than for them.[44] I'd communicated that domesticity and childcare were unmanly and that children don't need nurture from fathers. My spouse responded by conveying that this should be shared, and there was more to him, to me, and baby Lee.

There's an expectation to parent cisgender Black boys in proximity to the heteropatriarchy to make them tougher, responsible, "properly" masculine, and able to face and withstand antiblackness and white supremacist capitalist patriarchy. The gag is that white mothers are given the same charge, although it's to uphold the white power structure. I'll never forget having a friend over from out of town and baby Lee started crying because he was wet. My friend and I were getting dressed to leave for dinner, so I took him to his father to change. My friend was visibly undone. "Shouldn't the baby be coming with us? Men don't know how to take care of children! That's not their job," she exclaimed. My husband caring for the baby meant rigging the heteropatriarchy and thus harming our son and my spouse's masculinity. These are no small matters. Black mothers carry a special kind of weight in "safely" and "properly" raising Black cisgender boys to men.[45] We're required to nurture endangered "real" Black men-to-be, who will one day deflect white bullets, avoid police encounters and the criminal justice system, fight neofascist oppression, counter racial stereotypes, outsmart the racial hunt, carry the family name, maintain heterosexist black sex and gender ideologies, attain capital, and live till they're old—in an America that sees them as monsters.

And though I have the best coparenting partner I could ever dream of, as historical and cultural narratives go, Black mothers are too often blamed for the outcomes of Black boys seen as monsters and/or crises. When adversity hits, whether it be a fall, a fall from grace, or a fall by might, the collective question typically asked is, "Well . . . where was the mother?" When twelve-year-old Tamir Rice was murdered, many asked why he was playing in the park alone and with a toy gun in the first place, emphasizing negligent mothering as opposed to a militaristic police state. When twenty-five-year-old Freddie Gray was murdered, media placed emphasis on his heroin-addicted mother once expelled from middle school to frame Gray as troubled. This line of thinking occurs intracommunally as well. When protesting for Gray, a former student and organizer posted the following on Facebook:

> To Black men at [Black Lives Matter] protests that say "black queens, protect our children from this violence." First of all, why are children only the mother's responsibility . . . protect your kids and protect us! We been holding everyone down while being at risk for the same violence

you think is exclusive to Black men. We're getting killed and you never hear our names in any of these protests. . . . Black queer, trans, disabled, fat, etc. Black women been grindin' for liberation! We're on the front lines, posting on social media, writing, documenting, working behind the scenes, organizing logistics, creating the hashtags you dilute the meaning of, and creating whole movements you exclude us from. You keep telling us to show up for you . . . when are you gonna show up for us? We've been waiting for you to see our pain, humanity, and worth! When will you let Black women speak on the mic at these rallies that are dominated by Black men preaching misogynistic bullshit? When will Black women matter without our worth being connected to our relationship with men? When will you start a protest for Mya Hall the way you will for Freddie Gray? When can we speak for ourselves and be heard?[46]

It's easier to blame Black women and mothers for America than to face racial and gender realism: the same white supremacist capitalist patriarchy that produced the Three-Fifths Compromise produced the Fourteenth Amendment, which, regardless of language, deprives Black folks of privileges, equal protection, due process, and otherwise. Keeping Rice and/or Gray in the house wouldn't have necessarily saved them. Ask Breonna Taylor.

Underneath questions about Rice and the preceding exchange about Black cisgender women and mothers protecting Black cisgender men and boys are questions that I've been asked frequently and bluntly: "Doesn't being a *good* mother stop this sort of thing from happening?" and "Doesn't being a *good* mother first and foremost mean keeping Black children safe, and especially Black America's precious and endangered Black sons?" Rarely is this line of questioning asked in moments of triumph or of Black fathers. Stories about Black men's and boys' success often lust for seminal Black father figures while stories of their demise immediately note their absence, placing blame on deficient Black mothers. Such narratives are ample. As a new mother, I didn't want to be in this number, to be scrutinized for "bad" mothering. Yet, limiting "good" black mothering to heteropatriarchal performances and/or keeping Black children alive is a tall order.

Dani McClain writes in her article "As a Black Mother, My Parenting Is Always Political" (2019) in *The Nation*:

Black women have had to inhabit a different understanding of motherhood in order to navigate American life. If we merely accepted the status quo and failed to challenge the forces that have kept Black people and women oppressed, then we participated in our own and our children's destruction. In recent years, this has become especially evident, as dozens of Black women and men have had to stand before television cameras reminding the world that their recently slain children were in fact human beings, were loved and sources of joy. The mothers of those killed by police or vigilante violence embody every Black mother's deepest fears: that we will not be able to adequately protect our children from or prepare them for a world that has to be convinced of their worth. Many parents speak of feeling more fear and anxiety once they take responsibility for keeping another human alive and well. But Black women especially know fear—how to live despite it and how to metabolize it for our children so that they're not consumed by it.[47]

In *Birthing Black Mothers* (2021), Jennifer Nash argues that the political and cultural discourse on black motherhood recently shifted away from a crisis of pathology and poverty toward black motherhood as a site of cultural interest, empathy, fascination, and support, which locates Black mothers in the death world, casting black motherhood as suffering, traumatized, and tragic due to state-sanctioned violence against Black children. Meaning that Black mothers, who are literally dying while giving birth, also await the death of their children by the state. In this way, black motherhood becomes legible only because of being proximate to death. I hold that Black mothers' hyperlegibility as pathological, ill-equipped, and proximate to black death—as well as their illegibility as good mothers—continues to work in concert. White supremacist capitalist heteropatriarchy in America stains the black maternal story and vice versa, prompting Black mothers to choose heteropatriarchy as a strategy of survival and legibility.

My partner's resistance to my toxic femininity freed us, making me a better partner and mother as well as a powerful inscriber of what my future motherhood might be for me. Toxic femininity had me placing emphasis on what I thought were my partner's needs, which served him, though poorly, but not me or baby Lee. I prioritized and essentialized my husband in the household the same way that black social movements prioritize Black men and boys and pigeonhole black masculinity/ies. In parallel, I erased myself, my experiences and needs, and accordingly Black women and girls, trying to make self-designated sexism and extraordinary heteropatriarchal mothering compelling. I was on my way to terrorizing my family and others with a brand of femininity that was oppositional to Black girls' freedom, safety, autonomy, and emancipatory worldmaking. Moreover, enforcing heteropatriarchy as a normative paradigm for child-rearing not only limits identity, expression, and needs but harvests possibilities for reproducing and partaking in misogynoir, homophobia, transantagonism, effemiphobia, and otherwise, particularly intracommunally. To be clear, a proviso for "good" aspirational black heteropatriarchal mothering, particularly of Black boys, is keeping them cisgender and heterosexual.[48]

By the time my second son, Seth, was born, I'd found black feminism. When Lee and Seth were about three and one years old, I'd habitually wear a T-shirt that read, "ain't I a woman," in honor of Sojourner Truth. It intentionally welcomed difficult conversation around race, gender, and feminism. I was regularly asked some iteration of "What does it mean to be a black feminist mother raising Black boys?" This was almost always an antagonistic query rooted in anxieties around hegemonic effemiphobic heterosexist assumptions about black femininity, masculinity, and sexuality, as well as Black women's and mothers' duty to #protectblackmen and boys.[49] What I was really being asked was, as one person inquired during a routine visit to the local barbershop, are you raising "'real' Black men" (to be) or are you "feminizing future kings" with "white feminism"?[50] That is, am I raising Black boys to men—living under the constant threat of violence, police harassment, misrecognition, emasculation, depression, illness, a lack of health/care, poverty, an unjust criminal system, false accusation and imprisonment, hunger, substandard living conditions, a paucity of jobs and career opportunities, unemployment and/or low pay, a poor educational structure and preschool-to-prison pipelining, an overall lack of safety, and emotional neglect—to dominate, rule, lead, control, be strong, be hard, and under no circumstances show weakness, vulnerability, emotionality, femininity, or frailty? In other words, am I taking my job of rearing the race's precious cisgender hetero jewels seriously? My answer to the latter is categorically yes. I take mothering very seriously, which presently means, for me, rejecting toxic femininity, heteropatriarchy, Christocentric traditionalist black feminine-*ism*, structures of dominance, toxic masculinity, and otherwise.

To make it plain: toxic femininity may produce toxic children, and in my case toxic Black sons, who may in turn reproduce toxic worlds, which foremost harm themselves but also Black cisgender, transgender, nonbinary, and queer girls and people, especially as toxicity translates socially, politically, communally, culturally, and beyond. Toxic cisgender masculinities and femininities produce violence because the binary gender boxes folks are forced to live in are fraudulent. Facing the fact that cisgender heteronormativity is the tax paid to be semiaccepted here, as it's a tool of the "nuclear" religio-political project and empire, may be devastating to some and enraging for others. Still, the notion of cisgender heteronormative superiority hinges on the denial and dehumanization of whole populations. Our discomfort with the presences of Black transgender, gender-neutral, nonbinary, questioning, gender-fluid, lesbian, gay, bisexual, and queer folks leads to panic and thus violence, adding to the black genocidal story. Black cisgender folks can be endangering intraracially, too. Baldwin notes that as we try to limit the definitions and expressions of others, we concurrently create narrow, harmful, and destructive boxes for ourselves.[51] Circling back to current tensions between Black cisgender and transgender women, it's deeply troubling to watch Black cisgender women and mothers use social media platforms to fortify black binary heteronormative sex and gender ideologies against Black transgender women in particular, hence rallying a cult of toxic cisgender hypermasculine and hyperfeminine violence against Black transgender women. There are many ways of being, embodying, living, identifying, loving, and relating.

And mothers certainly aren't solely to blame for toxic children or adults. I dare not place all that on Black mothers' backs. All parents, kinships, histories, politics, media, along with other cultural mediums inform who we become. Some of us work counter to what we've been taught—for good or bad. We have an opportunity to maintain social place by doing the bidding of heteropatriarchy or something altogether radically different. Black heteropatriarchal "nuclear" futures won't stop racial suffering or make the governing structure value Black peoples' lives any more. Black people across genders, sexualities, and class are human, important, and invited into sanctuary because we say so. Black possibilities for knowing, valuing, loving, fulfillment, happiness, making and choosing kinships, and communing are expansive and meaningful because we say so.

Worldmaking in Anticipation: Revolutionary Mothering and Othermothering

I want a different world than the one I was imparted. I don't want a world shaped by traditional or reactionary toxic femininity. Neither do I want the past or the future that made Barrett, or that grounds the irony in her originalist claims. Primary slave sources and historical personal journals, medical accounts, and political notes concede what originalists thought of Black/African people, and particularly Black/African women, girls, mothers, and othermothers, and the kind of world they thought was most suitable. I don't want a world structured in neocoloniality, antiblackness, misogynoir, heteropatriarchy, legalized rape culture, forced pregnancies, hostagacy, death camps, trafficking, gun enthusiasm, neofascism, authoritarianism, socio-political-economic deprivation, manifest destiny, faux Christian virtue, toxic Christianity, Christian supremacy, "Christian" democracy, divine hierarchy, violence, homophobia, transphobia, xenophobia, white entitlement and fragility, and/or "true" or "real" womanhood or manhood.[52] Nor do I want a world that pretends to love and honor women and children through literacies on "pro-life" or that feigns white female and maternal virtue without critical historical nuance.[53]

This is the same world that vilifies fetal abortion while murdering living and breathing Black children in the street without cause or pause and that ripped nursing Black/African slave children from their mother's bosom to replace them with white babies whose mother's breasts were too sacred and delicate for the drudge work of feeding their own children. In this world, free and enslaved Black aunties, caretakers, and nurses knew white children better than their mothers did because they'd raised them. It's the same world where parents of over five hundred migrant children at the border couldn't be found and children from Guatemala, Honduras, and El Salvador were shoved into Mexico, a country that was not their own, without legal protections or, in many cases, guardians.[54] In this world, contrary to what some believe, neither Black nor brown children matter. This world, shaped by white supremacist capitalist heteropatriarchal conservative evangelical "true" womanhood and manhood, poses a threat to life, wellness, justice, and emancipatory world building because each requires a world informed by multiple interlocking and particularly antiblack oppressions.

A black feminist reading of both Barrett and my toxic femininity holds neither as the symbol of motherhood or pro-life. Pro-life "as is" is more honestly articulated as pro-heteropatriarchal-middle-and-upper-class-married-white-women's-pregnancy in the interest of empire and as emblematic of white male expansion, territory, and virility. What is pro-life in a context where Christian extremists pray for a neofascist legal structure that stands solidly against the rights of Black folks, women, and LGBTQ+ individuals while proudly justifying heteropatriarchal sexual assault and other violences?[55] Or, where Black women and girls lack reproductive justice? Or, where it's decided that innocent Black people, including children, deserve to die and are unworthy of safety or rights? I don't want a world where pro-life means white people, ends at birth for everyone else, is totalized by cisgender women's wombs, or is a sublimation for the moralizing of motherhood and naturalizing of patriarchy, each as patriotic duties. I want a world where Black girls, parents, and children in general live gloriously and freely into the future and where their futures are anticipated with goodwill.

Audre Lorde asserts that black mothering is a collaboration with the future—for children who aren't supposed to exist and need freedom from a violently destructive society. I hold that in contexts of rampant state-sanctioned and otherwise black genocide, revolutionary black mothering is a form of reproductive

FIGURE 5.1. This photo of me, Momma, my maternal grandmother, and my elder son is one of the few images I have of me pregnant and the only image of us together. The fat shaming I experienced in my youth and in high school in California led me to shun pictures. This was taken at my maternal grandmother's apartment in the Bronx River Projects in the Bronx, New York. I spent many days there with her. This was the last time I visited. Grandma fell ill not long after and moved to California with my parents. Photo taken by a family member.

justice, the zenith of pro-life.[56] Not only because Black people mother living socio-political-economically aborted children and adults every day but because revolutionary mothering intentionally centers collective freedom.[57] I want the world June Jordan dreamt of when she said that children are the ways the world begins again and again. In this world all Black people matter, black freedom is a virtue, the blackness of Black people is wonderful, the birth of all Black children is a cause for celebration into adulthood, the promise of mothering is in nurturing others into their own freedom, and the responsibility of all adults is to make love powerful, particularly in the face of a "dominating order that seeks to put love in opposition to power."[58] It's not enough to keep Black children alive and/or being anti–white supremacy or pro-black. When not radically intentional, pro-blackness can also be exclusive, essentialist, toxic, and aligned with the status quo, and in consequence a force of destruction. Bottom line: creating a more emancipatory world requires revolutionary practices.

FIGURE 5.2. This photo represents a release of my hair, body shame, and respectability politics. It was my first time wearing a bikini, early in my black feminist journey, and a vital turning point for me. I remember feeling so free but also wary of how I might be perceived in my relationships. My race, sex, gender, and sexuality politics were pressing against old traditional boundaries, and my father was particularly uncomfortable. We'd just had a very difficult conversation the day before. I was happy, but my heart was so heavy. Photo taken by my spouse.

In *Revolutionary Mothering: Love on the Front Lines* (2016), Alexis Pauline Gumbs posits, "Those of us who nurture the lives of those children who are not supposed to exist, who are not supposed to grow up, who are revolutionary in their very beings are doing some of the most subversive work in the world. If we don't know it, the establishment does."[59] The world I want reimagines black mothering, maternal politics, and maternal virtue as vital to abolition—the eradication of racism, misogynoir, homophobia, capitalism, transphobia, and more—and the birth of freedom. It takes its cues not from originalists, Barrett, "true" or "real" womanhood, the political economy, heteropatriarchy, or evangelical ministers but rather from the "Black midwives, granny midwives, unlicensed midwives who saved us as a people, and helped our communities give birth to revolutionaries, agitators, militants, freedom fighters," Sojourner Truth, Harriet Tubman, Ella Baker, Fannie Lou Hammer, Lorde, Jordan, and many others.[60] This isn't an overdetermination of black womanhood into motherhood. It's noting complementary communal interdependency, what Patricia Hill Collins means by othermothering—black mothering support networks rooted in colonial broken familial ties and the expansive pre- and neocolonial chosen kinships Black folks make in determining familial bonds and structures of support.[61] Concurrently, I mean to note the creative and necessary collective project of caring for Black folks in communities emotionally, financially, politically, physically, spiritually, and otherwise.

In the essay "The Meaning of Motherhood in Black Culture and Black Mother-Daughter Relationships" (1987) Collins asserts:

> One concept that has been constant throughout the history of African societies is the centrality of motherhood in religions, philosophies and social institutions. As Barbara Christian points out, "There is no doubt that motherhood is for most African people symbolic of creativity and continuity." . . . While the archetypal white, middle-class nuclear family conceptualizes family life as being divided into two oppositional spheres— the "male" sphere of economic providing and the "female" sphere of affective nurturing—this type of rigid sex role segregation was not part of the West African tradition. Mothering was not a privatized nurturing "occupation" reserved for biological mothers, and the economic support of children was not the exclusive responsibility of men. Instead, for African women, emotional care for children and providing for their physical survival was interwoven as interdependent, complementary dimensions of motherhood. . . . Finally, while the biological mother/child bond is valued, child care was a collective responsibility, a situation fostering cooperative, age stratified, women-centered "mothering" networks.[62]

Black othermothering moves across sex, genders, and sexualities and is inspired by the radical practices of mothers and othermothers (who welcome this designation) in the diaspora that provide extensive salvific, survival, creative, cooperative, and transformative networks, contexts, and sanctuaries for Black folks who weren't supposed to live, Black women who were never supposed to mother their own children, and Black children who were never supposed to survive.[63] Black revolutionary mothering and othermothering center the continuum and intersubjective relationships between Black girls, women, mothers, and othermothers and include and stand in the lineage of enslaved, impoverished, unmarried, trafficked, partnered, married, cisgender, transgender, nonbinary, and nonconforming folk who insisted on our freedom and stood as guardians over communities and political traditions, giving life to revolutions and revolutionaries—because all isn't settled.

In this way, othermothering may also be understood as otherparenting and/or otherloving. Dissimilar to originalists, I honor all representations and journeys to black motherhood and all Black mothers, othermothers, otherparents, and otherloves. I resist puritanical and punitive hegemonic gender ideologies that Black folks were exposed to during the triangular slave trade. And I welcome the radical perseverance and oppositional orientation toward the significant maternal virtue that is the advocacy for black love, freedom, and sanctuary building and realizing. This is the world I needed as a Black girl, young Black woman, and new Black mother, and the world I call on today. Though I may never experience it, like the ancestors I may as well speak it into the atmosphere.

Coda: Toward Sanctuary
(and *Loving Black Boys*)

Black Feminist Mothering, an Alternative Literacy,
Philosophy, and Practice

Alabama's gotten me so upset
Tennessee made me lose my rest
And everybody knows about Mississippi, goddamn . . .
I think every day's gonna be my last
Lord, have mercy on this land of mine
We all gonna get it in due time
I don't belong here, I don't belong there
I've even stopped believing in prayer . . .
You don't have to live next to me
Just give me my equality . . .

This is fighting, not dancing, music. We need both. Sometimes we do them in chorus. Occasionally our dance is just a dance. At other times it's a form of protest. But frequently our protest is a kind of dance. Surviving America as a Black girl and woman takes special skill. Our breath is political. Our bodies are powerful and multiply jeopardized at once. We're walking and breathing objections to the status quo—swaying, stomping, twirling, gyrating, swinging, two-stepping, bopping, and sparring—through time and generations, demanding the right to be here and to feel something, even if that something is rage. That's what I hear when listening to "Mississippi Goddam" (1964), by Nina Simone, released in response to the black genocide and general precarity of black life in 1963. Namely, the murder of Medgar Evers and the 16th Street Baptist Church bombing, which killed eleven-year-old Carole Denise and fourteen-year-olds Addie Mae, Carole Rosamond, and Cynthia Dionne. Sadly, Simone's passionate indignation remains relevant more than sixty years later.

While I was finishing up this book, two news stories captured my attention. The first is about the shooting of Ajike "AJ" Owens, and the second circles back to the shooting of Megan Thee Stallion, discussed briefly in chapter 2. Each story centers on violence against Black women, underlining the need for both *Freeing Black Girls* and *Loving Black Boys* (forthcoming) generally, and sanctuary/ies, black feminism, and black feminist mothering, specifically. On June 2, 2023, Susan Lorincz, a fifty-eight-year-old white Florida woman, fatally shot her Black neighbor, thirty-five-year-old Ajike Owens, through a locked metal door as Owens's nine-year-old son stood beside her. Owens's twelve-year-old son was tasked with calling 911 to say that his mother had been shot. The nine- and twelve-year-old Black boys awaited the Florida police, completely unprotected and endangered, as their mother lay dying outside of her killer's door, behind which Lorincz stood with a loaded handgun. Based on what we know, she didn't like Owens's Black children playing in an open field near her apartment door. Though Lorincz didn't own the land where the small Black children played, she assessed that they didn't belong and commenced to terrorizing them.

To mark her territory, colonize the outdoors, and convey her superiority and their undesirability, Lorincz closely monitored the children; directed racial slurs such as the N-word at them; threw an inline skate at them, hitting one in the foot and demanding he "fetch" it; swung an umbrella at them; referred to them as slaves while taunting that the outside space "wasn't the underground railroad"; and took their iPad after it was mistakenly left in the field.[1] When Owens's nine-year-old son knocked on Lorincz's door requesting the return of the iPad, Lorincz told him to go get his mother. Once Owens arrived, Lorincz shot her through the bolted door, leaving the four children, ages three, eight, nine, and twelve, to navigate the trauma, loss, Florida, and this world without their mother. While premeditation may be difficult to prove in the Florida court system, Lorincz researched the state's "stand your ground" law before requesting Owens's presence and killing her. Weaponizing white reactionary womanhood and the law, Lorincz called 911 prior to ending Owens's life, using buzzwords and phrases, for example, claiming that Owens's son threatened to kill her, that she feared for her life, and that Owens was trying to break down Lorincz's latched metal door with her bare hands. Witness statements and surveillance video reveal this wasn't true. "[Florida], goddamn!"

The children's crime: existing and playing while Black in Trayvon Martin's Florida. Owens's crime: being a loving and protective unmarried Black mother of four Black children in DeSantis's Florida. Though such proclamations are historically reserved for natural disasters, social unrest, and/or war, the NAACP released a statement saying that the state isn't safe for Black people due to DeSantis's white supremacist capitalist heteropatriarchal crusade against "wokeness." Meanwhile, white media framed Owens's homicide as the result of an ongoing "feud" rather than noting the execution as the expected outcome of armed white womanhood and fake fragility; unbroken racial hostility, intimidation, and rage toward Black people; persistent white historical violence against Black children; and a state operating under legalized antiblackness. The matricide of a Black mother of four Black children, who've now been uprooted from their home to live with their grandmother, is the crescendo. Terror, rupture, shattered kinships, upheaval, and death are by design, not fortuitous. As Simone rages, every day could be the last.

When asked if the governor or any elected officials reached out to offer condolences or support, Owens's mother, Pamela Dias, posited:

> No . . . I truly believe because Ajike was a single Black mother who resided in Ocala, Florida. Certain lives matter more than others. Her life doesn't matter to them, just like it didn't matter to Susan. . . . To them, she's a statistic because she had four children. She was single. She was Black. And where she resided. . . . What they don't know is she was such a beautiful person . . . she mentored other young women, single mothers, homeless women. She gave of herself. She was not just a statistic. She was my daughter. She was a mother of four precious children.[2]

The two oldest sons blamed themselves for their mother's death. The nine-year-old stated that if he hadn't left his tablet in the field for Lorincz to steal, his mother would be alive. The twelve-year-old bemoaned that he couldn't do anything to save her.[3] I wish they knew that Lorincz, Florida, and America are indisputably to blame for the death of their mother and the breakup of their family and home. Lorincz, sanctioned by Florida's war against Black, brown, and queer folks, didn't want the family as neighbors and therefore made it her business to get rid of them. Antiblack racial hostility, which misrecognizes blackness as problemed, out of place, sinister, and monstrous, is American. "[We] don't belong here, [we] don't belong there."

James Baldwin writes that part of maintaining the lie that whiteness is supreme in America is reproducing literacies on black iniquity, which informs fear and the shaping of the law, which is in turn deployed to enact and justify subjection, violence, genocide, and debasement, as necessary for safety, control, and dominance.[4] Though Florida is a unique and immoderate brand of baby fascism, what happened to Owens could happen to any of us in any state. In 2020, I was hired at an academic institution in the Midwest, which caused me to live between two states. I rented a loft and a private parking space in a renovated old factory building for my visits, which were at best one week every other month due to the global COVID-19 pandemic. Having a private parking space at the residence was a priority for me because I'd leave my car there to avoid the costs of having to rent one while in town. One day I received a phone call from the owner of the building (whom I'd never met or spoken to) saying that my car was "over the line" and I "needed to move it" or else he'd "have it towed." None of this made any sense. And yet it did within the context of white settler neocolonial domination, antiblackness, and white racial violence and entitlement. White-on-black harassment is at the same time anticipated, shocking, irrational, and sudden. And no, it's not general bad treatment that can happen to anyone. Antiblackness sets the rules for how quickly poor treatment might materialize and how far it may go. For example, in Owens's case it ended in extermination.

The owner of the apartment building moved from diktat to discipline straightaway, despite an active contractual agreement and no wrongdoing on my part. I explained that my car wasn't over any lines, that I primarily live out of state, that I had no intention of making a special ten-hour trip to move my car out of the parking space assigned to me by management that I paid a monthly premium for, and that I had a picture of the parked car—because being Black here requires collecting proof for the most humdrum things, just in case. Realizing that I had a photo of the vehicle, was out of state, and wasn't moving the car, the owner became audibly inflamed and began aggressively yelling into the phone, demanding that I "stop talking" and mail him my car keys or fly into town immediately and move the car to another space. After the mess of a phone call, he and his wife then double tag team harassed me with irate emails and more calls, including one to my job, where he tried to have me fired, and another letting me know that he wasn't renewing my lease when it ended. His mother's parking spot was next to mine, and she didn't want me parked next to her. Although I had a contract on my space and her space was free, she wanted to possess both her spot and mine, and she wanted me and my car gone. Perhaps the mother is a terrible person who likes to terrorize others to get her way. However, the explosive nature of the exchange, which was completely undeterred by any existing binding agreements, and the fact that I never saw a single other Black person on the property tell me much more.

My crime: parking my car while Black next to a white person's car and not scurrying to move it when told. My presence and refusal—the audacity to be Black and alive while declining to eagerly accommodate whiteness—required urgent and demeaning correction. Black women and girls know the signs of mushrooming white resentment and how rapidly it skyrockets to physical and other brutalities. Legitimately fearing for my life, family, and belongings, I moved out of the apartment shortly after, with several months left on the lease and the rented parking space. The building owner's mother eventually got her way. It costs to be a Black woman. Socioeconomic class doesn't stop antiblackness. It allowed a getaway. I ended up purchasing property down the street to avoid further stress with property owners. Notwithstanding, the state presented another form of antiblackness months later: unconscionable taxation. After closing on the deal, I learned that the property was highly desirable. The taxes increased over 1100 percent within twelve months. I was told that the hike was at the discretion of a single person in the tax assessor's office and would continue to climb. The real estate companies, the bank, the assessor, and the title agency were all on the same side. I was reminded of how Indigenous people lost their land and how Black people in Detroit and other cities historically lost their homes through predatory taxation, intimidation, and otherwise. I sold the property, which had a cash offer within six hours of listing, and have yet to find housing in the state where I work. White settler colonialism surveys the land and moves us from one structural violence to another. Howbeit, Owens didn't get to escape. She shouldn't have had to. Neither should I.

A connecting thesis between *Freeing Black Girls* and *Loving Black Boys* is that Black folks are collectively endangered. *Freeing Black Girls* has explored the devastating consequences of navigating a world where misogynoirist toxicity is normalized, inter- and intraracially and communally. My hope was to utilize personal narratives to lay bare and confront legacies of social, economic, sexual, political, cultural, systemic, institutional, communal, theological, psychological, emotional, and otherwise violence and render them fragile. I also wanted to connect the dots between interracial white supremacist capitalist heteropatriarchal terrorism and intraracial aspirational black patriarchal and communal warfare and predation. As Audre Lorde asserts, what's going on interracially and intraracially is connected. Furthermore, we "absorb" racism, heterosexism, and heteropatriarchy.[5] This creates a context for intraracial selectivity in terms of whose lives matter. Owens's mother's plea, "She was . . . a . . . person . . . she was my daughter," wasn't a message solely to Florida or America. It was for all of us. Perhaps because we're living in a post–Black Lives Matter America, or maybe because some of us saw Owens as a "baby momma" and/or "statistic" as well, there was little national upset. Might the response have been different if Owens was a wife? Or lighter skinned?

What *Freeing Black Girls* and *Loving Black Boys* hope to convey is that all Black people matter. Black freedom is for all of us. None of us can afford to be left out. And neither can we stand to leave anyone out. Just two months after Owens's murder, Tory Lanez, a Black Canadian male rapper charged with a felony count of assault with a semiautomatic firearm, negligent discharge of a firearm, and having a concealed and unregistered firearm in a vehicle, was sentenced to ten years in prison for shooting Megan Thee Stallion in the feet in July 2020. Talk about music that makes you dance! I fell in love with the sex-positive black feminist rapper when I first heard "Big Ole Freak" and "Cocky AF" in 2018. Stallion's[6] delivery, creative energy, and self-possessed reclamation of black humanity, black female power, sexuality, pleasure, joy, autonomy, her bag, bossing up, feeling good, and saying "yes" to herself spoke loudly and cogently to me. She was raging and twerking against the patriarchy and telling Black women and girls everywhere that we were inherently both everything and enough.

According to court reports, Stallion and Lanez became friends and sometime lovers after bonding over the loss of their mothers. As the story has been narrated, on the night of the shooting, Stallion, Lanez, and another friend, Kelsey Harris, argued in a car over who was having sex with whom, whose rap career was better than whose, and other matters. To assert dominance, Lanez called the women "bitches" and "hos" and critiqued Stallion's career. However, when Stallion, a Grammy winner and one of the most successful rappers today, told Lanez it was actually his career that was lackluster, not hers, he became incensed. Unable to rationally process his emotions and Stallion's critique, Lanez retrieved his gun, ordered her, "dance bitch," and fired five shots at her after they'd exited the vehicle.[7] Following the shooting, Lanez sent texts apologizing for what happened and promising Stallion $1 million to not go to the police because he was on probation for a prior weapons offense. Initially, Stallion didn't report the shooting. She explains, "This was at the height of police brutality . . . I felt like if I said this man just shot me, I didn't know if they might shoot first and ask questions later . . . in the black community . . . it's not really acceptable to be cooperating with police officers."[8]

Stallion told *Rolling Stone*, "In some kind of way, I became the villain. . . . And I don't know if people don't take it seriously because I seem strong. I wonder if it's because of the way I look. Is it because I'm not light enough? Is it that I'm not white enough? Am I not the shape? The height? Because I'm not petite? Do I not seem like I'm worth being treated like a woman?"[9] She further laments being disbelieved, feeling like Lanez and his supporters were trying to "break her," and the pornotropic emphasis placed on her sexual life. "This whole story has not been about the shooting. It's only been about who I been having sex with. . . . When people talk about Megan Thee Stallion getting shot, all the headlines are Megan Thee Stallion is on trial and I'm not on trial!"[10] Stallion asserts that at one point during the ordeal, she wished Lanez had killed her, given the hatred that she's experiencing, including one person who posited, "Damn, I would've shot that bitch too." Stallion testified, "This whole situation in the industry is like a big boys club. . . . Like I'm telling on one of y'all friends, now you're all about to hate me."[11]

The initial urge to protect herself and her harm doer from police violence while raising an iteration of Sojourner Truth's important question, "Ain't I a woman?," undergirds Black women's and girls' volatile place and layering of intersecting oppressions in America. Stallion became the villain for reasons similar to why Owens's mom thinks the governor never reached out: heteropatriarchal and misogynoirist literacies on black womanhood, which force Black women and girls to consistently prove their virtue, value, and worthiness of being treated as humans inter- and intraracially, lead to and rationalize violence, including death. Specifically, the violence toward Owens didn't happen independently of white supremacist capitalist heteropatriarchal violence. Her neighbor sought to conquer and get rid of her for taking up nearby space. Similarly, the sexual independence in Stallion's rap persona and her talking back to Black men in general in her music and to Lanez specifically in the car, made some feel that she deserved and/or incited heteropatriarchal disciplining. White supremacist capitalist heteropatriarchy and misogynoir produced the conditions for Lanez to shoot Stallion. The "big boys club" of aspirational black capitalist patriarchy turned him into the victim. "Lord, have mercy on this land of mine."

Stallion's audacity to resist heteropatriarchy and claim her body and sexual subjectivity as her own was and is her crime. And because some see the phallus as a symbol of male power and dominance, the emphasis on her sex life (rather than her trauma) with her shooter, who'd brought her to tears in social media and in court, highlights pleasure taken in the ultimate heteropatriarchal defeat. Misogynoirist sadism has no color. Sexual shaming enables violence. In addition, Stallion failed to shield Lanez from the law, thus "ruining" both his life and his young son's life. A fellow Black Canadian rapper, Drake, raps the following on "Circo Loco" (2022), "This bitch lie 'bout getting shots but she still a stallion." Lanez wrote an album about it as well, claiming his innocence. Two years later, a video surfaced online showing Lanez, flanked by several large bodyguards, sucker punching a fellow music artist for not shaking his hand. Lanez is seen smiling and high-fiving an excited onlooker after the attack. Heteropatriarchal violence is insatiable and impacts everyone, including Black men. It means to "break" all of us. Still, to this day, many continue to see Stallion as the menace and Lanez as the victim. Black diaspora, goddamn!

The everydayness and omnipresence of allied black endangerment makes us "lose [our] rest" and puts us on edge, sometimes constructing survival, coping, and processing mechanisms that harm each other intraracially and intracommunally. A main point in *Freeing Black Girls* and *Loving Black Boys* is this: we don't need to be surviving each other while also having to survive pervasive white supremacist harassment, discrimination, terror, and genocide. We need sanctuary/ies—emancipatory literacies, philosophies, relations, and safe places where nobody is prey. Granted, white supremacist capitalist heteropatriarchy is going to do what it does. Sanctuary aids us in standing together more forcefully against it, igniting us to collectively resist despair and "live hostile to hostility."[12] As a literacy and philosophy, sanctuary clarifies that Lanez deserves no more protection or support than Lorincz because sanctuary requires valuing, protecting, and empathizing with both Owens and Stallion. That said, sanctuary begins with a basic understanding and practice of respect for the autonomy of Black cisgender women and girls. All other points of recognition, such as genders and sexualities, extend from that.

We cannot insist on justice and mutuality for Black transgender women or nonbinary, gender-neutral, gender-fluid, or queer folk if misogynoir toward Black cisgender women and girls is considered allowable and/or insignificant. The source for vehemence against each of those collectives is hatred toward and misrecognition of Black cisgender women and girls. This is a baseline and practice, not a first step reminiscent of previous freedom movements that stated when Black men/white women get their rights all else will be alright. A[13] foundational politics for sanctuary is black feminism, which demands that we resist white racism, heteropatriarchy, heterosexism, misogynoir, homophobia, transantagonism, classism, and + at the same time. It offers a critical lens for seeing Owens and the women and mothers she mentored more wholistically and as especially endangered by the state, intercommunally, and intraracially. More, it opens up space to explore what's at stake and what it takes for each of them to survive. What can't be ignored, based on Owens's mother's account, is that she was surviving Florida and motherhood without a partner to offer financial, emotional, physical, and other support. Being an unmarried Black woman while mothering Black children—particularly in twenty-first-century post-Trayvon-Martin-conservative-right-wing-Florida—is a notable burden.

In addition, black feminism resists the notion that Owens needed to be a perfect victim, married, or male for collective outrage and social movement to ensue. Also, black feminism rejects any idea that Stallion got what she deserved, that her autonomy, talking back, and insurgency required correction. Black feminism holds that neither her sexual subjectivity nor her size nor her looks nor her color nor her rap prowess is to blame for Lanez's lack of self-control. It insists that Owens and Stallion matter unequivocally. And anyone who disagrees is both against Black women and girls, including those in their family, and antiblack—because you can't be for Black people or your loved ones and be against Black women's and girls' right to safety and autonomy. Furthermore, anyone who is antiblack and/or against Black women and girls resides outside of sanctuary. Black feminist sanctuary is both inclusive and exclusive in unison. The reader may be curious about my deployment of sanctuary in this way. Aside from places of spirituality, worship, and ritual, sanctuary historically offered protections for fugitives and could be ecclesial, political, communal, or legal. It was safe space as well as a place for plotting and negotiating freedom.

Creating safe space, whether ideological, representational, material, or otherwise, for Black women and girls to live, love, rage, and conspire for freedom is especially blessed work. Additionally, the enslaved ancestors provide an example of the power of imagining sanctuary/ies outside of institutions. Sacred communions, forces, rebirths, and oppositions sprung up wherever they deemed and willed them to be. My usage aligns with this practice. In the same way, sanctuary concomitantly serves as a critique of those sanctuaries that have failed to adequately respond to the ways that Black women and girls specifically and Black folks generally are socially and structurally endangered. More, my use of sanctuary calls attention to those who participate in harmful discourses on Black women and girls, for example, treatises on women's and girls' sexual impropriety, which dehumanized both Owens and Stallion. To this end, sanctuary in this context is also a critical commentary on the Black Church. Namely, its emphasis on otherworldliness and personal behavior (even as it centers itself in racial justice) when it comes to Black transgender, cisgender, nonbinary, gender nonconforming, and queer women, girls, and un/married/mothers requires a more ethical and humane reimagining.

Whereas *Freeing Black Girls* engages the sanctuary that I needed as a Black girl, *Loving Black Boys* explores the sanctuary/ies I'm trying to conjure and practice while mothering my Black sons. Owens's Facebook page shows a proud Black mother who loved her children fiercely and fought for them daily. *Freeing*

Black Boys began as a love/protest letter for and to Lee and Seth. It was me knocking on America's door and standing up for my and America's Black children. I didn't realize that I needed to write some love and protest notes to myself and Black girls, women, mothers, and othermothers everywhere, first. Loving and writing about Lee and Seth in the context of hatred, predation, and violence pushed me t/here. Like Wonder to Aisha, I wanted them to know that they're "lovely," "wonderful," "precious," the "angel's best," and the "product of love." I wanted them to know, see, and feel specifically black feminist motherly love, so that they'd love themselves, me as their momma, and all the Black girls and women—across genders and sexualities—that they'd one day encounter. I wanted that love to manifest in mutual respect, dignity, proper recognition, equity, and justice. I wanted them to connect the oppressions and violences they feel "out there" with those constructed intraracially and intracommunally. I wanted them to help build sanctuary rather than be the reason why we need sanctuary. Of course, that story is still being told.

A[14] requisite critical gaze within black feminism for building sanctuary/ies is revolutionary mothering, what I refer to in *Loving Black Boys* as black feminist mothering. Black feminist mothering, which is for all of us, is an offering that's been in process for a lifetime and that shifts and changes through time as I and we continue to confront life's challenges. It notes the precarious place of Black cisgender, transgender, nonbinary, gender nonconforming, and queer girls, women, mothers, and othermothers trying to survive white supremacist capitalist heteropatriarchy, aspirational black patriarchy, and otherwise, while also taking seriously the particular multiple imperilments of Black cisgender, transgender, gender-neutral, nonbinary, queer, and + Black men and boys.[15] It's the cultivating work, survival dance, soul nurture, black living hope, radical perseverance, oppositional orientation, and collective transformation that create contexts for children to grow, despite threats and realities of antiblack oppression, war, neofascism, communal disinvestments, abandonment, and/or vulnerabilities to violence, exploitation, trauma, black death, and more. It's talking back and an insertion of warrior strength and partnership. Not because war defines black power, community, and/or identity, but because emancipation requires contention.

Black feminist mothering is thus a revolution of values.[16] It's a direct confrontation with the status quo, and an ethics of care that recognizes Black mothers and othermothers participating in this work as powerful oracle shapers and transmitters of culture and politics; Black women and girls as sacred; and the future that we make together as both possible and a promise.[17] As June Jordan says, Black women and girls must invent the power that freedom requires.

And if children learn the politics of hate at home, why not revolutionary love? To be clear, revolutionary love isn't heteropatriarchy in blackface, ride or die, or unchecked loyalty. It's the work of raising agitators and freedom fighters or, at minimum, children who care about equity and justice across sex, genders, sexualities, class, and so on. Such work is rooted in the destruction of all systems of oppression, and what Alexis Pauline Gumbs refers to as the practice of valuing ourselves and each other and creating the world we deserve.[18] It requires neither empire nor oppression to thrive, noting each as antiblack and opposed to black freedom and survival. I owe it to Lee, Seth, my spouse, and myself to co-imagine a world where we aren't left breathless under white supremacist capitalist heteropatriarchy or preexisting masks of toxic femininity or masculinity.

Some readers of *Freeing Black Girls* or *Loving Black Boys* may question the possibilities of such worldmaking or black feminist mothering due to my social location as an economically privileged, cisgender, heterosexual, married, and, though radically left, Black Christian woman and black feminist scholar of black religion.[19] My place and understanding of the world are significantly shaped by my race, gender, heterosexuality, and faith but are not limited to them. My station as a wife and mother grants liberties that require consistent naming. And though my economic advantages, which began two generations before mine, may seem to place me in opposition to impoverished, working-class, and unmarried Black mothers and othermothers, they may also allow freedoms for me to take more risks. Simultaneously, I reject colonizing epistemologies and sociopolitical moral frames that problematize and/or demonize Black women, mothers, and othermothers, or that turn us into foes. I also welcome class, gender, and otherwise critiques of my analyses. I understand that I'm not the standard of black feminism, black mothering, or black feminist motherhood. Still, none of this lessens my loyalty to insurgent black feminist theories, philosophies, and practices. And none of it changes the fact that I'm a Black girl turned woman turned Black feminist/mother attempting to think nontoxically about a more emancipatory world. Black feminism is a politics, not a gender, sexuality, biology, or socioeconomic class. The structural constraints of white supremacist capitalist misogynoirist patriarchy are universal. The "black" disables the guarantee of safe passage to adulthood for all of us. Neither marital nor class status changes that. We are collectively yet differently vulnerable to uncertainty.

Further, black feminist mothering is a site of reproductive virtue that provides opportunity for restoration and resistance, not perfection. It's shaped by the idea that nurturing humans born into combat zones from fugitivity to freedom is a sacred act of love. It recognizes the fragility of black breath and specifically the constant threat of violence and losing loved ones, children, power, humanity, and stability, and attends to all the ways Black folks survive and deserve to be free and whole in safe, healthy, just, and productive environments. Consequently, it actively pushes against inherited investments in antiblackness and empire, including white supremacy, "real" manhood and womanhood, and motherhood as a neoliberalist moralist individualist heteropatriarchal race, class, and gender-based project.[20] Synchronously, it seeks and embraces a freedom to becoming rather than an imprisonment to what is "real."[21] It repudiates toxicity from all angles and at all levels and being unwhole and unwell. It insists on a world where neither the black nor the feminine is seen as a threat and/or demonic; where Black cisgender, transgender, nonbinary, gender nonconforming, heterosexual, and queer girls and women are safe and powerful; where Black cisgender, transgender, gender nonconforming, heterosexual, and queer men and boys longing for equity, to be seen, for fathers, or otherwise, can safely note loss, isolation, hurt, resentment, trauma, and rejection, rather than Black girls', women's, or mothers' deficit; where Black cisgender heterosexual men and boys can say that they're afraid and feel powerless without being judged; and where Black women and girls across sexualities and genders can articulate to Black men and boys how they've hurt them without them becoming violent and/or patronizing in return.

Finally, it's my hope that revolutionary black feminist mothering proffers an alternative mother tongue on black knowing, loving, and socialization, and in the process murks (kills, ends, gets rid of) originalists' claims and all the ways that we're collectively endangered.[22] This is more than changing our language. It's seeing, doing, growing, and holding accountable, differently. For me, this gaze and work are political, spiritual, aggressive, loud, and nasty, particularly as they demand deep and thick structural change of all sexual, gender, racial, class, and ability + hierarchies that deny people the freedom to thrive emotionally, intellectually, and bodily. This is the heart of the new egalitarianism, and it's necessary for Black peoples' survival, and, most notably, Black girls.

Notes

AUTHOR'S NOTE

1   I'll say more later. For now, *Freeing Black Girls: A Black Feminist Bible on Racism and Revolutionary Mothering* and *Loving Black Boys: A Black Feminist Bible on Racism and Revolutionary Mothering* were written together and are meant to be engaged in conversation. *Loving Black Boys* is on the way!

2   For more on the *B* in *Black*, see "AP Changes Writing Style to Capitalize 'B' in Black," Associated Press, June 19, 2020, https://apnews.com/71386b46dbff8190e-71493a763e8f45a; Mike Laws, "Why We Capitalize 'Black' (and Not 'White')," *Columbia Journalism Review*, June 16, 2020, https://www.cjr.org/analysis/capital-b-black-styleguide.php.

INTRODUCTION

1   *Othermothering* refers to Black people who mother beyond gender and blood ties. See Patricia Hill Collins, "The Meaning of Motherhood in Black Culture and Black Mother-Daughter Relationships," *Sage* 4, no. 2 (Fall 1987): 3–5.

2   bell hooks, "The Oppositional Gaze: Female Spectators," in *Black Looks: Race and Representation* (Boston: South End Press, 1992), 115–31.

3   In *The Souls of Black Folk*, originally published in 1903, W. E. B. Du Bois refers to the verbal and nonverbal enthusiasm in black churches in response to the sermon as "the frenzy," also a call-and-response between congregants and podium, a distinguishing marker of what makes the institution "black." W. E. B. Du Bois, *The Souls of Black Folk* (Greenwich, CT: Fawcett, 1961).

4   I use the King James Version (KJV) throughout this text for consistency.

> **16** Then came there two women, that were harlots, unto the king, and stood before him. **17** And the one woman said, O my lord, I and this woman dwell in one house; and I was delivered of a child with her in the house. **18** And it came to pass the third day after that I was delivered, that this woman was delivered also: and we were together; there was no stranger with us in the

house, save we two in the house. **19** And this woman's child died in the night; because she overlaid it. **20** And she arose at midnight, and took my son from beside me, while thine handmaid slept, and laid it in her bosom, and laid her dead child in my bosom. **21** And when I rose in the morning to give my child suck, behold, it was dead: but when I had considered it in the morning, behold, it was not my son, which I did bear. **22** And the other woman said, Nay; but the living is my son, and the dead is thy son. And this said, No; but the dead is thy son, and the living is my son. Thus they spake before the king. **23** Then said the king, The one saith, This is my son that liveth, and thy son is the dead: and the other saith, Nay; but thy son is the dead, and my son is the living. **24** And the king said, Bring me a sword. And they brought a sword before the king. **25** And the king said, Divide the living child in two, and give half to the one, and half to the other. **26** Then spake the woman whose the living child was unto the king, for her bowels yearned [1] upon her son, and she said, O my lord, give her the living child, and in no wise slay it. But the other said, Let it be neither mine nor thine, but divide it. **27** Then the king answered and said, Give her the living child, and in no wise slay it: she is the mother thereof. **28** And all Israel heard of the judgment which the king had judged; and they feared the king: for they saw that the wisdom of God was in him, [2] to do judgment.

For more, see "Solomon's Wisdom and Prosperity," Christianity.com, accessed July 2022, https://www.christianity.com/bible/kjv/1-kings/3-16-28.

5 I aspire to be inclusive. I say "aspire" because sometimes my unconscious bias as a Black cisgender heterosexual woman peeks through. Notwithstanding, when I use the words *women* or *girls*, this includes all self-identifying women and girls (cisgender, transgender, queer, nonbinary, gender nonconforming, gender-neutral, pangender, asexual, questioning, fluid, . . .). And while the word *woman* in particular is too often deployed reductively, it's also a subversive political and organizing category used to articulate collective and nuanced experiences necessary for liberation. Both *Freeing Black Girls* and *Loving Black Boys* use gendered terms such as *girls*, *women*, *boys*, and *men*. Both will and will not use designations. When referring to history or social beliefs, I may add *cisgender* and/or *heterosexual* to drive the point home. When I want to further highlight inclusion, I may add *transgender* et al. For some readers, this may be confusing and/or off-putting. "Why not just write Black 'girls, women, boys, and men'?" Because this may be the first text a reader encounters on race and gender, and I'd hope that meeting is radically inclusive. As a baseline I offer the following: *cisgender* describes those whose sense of personal and gender identities corresponds with the sex they were assigned at birth. For example, I'm a cisgender woman. Janet Mock is a transgender woman. *Transantagonism* notes hostility toward transgender people just as *racism* notes hostility toward Black people. However, neither *cisgender* nor *transgender* names sexual identity (homo, hetero, bi, questioning, inter, undefined, nonconforming). For example, I am a cisgender heterosexual woman. Mock is a transgender heterosexual woman. We're both women.

6 Misogynoir articulates a form of misogyny (contempt against all women) that overwhelmingly and intentionally impacts all Black women and girls. For more, see

Moya Bailey, *Misogynoir Transformed: Black Women's Digital Resistance* (New York: New York University Press, 2021). On differentiating among Black women and girls, see Tamura Lomax, "These Hos Ain't Loyal: White Perversions, Black Possessions," in *Jezebel Unhinged: Loosing the Black Female Body in Religion and Culture* (Durham, NC: Duke University Press, 2018).

7 I define *pornotroping* or *pornotropic gazing* as a way of "seeing" with both the eyes and the psyche that is simultaneously "othering," and particularly sexualizing. It's a mapping of racial, gendered, and sexual stereotypes onto others, namely, Black women and girls. For more on pornotroping, see Lomax, *Jezebel Unhinged*. Additionally, the story presented here follows the account of Solomon's dream at Gibeon where God promises to give him unprecedented wisdom.

8 This brief interjection deserves a lengthy prediscussion as *Freeing Black Girls* is a decidedly black feminist text that (1) deploys a black feminist study of religion critical gaze and (2) converses with both black feminists and womanist theologians when discussing the Bible, religion, and theology. I examine distinctions and similarities between womanist theologians and black feminists and why I identify as a black feminist in *Jezebel Unhinged* (86–93). More, there are different kinds of womanism with different histories, beliefs, and so on. Thus, when asked, "Why black feminism and not womanism?" I always respond with "What kind of womanism?" Because the distinctions matter. *Jezebel Unhinged* lays those out and answers the question. Additionally, in my work/s, I'm specifically engaging womanist scholars within the study of theology and religion when I use the term. This isn't an either-or for me. As a black feminist scholar of religion, I'm indebted to womanist theologians, ethicists, and biblical scholars. In fact, womanist theology is my entry point to black feminism. My politics as a black feminist scholar, theorist, mother, and so on, is a matter of theoretical and methodological distinction. That said, I am and will always be in conversation with and inspired by womanism in religion. The idea that womanist theologians and black feminists are oppositions is the result of capitalism, which requires winners, prizes (jobs, departments, book deals, funding, etc.), and losers. Noting difference doesn't have to mean framing hostilities. At least it shouldn't. Each discourse is invested in cultivating wholeness for Black folks and is rooted in black struggles for freedom. This isn't a zero-sum game where Black women cannot coexist.

As Patricia Hill Collins stated on a 2020 womanism/feminism "verzus" panel that we were on together, "There is plenty of room and space for differences that don't have to be framed in verzus. . . . Black people are New World black populations, not a continuum of African populations because we have many African populations within us. We have been involved in the freedom struggle from captivity. But this struggle for freedom is not something we experience the same way. . . . [This is the foundation to] specialization for a freedom struggle where we can look at various aspects of that." For example, gender, sex, class, sexuality, community, and religion. Collins continues:

> [This is the] foundation for building community—intellectual, ethical, political community—that can deal with captivity. . . . These are the origins of what we are calling black feminism and womanism. . . . Black feminism

doesn't come from a feminism that is derived from white women. . . . It comes from the fusion of blackness and women that said we need a political response to this in the secular sphere. . . . Many early Black women thinkers were theologians or leaders of their churches. They were cultivating communities to push the freedom struggle forward. However, the freedom struggle was never disconnected from the mind and the depth of thinking about freedom and politics against racism, sexism, classism, or heterosexism (Ida Wells Barnet talks about sexuality though never identifies as feminist or womanist).

Collins posits, the naming and framing, black feminist and womanist, "comes from not only 1950s and '60s social movement but the move to specialization. . . . Black women politicized and became politically active . . . [in] social change and dealing with body politics." This included, for example, reproduction, families, economic conditions, and access to the vote. All of this was a part of Black women's empowerment. According to Collins, "What we see in the '70s and '80s is more specialization and how we continue to work for those things. . . . Something as broad as the freedom struggle and Black women's empowerment requires us to think more expansively." Heterogeneity is unhelpful here. We need both critical lenses. Simultaneously, Collins cautions:

> We can't look too closely at any one group of women to the exclusion of other women. . . . It is not enough to say that women in the church are somehow accessing a southern womanist tradition that is sort of grounding the entire enterprise. There are many, many, many Black women in this country who did not grow up in the South . . . who do not have access to that tradition. . . . At the same time, black feminists cannot say there is a litmus test for black feminism. There's a problem for both discourses and its boundaries and how it's going to differentially serve the needs of Black women. . . . Pay attention to the external politics and the times that we are in. . . . We have to look back and forward . . . we need to also attend to the fight from the far right . . . and in many terrains. . . . Womanist claims of ethics and Black women's humanity is essential for dealing with religious fundamentalism and oppression in our sacred institutions. . . . Black feminism and womanism can be inhabited in the same body. To think about these as identity categories is limiting. . . . The verzus framework aggravates the ability to form coalitions and alliances to do this work.

"Verzus Panel: Womanism v. Black Feminism," Union Presbyterian Seminary Center for Womanist Leadership spring conference (virtual), April 9, 2021. In view of Collins's analysis, *Freeing Black Girls* is a form of specialization with emphasis on Black girls, mothers, and religion in the movement to empower Black women, girls, and folks.

9 I explain the historical racializing and gendering of the term *ho* in *Jezebel Unhinged*.

10 One can say the same for Black men and boys. All minoritized people are surviving the patriarchy and the state, however differently. *Freeing Black Girls* and *Loving Black Boys* hope to get at some of these differences.

11 On the reduction to historical racial tropes, see Lomax, *Jezebel Unhinged*.

12 *Semi* means to distinguish between my girlhood heteronormativity and sex and gender biases taught in the Black Church and conservative white Christianity, which usually includes antiblackness, sexism, transantagonism, homophobia, classism, and more.

13 I'll say more about traditional womanhood in later chapters. For now, heteropatriarchal-centered womanhood moves across racial and ethnic lines.

14 Lomax, *Jezebel Unhinged*.

15 Misogynoir wrapped in religion, blackness, political consciousness, art, humor, the arms of a knight in shining armor, and/or whatever else is still misogynoir. It's just a more succulent form of toxicity.

16 The distinction between *inter* and *intra* is significant. While *interracial* denotes interactions between different racial and ethnic bodies, *intraracial* highlights engagements within a racial body. I deploy it to engage happenings within and among Black folks, sometimes interchanging it with *intracommunal*. This isn't meant to absolve what happens interracially due to white racism and white supremacist capitalist heteropatriarchy, however. Simultaneously, this book deploys *black community* and *intracommunal* not in terms of a monolith or singular entity but instead as a range of spaces where Black folks gather. They're communities within communities where Black people live, connect, work, build, encounter each other, and make meaning and sense of their lives. While *community* and *communal* can be about a certain district, zone, or four-block radius, it's much more than that. More, it's both tangible and imagined.

17 See Lomax, "These Hos Ain't Loyal."

18 *Single Black mothers* is often used as a trope to blame pathology on unmarried Black women and girls. However, one can be unmarried and not be single. Moreover, Black women and girls aren't the root or face of black pathology. Further, blackness isn't innately pathological.

19 In *Jezebel Unhinged*, in the chapter "The Black Church, the Black Lady, and Jezebel: The Cultural Production of Feminine-*ism*," I write about the religio-cultural preoccupation with distinguishing between "hos" and "housewives." Underlining this binary is the directive for girls and women to be "good"/"proper" so that they're chosen for marriage. Ironically, whereas "proper" femininity and being a "good" woman or girl centers heteronormative gender ideology and sexual respectability for women and girls, being a "good" Black man or boy ofttimes means the assertion of heteropatriarchal dominance and regular things like taking care of offspring or paying personal bills.

20 Not all families include a mother for a range of reasons—for example, divorce, death, abandonment, sexuality, or gender identity.

21 Establishing "the" Black (heteropatriarchal) family became a political and religious campaign after slavery not solely for the sake of reuniting with lost loves or formally establishing bonds between the newly freed, but also for countering stereotypes, establishing a moral order and respectability, rebuking other kinds of familial makeup and identities, and configuring black aspirational politics. Lomax, "The Black Church, the Black Lady and Jezebel." I write the following in *Jezebel Unhinged*:

> I use (black) "progress" and "racial uplift" interchangeably throughout this text. Both articulate the plight, passage, and hopeful advancement of Black Americans after slavery. "Racial uplift" is the Du Boisian ideology that an

educated "talented tenth" was responsible for the progress of most the race. The best (men) of the race were accountable for guiding the worse to a better state. Similarly, "black progress" is the idea that improvement for those categorically cut off from opportunity due to race, comes by way of civil and political rights accessible through classical education, which produces not merely workers of trade and bread winning but knowledge, culture and character. Those who did not have this training remained in the underclass and on the underside of the veil of blackness. Du Bois's "talented tenth" has been critiqued for sexism, elitism, paternalism, and exceptionalism. He later changed his thinking, noting that progress and uplift could arise from many efforts to include and exceed higher education. Nevertheless, Du Bois's idea continues to thrive. An unintended consequence is how the advancement of knowledge, culture and character, and distinctions between the "tenth" and the rest and the best and the worst, simultaneously hinge upon the performance of "proper" bodies, sexualities, sexual liaisons, and relations. The discourse on black womanhood, which requires a highly regimented body along with a role in the black "nuclear" family, has been significant for establishing the latter. (219)

22 The word *real* has cultural meaning. The angst around establishing "real" black womanhood or manhood arises out of the history of North American slavery, which defined the Black/African slaves as cattle, partially human, and undeserving of legal and political rights. "Real" black manhood typically articulates a quest for humanity, power, citizenship, patriarchal rights, and political power. "Real" black womanhood often notes the "proper" performance of femininity in relation to Black men. "Real" is distinct from "true," however. As I posit in later chapters and in *Loving Black Boys*, "true" manhood, akin to "true" womanhood, refers to white manhood and white supremacist capitalist patriarchy. *Freeing Black Girls* and *Loving Black Boys* radically critique the terms *real* and *true*. There's no singular authentic way to express race, sex, gender, or sexuality just as there's no one group of people who are more human than others.

23 "Natural hierarchy" informs the patriarchy. "The" patriarchy isn't new or particular to North America. It's been operative for several thousand years all around the world. Especially significant is its role in the "nuclear" family and thus society. Patriarchy is in essence the rule of the father. Meaning that if you're a man, you should have dominion over the household—*and in society*. If you're a woman, you should be subject to the dominion of the man—*within and outside of the home*. For more on my framing of race, religion, and "natural hierarchy," see Tamura Lomax, "Black Venus and Jezebel Sluts: Writing Race, Sex, and Gender," in *Jezebel Unhinged*, 13–33.

24 I deploy *African* rather than *Black* in this sentence because blackness as a racial category and identity is primarily a twentieth-century conception. W. E. B. Du Bois writes about the interpretive shift from *African* to *Negro* to *Black* in *The Souls of Black Folk*. However, some slave sources use *negro*. Some also deploy *nigger*. It's not hard to imagine some slaves felt less African over time. Slave sources speak to that as well. I use *African* when referring to slaves for consistency. However, in some instances, I deploy *Black/African* to highlight the line and/or continuum between African slaves, Black folks, and black thought, ideas, and indignities.

25 Lomax, *Jezebel Unhinged.*

26 There's much political and academic discussion around whether or not to use *slave* or *enslaved. Enslaved* means to humanize and note the dehumanizing structure of slavery, particularly as Black/African bondspeople weren't seen as human. I've worked with many ancestral accounts in which they refer to themselves as "slaves," not because they were unsure of their humanity but because they were clear about it as well as the system they were attempting to survive. I lean toward their deployment.

27 Lomax, *Jezebel Unhinged.*

28 Lomax, "The Black Church, the Black Lady and Jezebel."

29 I argue in *Jezebel Unhinged* how slave women and girls were called "jezebels" (I reserve the lower case *j* for stereotyping and the uppercase for the biblical figure of the same name) to distinguish them from free white women and how this relates to calling contemporary Black women and girls "hos" and/or sexualizing them as the pastor did in the Mother's Day sermon.

30 Some may read this as me creating a binary. However, while there's always nuance and though Black women and girls refuse totalization in reductive binaries, the construction and the saying "you can't turn a ho into a housewife" are still deployed in religion and culture.

31 In the Bible and religious culture, Jezebel is blamed for the demise of her husband and children. It's argued that her alleged pathology (worshipping other deities and wielding power over men) led to corruption in her son in particular and to his being killed by the state. As I discuss in *Loving Black Boys*, Black mothers are also often blamed when their sons are killed by the state. More, as I posit in later chapters, Black mothers are generally blamed when Black children don't live up to certain expectations.

32 Patricia Hill Collins argues, "The cult of true womanhood, with its emphasis on motherhood as women's highest calling, has long held a special place in gender symbolism of white Americans. From this perspective, women's activities should be confined to the care of children, the nurturing of a husband, and the maintenance of a household. By managing this separate domestic sphere, women gain social influence through their role as mothers, transmitters of culture and parents for the next generation." See Collins, "Meaning of Motherhood in Black Culture," 3. Simultaneously, ministers like Bishop T. D. Jakes have argued cisgender heterosexual mothers are the safeguards of morality and virtue. Namely, virtuous mothers raise children of virtue because it's their job to pray for the children and steer them away from trouble. However, Black women have historically and predominantly been laborers, particularly since North American slavery, thus constructing gender identities within and beyond the home.

33 Melissa Harris-Perry, *Sister Citizen: Shame, Stereotypes, and Black Women in America* (New Haven, CT: Yale University Press, 2011).

34 In both *Freeing Black Girls* and *Loving Black Boys*, I lean into survival for reasons explained throughout both texts. As Audre Lorde once said, survival isn't theory. It's lived work. It's enough by itself. However, I also deploy *thriving* because, as Maya Angelou once stated, her "mission in life is not merely to survive, but to thrive; and to do so with some passion, some compassion, some humor and some style." See "Maya Angelou: In Her Own Words," BBC, May 28, 2014, https://www.bbc.com/news

/world-us-canada-27610770. Black surviving and thriving in this text both name access to living, full humanity, recognition, freedom, liberation, love, restoration, community, accountability, equity, justice, spirit, joy, safety, resources, bloom, creativity, imagination, wellness, healing, nourishment, balance, empowerment, self-articulation, autonomy, radical sociopolitical and communal transformation, flourishing, and so on.

35 *Effeminophobia* is fear of the feminine, womanliness, and/or the behaviors, gestures, presentations, and otherwise associated with women and/or femininity.

36 White supremacist capitalist heteropatriarchal masculinity is a critique of white imperialist settler masculinity, which stands against any form of race, gender, labor, sexual, sex, or class equity. For more, see Democracy Now, "Remembering bell hooks & Her Critique of 'Imperialist White Supremacist Heteropatriarchy,'" YouTube, accessed June 2023, https://www.youtube.com/watch?v=DkJKJZU7xXU. Additionally, if "the" patriarchy is the rule of the father within and outside of the home and equates to power, empire, and dominance, race makes *black* patriarchy at best aspirational (some would say oxymoronic) because Black men don't collectively hold dominion in American society. *Freeing Black Girls* and *Loving Black Boys* argue that though patriarchy has different points of access and rewards, aspirational black patriarchy is no less material intracommunally. Its impact is still operative and felt.

37 The word *girls* is inclusive. Simultaneously, *Loving Black Girls* is a collection of stories about my journey from girlhood to motherhood as a cisgender heterosexual Black woman.

38 I deploy *love* throughout this text to refer to romantic partnerships, family, friends, and more, but also to engage a love ethic rooted in justice, which requires rebellion or, as Dr. Martin Luther King Jr. would say, direct confrontation with the status quo. This demands seeing the inherent dignity, value, and "somebodiness" in others, and specifically in Black folks.

39 I'm emphasizing motherhood not because this work isn't for fathers but because I'm writing out of experience, which is personal and political, not ontological.

40 This book is about building emancipatory communities among Black folks to help us be, live, thrive, survive, and fight oppression better. It's disinterested in appealing to white folks to see our humanity. The 2016 and 2020 elections say plenty about why that's not a useful strategy for black survival. White people will need to face their own music and do their own work to stop white supremacist capitalist patriarchal oppression.

41 Aimé Césaire, *Discourse on Colonialism* (New York: Monthly Review Press, 2000), 39.

42 The spiritual and political right to expansion and empire.

43 Megan Zahneis and Beckie Supiano, "Fear and Confusion in the Classroom," *Chronicle of Higher Education*, June 9, 2023, https://www.chronicle.com/article/fear-and-confusion-in-the-classroom. See also Eva Surovell, "Diversity Spending Is Banned in Florida's Public Colleges," *Chronicle of Higher Education*, May 15, 2023, https://www.chronicle.com/article/diversity-spending-is-banned-in-floridas-public-colleges.

44 *Freeing Black Girls* and *Loving Black Boys* aren't about increasing agitations. These works are interested in facing intracommunal differences and violences in an effort to build bridges and sanctuaries.

45 Zakiyyah Iman Jackson, "Losing Manhood: Animality and Plasticity in the (Neo) Slave Narrative," *Qui Parle: Critical Humanities and Social Sciences* 25, no. 1–2 (2016): 95–136, www.jstor.org/stable/10.5250/quiparle.25.1-2.0095.

46 Ta-Nehisi Coates, *Between the World and Me* (New York: Spiegel and Grau, 2015).

47 bell hooks, *We Real Cool: Black Men and Masculinity* (New York: Routledge, 2004), 88.

48 Mark Anthony Neal, *New Black Man* (New York: Routledge, 2015). While not all Black men interpreted Black women's rights as secondary to their own or assumed racial rights were synonymous with Black men's rights, the centrality of cisgender heterosexual men's rights in black liberative efforts is well documented. Sojourner Truth, Anna Julia Cooper, Ella Baker, Michele Wallace, Elaine Brown, Audre Lorde, and others articulate this reality.

49 It's important for me to note the specialness and particularity of Black fathers, especially in terms of affirmation, experiences, and identity. *Freeing Black Girls* and *Loving Black Boys* both take this very seriously.

50 James Baldwin, "On Being White . . . and Other Lies," *Essence*, April 1984, Anti-Racism Digital Library, https://sacred.omeka.net/items/show/238.

51 Audre Lorde and James Baldwin, "Revolutionary Hope: A Conversation between Audre Lorde and James Baldwin," *Mosaic Literary Magazine*, no. 39 (Fall 2016): 43–44, ProQuest.

52 Lorde and Baldwin, "Revolutionary Hope," 43–44.

53 bell hooks, *The Will to Change: Men, Masculinity, and Love* (New York: Atria Books, 2004).

54 Luis Andres Henao, "Black Protestant Church Still Vital Despite Attendance Drop," *AP News*, May 1, 2023, https://apnews.com/article/black-protestant-church-attendance-youth-covid-pandemic-5d854b4db73e118cb22767220573455f.

55 Albert J. Raboteau, *Slave Religion: The "Invisible Institution" in the Antebellum South* (New York: Oxford University Press, 1978).

56 Eddie S. Glaude Jr., *African American Religion: A Very Short Introduction* (Oxford: Oxford University Press, 2014).

57 Glaude, *African American Religion*.

58 Lomax, *Jezebel Unhinged*.

59 Black sovereignty for me has to do with building more emancipatory love- and justice-centered communities and relations among Black folks while also collectively and individually surviving and resisting the white supremacist capitalist patriarchal state. I say more about that in the essay "The Black Church Movement Profile Is Dead: The Audacious Absurdity of Transgressive Imagination between 'The American Dream' and the Nightmare," in *Moved by the Spirit: Religion and the Movement for Black Lives*, ed. Christophe D. Ringer, Teresa L. Smallwood, and Emilie M. Townes (Lanham, MD: Lexington Books, 2023), 117–34.

60 Raboteau's *Slave Religion* reveals North American Black Christians have always had progressive and regressive profiles. The Black Church has historically been a source of both freedom and oppression. As a source of freedom, it serves as a critique of white supremacy and thus redeems the profaned faith of the slavers. As a tool of oppression, it maintains many of the ideologies, representations, and theologies of the imperial project. For more, see Lomax, "Black Church Movement Profile Is Dead."

61 When writing this book, I likened it to a course on black feminism and black girlhood and often queried what that might look like if I were teaching it as a Black
feminist scholar of religion. Specifically, what categories of analysis would (must)
I include? Foremost, race, sex, class, gender, and sexuality, and because of my
research in black religion and black popular culture, I'd also necessarily incorporate
that. Truthfully, any study on Black girls and how they interface with the world,
and how the world in turn shapes them, requires these additions. Anyway, each
chapter attempts to weave all of this together, sometimes presenting a "big" category of analysis over others. For example, chapter 2 emphasizes sexuality and the
body by way of *P-Valley*, history, theory, and personal narrative, whereas chapter 3
centers race and heteropatriarchy. Additionally, the stories aren't rigidly chronological. For example, I begin at the time I was fourteen years old in chapter 1, then move
to a story that happened at age twelve in chapter 2. Chapter 3 moves through time,
from age fourteen to adulthood. Finally, the chapters have distinguishing tones.
This is intentional as each chapter came alive in distinct historical moments. The
flow and mood of the writing mirror that.

62 April Baker-Bell, *Linguistic Justice: Black Language, Literacy, Identity, and Pedagogy* (New
York: Routledge, 2020).

1. BLACK GIRLS MATTER

1 I use *Black Girl* in this letter and subsequent mini-letters to speak to my younger self
because that is how I refer to me in my early years. Simultaneously, I dedicate these
words, letters, and chapters to my very special nieces: Alexa, Chela, Kacey, Ky, and
Jasmine. When writing this book, I thought about the world that I wish I had when
growing up, as well as the one I want for them and all Black girls more generally.
This in mind, "Dear Black Girl" is also an address to all Black people who identify as
a girl, presently, past, in the future, et cetera. And though I'm a full-grown woman
today, I'm still a "Black girl," as in the colloquial way Black women and girls inscribe
it when we truly love you, have something juicy and/or ridiculous to share, and feel
completely at home. When we enter this space, it's often "girrrrrrrrll." This isn't for
non-Black folks to try. A white woman married to a Black man once referred to me
in this way and it stopped me in my tracks. "Please don't," I responded, and as a sharp
boundary I requested that she refer to me as "Tamura" or "Dr. Lomax" going forward. I don't like "Ms." or "Mrs." And typically only my students refer to me with my
academic title. However, I needed to make the distance between her and me and the
use of Black Language such as "girrrrrrrrll" clear and firm. I know this is a nonissue
for some. In the words of Bobby Brown, "It's my prerogative."

2 This and the following italicized messages are my "ten commandments" to myself
and all Black women and girls.

3 Like "love bombing," "pretty bombing" is when someone manipulatively over-
whelms a person with faux compliments only to get something in return, typically sex or some other goal. For example, when boys catcall, in person, digitally,
or otherwise, saying how "fine" a person is, sometimes it's a genuine compliment.
Other times, it's a means to an end. If the end is sex or something sexual, I refer to

this as "pretty bombing." I'm reminded of the song "Beautiful" (2003) by Pharrell Williams and Snoop Dog. The song goes, "Beautiful, I just want you to know, you're my favorite girl." However, as T. Denean Sharpley-Whiting writes in *Pimps Up, Ho's Down: Hip Hop's Hold on Young Black Women* (New York: New York University Press, 2008), the compliment is so good one might miss the insult. Favorite girl for what? The song lets us know.

4 I changed the name in this account, and no formal charges were filed.

5 This speaks to the adultification of Black girls, not gender.

6 Deborah Gray White, *Ar'n't I a Woman? Female Slaves in the Plantation South* (New York: Norton, 1999).

7 In *Rethinking Rufus: Sexual Violations of Enslaved Men* (Atlanta: University of Georgia Press, 2019), Thomas A. Foster posits that while the slaves strove for agency and intimacy and though intracommunal sexual violence between slaves on plantations wasn't systemic, Works Progress Administration interviews note sexual abuse, particularly as sexual prowess correlated to manhood. Foster argues that intracommunal sexual violence, breeding, and otherwise were a source of shame for men and women. Research also suggests sexual assault and violence were sometimes a source of male power. That is, sexual coercion during slavery must also be engaged in terms of intracommunal masculine dominance, not solely interracial oppression, powerlessness, victimization, or emasculation. While there were many loving Black/African slave men, there were also at times constructions of intracommunal hierarchy, which enabled violence.

8 bell hooks, *Salvation: Black People and Love* (New York: Harper Perennial, 2001), 134–46.

9 As an example, see Mirhir Zaveri, "Body Camera Footage Shows Arrest by Orlando Police of 6-Year-Old at School," *New York Times*, February 27, 2020, https://www .nytimes.com/2020/02/27/us/orlando-6-year-old-arrested.html.

10 Of course, Black people aren't a monolith. This book isn't calling for black essentialism or ontology. It's exploring possibilities for some sociopolitical consensus around concepts like "freedom," however.

11 Kimberlé Crenshaw, "The Precarity of Black Girls' Lives," *Essence*, July 10, 2020, https://www.essence.com/articles/watch-essence-festival-2020-live/.

12 Psalms 139:14.

13 As I note elsewhere, Black girl vernacular language and play allow for nuance here. As Queen Latifah says in her song "U.N.I.T.Y.," "Who you calling a bitch? (You ain't a bitch or a ho)." However, as she raps, there's a distinction between mutual play within social groups and among friends—and projections and misrecognitions outside of friendships and mutual agreements, which mean to structure relationships and experiences. As I argue in *Jezebel Unhinged*, while the former, mutual play, notes "the complicated ways Black women and girls negotiate community, love, dis/respect, play, sexuality, and sexualization, often simultaneously," the latter highlights "calling [us] out [our] name." The former is no different than black vernacular uses of *nigga*. This book makes room for mutual play. Black girl vernacular language is a powerful tool for renegotiating meaning and opposition. However, this is distinct from what I experienced in my new environment and my introduction to pimp/ho culture and gangsta rap. When the Black boys called the Black girls bitches and hos,

it was felt, and it stung. They were emphatically structuring black masculine dominance, specifically talking down to us, explicitly scrutinizing our sexual identity and experiences, and unabashedly foretelling how they saw us sexually and otherwise. Simultaneously, this representation of violent black masculinity was not consumed only by Black men and boys but also by Black girls. Tupac Shakur, a friend I went to high school with, struggles through this dynamic here: Historic Films Stock Footage Archive, "Tupac Shakur 1988 High School Interview," YouTube, accessed July 2022, https://www.youtube.com/watch?v=v_XT9-C5Qu8, 33:45–35:48.

14 The reader may notice my language in this letter isn't always sex and gender inclusive. Certainly, these challenges move across genders and sexualities. However, I'm trying to write in a way my fourteen-year-old self might understand. We didn't have these categories of analysis then. I'm also attempting to keep laser focused on one particular cisgender heterosexual Black girl—me—while also inviting others in. Notwithstanding, I paused here and reread this sentence again and again. It demands further conversation. My first conscious encounter with Black transgender women was after I moved to California. They were sex workers whose track ran in front of our church in Oakland. They often rested on the church steps. They were both unwelcome and unsafe. Yet no one spoke of the violences against them, only how their presence was a nuisance, how their work and identity were sinful and abnormal, and how they were dangerous. No one attempted to engage their endangerment and survival mechanisms. And no one cried for them when they went missing or were violated, robbed, or murdered. Yet they were also subjects of history surviving white supremacy, heteropatriarchy, and capitalism on the margins. Further, just like pimp/ho and gang culture created a heightened context for misogynoir that led to violence against Black cisgender girls, it enabled an even more vicious cult of violence against Black transgender women. And even fewer people cared.

15 This book is significantly influenced by June Jordan and the work Alexis Pauline Gumbs, China Martens, and Mai'a Williams do in *Revolutionary Mothering: Love on the Front Lines* (Oakland, CA: PM Press, 2016). See also June Jordan, "The Creative Spirit: Children's Literature," in *Revolutionary Mothering*, 12–13.

16 In *The Second Sex*, first published in 1949, Simone de Beauvoir writes, "One is not born, but rather becomes, a woman," noting how gender is learned and is thus distinguished from sex rather than overdetermined by biology. Similarly, this book holds one is not born but rather becomes a participant in the patriarchy and thus a patriarchal threat. I suggest this learned behavior and politics can be unlearned and/or resisted. And thus, while we are born into a forceful patriarchal context, there're emancipatory possibilities for resistance in revolutionary parenting, mothering, and othermothering. Simultaneously, this letter posits (1) had I and other Black girls and women had these "commandments," we'd have more ways to resist the violences we experience, and (2) had Black men and boys (and women) understood these lessons/commands, they may have been less violent. This isn't to say Black men and boys or nonbinary and nonconforming folk don't experience violence or that Black women and girls and nonbinary and nonconforming folk don't participate in violence. For more on Simone de Beauvoir, see *The Second Sex* (New York: Vintage, 2009).

1   There won't be trigger warnings in this book. Notwithstanding, I feel it imperative to note that this chapter contains specific cases of childhood sexual violence.
Rape culture is the ordinariness, everydayness, and normalization of rape, sexual
assault, sexual predation, and otherwise, often typical of environments where sex-
and gender-based domination and violence are customary. Normalization occurs
through language, culture, education, advertising, religion, politics, practices, and
so on. More specifically, it's the standardization of violence as well as objectifica-
tion/thingification that enables victim blaming; slut-shaming; street harassment;
a culture that teaches girls to not get raped rather than teaching everyone not to
rape; the hypersexualization of girls and women; defining manhood in terms of
conquest and womanhood in terms of sexual acquiescence; disbelieving cisgender
heterosexual men and boys can be assaulted; discrediting and shaming survivors;
and more. Movements against rape and sexual assault exist on a continuum. The
most recent and/or popular iteration is #MeToo, founded by Tarana Burke. Previous
organizations, particularly those emphasizing Black and POC survivors, include the
National Organization of Sisters of Color Ending Sexual Assault (SCESA); INCITE!
Women and Trans People of Color against Violence; Women of Color Network;
Black Women's Blueprint; What About Our Daughters; and many others. Sexual
violence awareness has been pivotal to black feminist/womanist theory, organizing,
and social movement; the 1960s women's movement; and women's studies departments founded in the 1970s. They gave us the language "rape culture." Movement
workers like Aishah Shahidah Simmons, creator of NO! The Rape Documentary
(2006); Kimberlé Crenshaw, author of "Mapping the Margins: Intersectionality,
Identity Politics, and Violence against Women of Color" (Stanford Law Review 43,
no. 6 [1991]: 1241–99, doi:10.2307/1229039) and cofounder of the African American
Policy Forum, which coined #SayHerName; sisters Salamishah and Scheherazade
Tillet, cofounders of A Long Walk Home; and more proffer foundational works
necessary for understanding and organizing against rape culture, particularly in
black communities. In addition to these cultural, legal, and political workers and
works are some of the initial writers, theorists, and activists, such as Harriet Jacobs,
author of Incidents in the Life of a Slave Girl (originally published in 1861), and Rosa
Parks, who covered Recy Taylor's story after she was gang-raped by six white men
in 1944. Other important texts include Toni Cade Bambara, The Black Woman: An
Anthology (New York: Washington Square Press, 1970); Angela Y. Davis, "Rape,
Racism, and the Myth of the Black Rapist," in Women, Race, and Class (New York:
Vintage, 1983); Darlene Clark Hine, Hine Sight: Black Women and the Re-construction of
American History (Bloomington: Indiana University Press, 1994); Saidiya Hartman,
Scenes of Subjection: Terror, Slavery, and Self-Making in Nineteenth-Century America (New
York: Oxford University Press, 1997); Tera Hunter, To 'Joy My Freedom: Southern Black
Women's Lives and Labors after the Civil War (Cambridge, MA: Harvard University
Press, 1997); and Danielle L. McGuire, At the Dark End of the Street: Black Women,
Rape, and Resistance—a New History of the Civil Rights Movement from Rosa Parks to the
Rise of Black Power (New York: Vintage, 2011). This is not a comprehensive list. It's a

listing of sources that may be useful for thinking through Black women's and girls' legal, cultural, social, political, and otherwise vulnerability to rape culture and their erasure from the discourse as victims. These sources aid us in interrogating how networks of predation have operated in Black women's and girls' lives.

2 Though Chucalissa, Mississippi, is fictional, there's a Chucalissa Village, a Mississippian Period archaeological site, at T. O. Fuller State Park in Memphis, Tennessee. It's said the original location was occupied, abandoned, and reoccupied between 1000 and 1400 CE. The history of occupation and abandonment serves as a backdrop for the show. See Carroll Van West, "Chucalissa Village," *Tennessee Encyclopedia*, October 8, 2017, https://tennesseeencyclopedia.net/entries/chucalissa-village.

3 For example, The Pynk faced foreclosure due to a $55,128.34 debt, an exploitative convenience for Promise Land, a group of white investors hoping to build a casino in its place. Although the investors told the locals that they're rebuilding the struggling town, they actually planned to gentrify it and displace impoverished Black people.

4 While dirty politicians and Bible thumpers, who happen to be Black folks, seem to be raising hell for The Pynk, the city is run at the state level by white wealthy southerners with roots in North American slavery.

5 I'm less interested in defining *sex work* and more concerned with noting how entering the sex industry and/or offering sex for pay isn't always a choice, or rather, it's a choice based on context and need, such as when Patrice says she had to "ho" because the city gave her no other choice.

6 This was a hard chapter to write. I struggled with articulating what some may read as dangerous or politically incorrect. How do we engage Black girls as autonomous and powerful sexual subjects without sexualizing them or trafficking in historical narratives that suggest they're "fast" or rape-able? At a minimum, this chapter is trying to acknowledge that Black girls think, imagine, and feel things, too—because they're human. And affirming this rather than hiding or shaming it defends Black girls more wholistically. I can't stress enough that this is absolutely not an invitation for sexualization, exploitation, partnering, or violence for Black girls—unable or able to consent. Sexual subjectivity is an assertion of full humanity. Bodily autonomy, which I sometimes deploy interchangeably, speaks to the power one should have over their own bodies. I deploy erotic power mostly when engaging Black women rather than Black girls to explore how consenting women might decide to act on their creative energies.

7 While in jail in season 1, Patrice states, "You called me a pimp, but I started lower than that, on my knees," alluding to prostituting to help raise Mercedes. She repeats this claim in season 2, episode 8. Patrice is also the ultimate panderess. She knows how to squeeze money out of the hands of dancers, business owners, politicians, and otherwise.

8 In Black Church culture, heterosexual married mothers symbolize possibilities for virtue and ladydom. Patrice's access to virtue is through Christianity, rather than motherhood, wifedom, or the black "nuclear" project. This in mind, everything she's done in the past to harm Mercedes or that's out of line with virtue and respectability has been "washed by the blood of Jesus," thus making her anew and allowing her to feel as if she's superior to Mercedes.

9 In *Birthing Black Mothers*, Jennifer C. Nash posits that "unmothering" is a "hallmark of the black maternal," rooted in slavery. It's the theft and loss of children and the uncertainty of mothering due to violence, captivity, alienation, sale, regulation, devaluation, commodification, forced surrogacy, biocapitalism, and so on. For more, see Jennifer C. Nash, *Birthing Black Mothers* (Durham, NC: Duke University Press, 2021).

10 For example, Uncle Clifford is an othermother to club workers and a caretaker for her mother.

11 Played by Skyla I'Lece.

12 There was and continues to be resistance toward openly discussing both inter- and intraracial sexual violence because some believe it validates hypersexual stereotypes and thus limits possibilities for establishing respectable manhood and womanhood and rights in the political economy. Simultaneously, sexual violence was and is seen as a women's issue and thus not pivotal to black political rights. This enabled and maintains the construction of a male-centric black liberation struggle. I write more about this in *Loving Black Boys* when discussing the 2020 presidential election and rapper Ice Cube's "Contract with Black America."

13 bell hooks, *We Real Cool: Black Men and Masculinity* (New York: Routledge, 2004), 88.

14 Respectability wasn't solely a middle-class phenomenon. There were also working-class women who forged their own notions of sexuality and respectability. Patrice serves as an example of this. Additionally, there's a thin line between respectability as performance of model citizenry to gain rights and possibly decrease violence and the threat thereof as deployed by civil rights activists as a strategy, and using respectability as a way of being "uppity" and/or policing other Black folks intracommunally, thus segregating "proper" and/or "good" Black people from others. The latter may also become a kind of placation to whiteness. See Evelyn Brooks Higginbotham, *Righteous Discontent: The Women's Movement in the Black Baptist Church, 1880–1920* (Cambridge, MA: Harvard University Press, 1993); and Darlene Clark Hine, "Rape and the Inner Lives of Black Women: Thoughts on the Culture of Dissemblance," in *Hine Sight: Black Women and the Re-construction of American History* (Bloomington: Indiana University Press, 1994), 37–48. Additionally, in many stories in the Bible, the rape of women and girls brings shame on the father, brothers, and other members of the victim's family rather than the victimizer. This plays out in culture as well.

15 Mikki Kendall, *Hood Feminism: Notes from the Women That a Movement Forgot* (New York: Viking, 2020).

16 While there's overlapping, I want to distinguish between being internally ashamed and externally projecting that shame onto others. One can feel ashamed without subjecting someone else to their feelings. Thus, shame and reputational ruin may also differ from slut-shaming. Namely, feelings of disgrace, inadequacy, or embarrassment can be solely internal—meaning that I can feel a certain way without making others aware of how I'm feeling.

17 Tamura Lomax, *Jezebel Unhinged: Loosing the Black Female Body in Religion and Culture* (Durham, NC: Duke University Press, 2018), 62.

18 In the essay "Rape and the Inner Lives of Black Women: Thoughts on the Culture of Dissemblance," in *Hine Sight*, Darlene Clark Hine argues that Black women concealed their inner sexual lives, thoughts, identities, feelings, and desires in response

to stereotypes about promiscuity, which they believed increased possibilities for rape. Disidentifying with their sexual selves, they made themselves over to the public to appear more respectable in hopes of decreasing sexual violence and demanding respect and autonomy.

19 Armtrice Cowart, "Most predators pick the girls y'all call fast . . . ," Facebook, June 14, 2023, https://www.facebook.com/armtrice/posts/10231004857683800.

20 Preezy Brown, "YK Osiris Accused of Sexual Assault, Apologizes after Forcibly Kissing Sukihana," *Vibe*, June 15, 2023, https://www.vibe.com/news/entertainment/yk -osiris-accused-sexual-assault-forcibly-kissing-sukihana-1234765031/.

21 On Sukihana leading YK on, see Unwinewithtashak, "Mmhmm now this $hit makes sense!! If I was #ykosiris I would TAKE MY APOLOGIES back ASAP!! . . . ," Instagram, June 15, 2023, https://www.instagram.com/p/CthY9gMuYYx/. For the longer quotation from Tasha K, see Unwinewithtashak, "LET'S TALK ABOUT IT!! Over the last couple days people have been painting a picture like #sukihana is a victim & needs to be saved . . . CAP!! . . . ," Instagram, June 15, 2023, https://www .instagram.com/p/CthLiv2gQ9T/.

22 Shannon Power, "Meek Mill Slammed for Supporting Rapper over Unwanted Sexual Behavior," *Newsweek*, June 15, 2023, https://www.newsweek.com/meek-mill-rapper -sexual-assault-sukihana-yk-osiris-1806830.

23 Nash argues that black sexual images and performances excite, arouse, and generate intensities. For more, see Jennifer C. Nash, *The Black Body in Ecstasy: Reading Race, Reading Pornography* (Durham, NC: Duke University Press, 2014), 54–58, 96–106, 147–51. Sexual safety is more than consent. It's also about mutuality.

24 Coach's wife, Farrah, urges him to pay Mercedes what they agreed to. She later pays Mercedes $30,000 for royalties from pictures she took of her.

25 Sexually exploiting and assaulting a child by having them bend over for adult men for favors and being a consenting adult erotic dancer are oppositions.

26 T. Denean Sharpley-Whiting, *Pimps Up, Ho's Down: Hip Hop's Hold on Young Black Women* (New York: New York University Press, 2008).

27 Mireille Miller-Young, *A Taste for Brown Sugar: Black Women in Pornography* (Durham, NC: Duke University Press, 2014), 10.

28 As Sharpley-Whiting asserts, financial stability and/or wealth/capital building is volatile as erotic performances for pay are also based on desirability, conventional beauty industry expectations, and so on. For more, see Sharpley-Whiting, *Pimps Up, Ho's Down*.

29 A "pick me" is a girl or woman willing to do anything, including throw other women and girls under the bus, deny sexism, and participate in patriarchy to gain male approval and attention. It's simultaneously a toxic form of femininity.

30 Lomax, *Jezebel Unhinged*, 139.

31 We still shame Black women and girls for having too many sexual partners and/ or encounters, twerking, sex work, and so on. See Tamura Lomax, "Black Venus and Jezebel Sluts: Writing Race, Sex and Gender in Religion and Culture," in *Jezebel Unhinged*; Tamura Lomax, "#BlackSkinWhiteSin: From Pernicious Editing to Audacious Rescripting (Benediction)," *Feminist Wire*, February 17, 2017, https:// thefeministwire.com/2017/02/blackskinwhitesin-from-pernicious-editing-to -audacious-rescripting-benediction/.

32 White supremacist capitalist patriarchy notes "the" patriarchy—white male rule of empire; the ultimate keepers of patriarchal dominance in society and within the home, a position enjoyed under North American slavery and its afterlife through legalized, state, and other violence and repressive laws.

33 Audre Lorde, "Uses of the Erotic: The Erotic as Power," in *Sister Outsider: Essays and Speeches* (Berkeley: Crossing Press, 2007), 53–59.

34 We can't undo white supremacist capitalist patriarchy. Yet there is power to resist participating in it and interrogating the parts we've absorbed.

35 Tamura Lomax, "#MeToo for the Wood," April 21, 2018 (unpublished sermon).

36 I use *racist misogyny* and *misogynoir* sometimes interchangeably to note collective historical degendering of all Black folks during slavery. For example, I argue in this chapter that plantation sexual violence toward Black men and boys was also a form of misogynoir. Simultaneously, racist misogyny can be more inclusive and misogynoir more particular as it speaks to biases specifically directed toward Black women and girls.

37 Sowande' M. Mustakeem, *Slavery at Sea: Terror, Sex, and Sickness in the Middle Passage* (Urbana: University of Illinois Press, 2016).

38 When thinking about breeding, we typically reduce the discourse to sexual violence against Black women and girls. However, Thomas A. Foster argues that all parts of breeding were exploitative and sexually violent. Male breeders were hired out like prostitutes, which he refers to as "third party rape," as they too were not allowed to reject or consent to the sexual encounters. See Thomas A. Foster, *Rethinking Rufus: Sexual Violations of Enslaved Men* (Atlanta: University of Georgia Press, 2019).

39 Leslie Howard Owens, *The Species of Property: Slave Life and Culture in the Old South* (New York: Oxford University Press, 1976), 189–90.

40 Owens, *Species of Property*, 192–93.

41 George P. Rawick, ed., *The American Slave, Texas Narratives*, supplement, no. 2, vol. 7, pt. 6 (Westport, CT: Greenwood Press, 1977), 2531.

42 Rawick, *American Slave*, 2531.

43 Rawick, *American Slave*, 2531.

44 African slaves weren't seen as men or women.

45 See also Caroline Randall Williams, "You Want a Confederate Monument? My Body Is a Confederate Monument," *New York Times*, June 26, 2020, https://www.nytimes.com/2020/06/26/opinion/confederate-monuments-racism.html.

46 For more on "plantation sexual politics," see Lomax, "Black Venus and Jezebel Sluts," 20–32.

47 Auction blocks and slave beatings included forms of sexualized violence, given bodily exposure, touching, et cetera.

48 Strip Search @ProtectOurBoys_, "Milwaukee Police Department (MPD) molested 74 (SEVENTY FOUR) Black men . . . ," Twitter, November 22, 2022, https://twitter.com/protectourboys_/status/1591135675453435904?s=42&t=NEoN4EX_2pIjL3x-y13gCw.

49 This isn't to say Black folks have equitable access to colonizing structures, for example, conquest, dispersal, enslavement, and/or sale. There's nothing more reprehensible than the transatlantic slave trade and/or the ensuing colonial apparatus that emerged in its afterlife. More, Black folks are its immediate and primary victims and survivors. Still, the slave system simultaneously had and continues to have cosmic

intraracial and intracommunal ramifications. For more on "Black possessions," see Tamura Lomax, "'These Hos Ain't Loyal': White Perversions, Black Possessions," in *Jezebel Unhinged*, 34–58.

50 Audre Lorde and James Baldwin, "Revolutionary Hope: A Conversation between Audre Lorde and James Baldwin," *Mosaic Literary Magazine*, no. 39 (Fall 2016): 45, ProQuest.

51 A quick word on Lorde's point about the absorption of white racism by Black folks. This isn't to say Black folks are racist. Racism is structured in systemic and structural oppressions. It's to note how white racial ideologies are operative and/or possessed and often forceful within Black collectives. Lorde and Baldwin, "Revolutionary Hope," 46.

52 Lorde and Baldwin, "Revolutionary Hope."

53 Lorde and Baldwin, "Revolutionary Hope."

54 Audre Lorde, "Age, Race, Class, and Sex," in *Sister Outsider*, 123.

55 We must discuss the adultification, sexualization, and rape of young Black girls by older boys. These aren't strangers in a dark alley. They're often beloved members of the community. What I mean to emphasize isn't some sort of inherent sexualization of Black boys and men but rather the normalcy with which rape culture occurs for young Black girls everywhere. For example, in 2017, the radio personality Charlamagne noted that he just realized "that many men have been raised on rape culture in this country" and how getting women drunk or high, spying on them, and touching their bodies in a sexual manner were normalized. Sam Valorose, "Charlamagne Finally Realizes Men Have Been Raised on Rape Culture," *Breakfast Club*, November 10, 2017, https://thebreakfastclub.iheart.com/content/2017-11-10-charlamagne -finally-realizes-men-have-been-raised-on-rape-culture/.

56 We felt "grown." Twenty-first-century age of sexual consent ranges between sixteen and eighteen years old, depending on the state. However, the messy gray areas of life require more honest conversation, and in a way that refuses both hypersexualization and victim blaming around desire and curiosity. Sexual thoughts begin when they begin, and we need more conversation about that. Yet having thoughts do not mean Black girls should be or want to be having sex or that the age of consent should be lowered. Nothing in this chapter argues that. In fact, the argument here isn't about having sex. It's about honoring Black girls' sexual being enough to protect them rather than shaming or alienating them. Concomitantly, honest talk calls for attention to how Black women and girls have historically and contemporarily resisted sexual exploitation, using their bodies and/or bartered sex as a form of survival—for shelter, protection, food, money, clothing, and so on. This may have been the case for Mercedes and Cortez, even if she loved him. Autonomous sexual decision-making may occur in exploitative economies. The conditions of America made it so Black women and girls have always had to construct alternative values, unions, and systems of survival.

57 This calls to mind the statement "No means no." However, some are taught that "no" sometimes really means "yes." Thus, rape prevention can't stop at "no means no." Power dictates that verbal communication isn't always believed or accessible. Simultaneously, physical resistance such as fighting can get you killed. I risked my life that night in the car. I was either going to be raped, again, beaten up, or

abandoned. This is also why resistance is sometimes silent and why some survivors "check out." "Checking out" isn't consent. It's survival.

58 I document one of my first predatory encounters in the Black Church in the prolegomenon of *Jezebel Unhinged*; this event occurred when I was eleven years old.

59 Some readers may be wondering, "Why not go to the police?" I didn't even think to do so because I was sure I'd "sinned" because I was "fast."

60 I discuss the fear of sexual shame at length in *Jezebel Unhinged* and "Theorizing the Distance between Erotophobia, Hyper-moralism, and Eroticism: Toward a Black Feminist Theology of Pleasure," *Black Theology: An International Journal* 16, no. 3 (2018): 263–79, https://doi.org/10.1080/14769948.2018.1492305. As mentioned, Black women and girls carry "proof" of sexual immorality and shame in their bodies through rumors, pregnancies, and childbirth while Black cisgender heterosexual men and boys are permitted to have as many sexual encounters as possible without stigma. Sociopolitical and sociocultural narratives and policies on Black "teen pregnancy" have historically centered the teen mother, not the father. Noting this distinction, Lorde posits the following in her exchange with Baldwin: "There are little Black girl *children* [italics mine] having babies. But this is not an immaculate conception, so we've got little Black boys who are making babies, too. We have little Black children making little Black children. I want to deal with that so our kids will not have to repeat that waste of themselves." Lorde and Baldwin, "Revolutionary Hope," 45.

61 See Joan Morgan, "Why We Get Off: Moving towards a Black Feminist Politics of Pleasure," *Black Scholar* 45, no. 4 (Fall 2015): 36–37; Joan Morgan, *When Chickenheads Come Home to Roost: A Hip-Hop Feminist Breaks It Down* (New York: Simon and Schuster, 1999).

3. "BREAK MY SOUL"

1 Please check your mobile phone manufacturer's safety guidelines. Keeping your phone in your bra may be hazardous to your health.

2 By now the school year has passed and Seth is doing amazing. He didn't return home the following summer. The kitchen fire and the upset it caused still gives Seth angst. He got a wonderful internship out of state instead. He's now a graduate student out of state and is working in his field.

3 I diagnosed myself with obsessive-compulsive personality disorder when my children, who were in middle school, pointed out my fixation with cleanliness and straight lines. It's interesting how my very fluid view of life and people is countered with perfectly linear lines and structures in terms of objects, for example, furniture, pictures, and otherwise.

4 The hymn "Take Me to the Water" is often sung during baptism in the Black Church. The ritual and water are believed to have sanctifying powers. In my case, my tears were the water in response to the powerful lyrics.

5 In the opening letter of this chapter, I note "different freedoms" because "Break My Soul" responded to the freedom to be outside postpandemic isolation; threats of racial, gender, sexual, and economic injustices in America; the great resignation due to dissatisfaction with wages and labor conditions; and freedom to inspire, seek, and

experience joy. Beyoncé posits, "Creating this album allowed me a place to dream and to find escape during a scary time for the world. It allowed me to feel free and adventurous in a time when little else was moving. My intention was to create a safe place, a place without judgment. A place to be free of perfectionism and overthinking. A place to scream, release, feel freedom." In *British Vogue* she asserts, "Fun can feel like a radical act right now." See Danielle Chilosky, "Beyoncé Shares a Statement before the 'Renaissance' Release: 'It Was a Beautiful Journey of Exploration,'" *Uproxx*, July 28, 2022, https://uproxx.com/pop/beyonce-renaissance-statement-leak /; Edward Enninful, "'I've Decided to Give Myself Permission to Focus on My Joy': How Beyoncé Tackled 2020," *British Vogue*, November 1, 2020, https://www.vogue.co .uk/arts-and-lifestyle/article/beyonce-british-vogue-interview. Additionally, "Break My Soul" has explicit roots in black queer communities, introduced to Beyoncé by her "Uncle" Jonny, her gay cousin and godmother, who designed clothes for her and aided her mother, Tina, in raising her until their death during the AIDS epidemic.

6 See Albert J. Raboteau, *Slave Religion: The "Invisible Institution" in the Antebellum South* (New York: Oxford University Press, 1978); Lawrence Levine, *Black Culture and Black Consciousness: Afro-American Folk Thought from Slavery to Freedom* (New York: Oxford University Press, 1977).

7 Evangelicalism highlights Protestant Christians who believe Jesus died on the cross for their sins and rose from the dead; because of this he is the Lord, and they too may be "born again" if they profess the former. Evangelicalism places emphasis on individual experience, biblical inerrancy and moral authority, personal conversion, and evangelizing others. My emphasis in this chapter is on how white evangelical theology is oppressive to Black people. For more on evangelicalism in America and its relation to Black folks and specifically North American slavery, Raboteau's *Slave Religion* is particularly insightful. Additionally, though evangelicalism is interdenominational, the Southern Baptists, descendants from the Baptists who broke away due to the Southern Baptists' interests in slavery, are the largest evangelical Protestant group in the United States. They are predominantly white, theologically conservative (namely, on issues of gender, identity, abortion, and sexuality), and Republican. See Dalia Fahmy, "7 Facts about Southern Baptists," Pew Research Center, June 7, 2019, https://www.pewresearch.org/fact-tank/2019/06/07/7-facts-about -southern-baptists/. For more on evangelicalism and racism, see Anthea Butler, *White Evangelical Racism: The Politics of Morality in America* (Chapel Hill: University of North Carolina Press, 2021).

8 Tamura Lomax, "Whose 'Woman' Is This? Reading Bishop T. D. Jakes's *Woman, Thou Art Loosed!*," in *Jezebel Unhinged: Loosing the Black Female Body in Religion and Culture* (Durham, NC: Duke University Press, 2018).

9 Not all Black girls survive. Some Black girls die. Some never get to grow to be women. More, not everyone loves oneself or others, or is fighting for oneself or others. Some spend their lives antagonizing, demonizing, and bullying Black girls worse than the patriarchy. When I speak of sacredness, I'm referring to those who love themselves and us, who fight for self and us, as well as those that want to but can't or weren't allowed to, given context, including death. I'm noting potential as well as the material and historical.

10　See Toni Morrison, "Home," in *The House That Race Built: Original Essays by Toni Morrison, Angela Y. Davis, Cornel West, and Others on Black Americans and Politics in America Today*, ed. Wahneema Lubiano (New York: Vintage, 1998), 3–12.

11　I'm here for joy, dancing, self-care, soft life aspirations, and more. I also note some forms of joy may be superficial without doing the other liberating work. Yet, superficial joy may at times be all we can grasp. And in that case, we must grab hold to whatever we can.

12　A note on the title of this section: in the Bible, the land of Canaan (aka the promised land) is promised to Abraham and his descendants and specifically Moses and the children of Israel after Exodus. It was the fulfillment of God's promise that they would have a place where they could settle and that would be flowing with milk and honey. However, after wandering in the wilderness and eventually gaining the courage to invade Canaan, which was already occupied and not flowing with milk and honey, the children of Israel faced several battles instead. Similarly, W. E. B. Du Bois writes in *The Souls of Black Folk* that newly freed Black people in North America believed emancipation would establish America as a kind of promised land. However, history tells us that Black folks have been battling for their freedom and humanity since arriving in America and unfortunately that battle has not yet been won. I use the terminology here to highlight the hope that our move to California posed for our family as well as the battles that lay ahead for me. Additionally, I use Black Language, *be*, to note my place as an outsider and Black girl from the East Coast often scolded for my speech and particularly my use of the "to be" verb. I say more about this later. W. E. B. Du Bois, *The Souls of Black Folk* (Greenwich, CT: Fawcett, 1961).

13　A participant in Hip-Hop culture.

14　In the 1970s and 1980s the Bronx was defined by fires, poverty, incinerated neighborhoods, racism, economic disinvestments, redlining, rats, displacement, sanitation cuts, trauma, broken kinships and communities, and more. There were always burned abandoned high rises whenever we visited. The rubbish was rarely removed. Tenants were often blamed for setting the buildings on fire. However, landlords would burn the buildings to get the insurance money. Concurrently, the Cross Bronx Expressway was eventually built in their place. For more, see Democracy Now, "Who Burned the Bronx? PBS Film 'Decade of Fire' Investigates 1970s Fires That Displaced Thousands," YouTube, accessed August 4, 2022, https://www.youtube.com/watch?v=x3Tyj0AQu00. See also David Gonzalez, "How Fire Defined the Bronx, and Us," *New York Times*, January 20, 2022, https://www.nytimes.com/2022/01/20/nyregion/bronx-fires.html.

15　bell hooks deploys this idea to refer to men who are dominant yet kind protectors and providers. bell hooks, *Communion: The Female Search for Love* (New York: Harper Perennial, 2002).

16　Momma got her self-care and idle time through us. This was a major point of contention between us several years ago. I expressed this was not our job, especially childcare. Momma responded frustratingly and later affirmatively. It was what she learned as a girl.

17　As I write in the introduction of this book, "natural hierarchy" informs the patriarchy, which is in essence the rule of the father.

18 hooks, *Communion*.

19 As I write in *Loving Black Boys* and later in this chapter, Daddy's love was steady and vital but complicated and flawed. Notwithstanding, it stabilized me in countless ways.

20 Frantz Fanon, *Black Skin, White Masks* (New York: Grove Press, 1967).

21 I was introduced to the Oakland-based rapper Too Short and West Coast rap my first day of high school. The Black students from Marin City who drove to school circled the quad blasting "Dope Fiend Beat" and "Freaky Tales" on repeat. These songs informed our interactions and how the Black girls were seen and treated.

22 Despite racist connotations, Marin City was lovingly called "The Jungle" by Black folks who lived there when I was in high school. I saw this as a deployment of Black Language and a political play on words, which can be messy when in the wrong hands. Marin City, which was initially built to house Black men who were shipyard workers during World War II, was a mix of public and private housing for predominantly Black folks. Interestingly, while it sits within one of the wealthiest counties in the nation, Marin City was literally fenced in, as in a circular partition, when I lived in California. However, unlike a gated community where there's a security guard to keep people out, the partition was intended to communicate racial and class "Otherness" therein. Gentrification has changed much of this today.

23 See Michel Foucault, *History of Sexuality, Volume 1: An Introduction* (New York: Vintage, 1990).

24 Lomax, *Loving Black Boys*.

25 Lomax, *Loving Black Boys*. In the text, I also wrestle with my own mechanisms of punishment during Lee's and Seth's early years. See also Stacey Patton, "Why Are We Celebrating the Beating of a Black Child," *Washington Post*, May 1, 2015, https://www.washingtonpost.com/opinions/2015/05/01/cca770dc-ef9f-11e4-a55f-38924fca94f9_story.html.

26 This is not a nod to romantic nostalgia. I'm well aware of the socioeconomic challenges in these cities. What I'm referring to is the way we still found freedom, love, acceptance, home, and each other.

27 There are many good parts to specifically liberationist black churches, for example, how it's safe to be fully Black, how blackness is affirmed there, and how blackness needs no explanation. It's a source of historical and cultural awareness and a community, though imperfect, within an antiblack world. The religious and spiritual aspect of the church, wherein many find value, is intertwined with black culture. That said, the Black Church can be a cultural source and family reunion.

28 See Walter B. Shurden, *Struggle for the Soul of the SBC: Moderate Responses to the Fundamentalist Movement* (Macon, GA: Mercer University Press, 1994).

29 The "unvirtuous" wrongs include abortion, women's rights, LGBTQ+ rights, affirmative action, and entitlements for poverty-stricken people and communities. The Southern Baptist Convention, an evangelical religious right conservative body, is one of the country's most politically influential organizations and has long aligned itself with conservative causes and political candidates.

30 Ronald Reagan, a Hollywood actor turned union leader turned thirty-third governor of California turned fortieth POTUS turned architect for the original "Making America Great," proudly rolled back significant civil rights gains made in the 1960s

via law-and-order policing and ideology, mass incarceration, and the depletion of social services, public education, and economic opportunities. The emptying of socioeconomic entitlements is pivotal to both "draining the swamp" and "making America great"—for economically advantaged white people. In this way, MAGA, then and now, means making all others disproportionately vulnerable to a host of risk factors that increase the likelihood of sociopolitical and socioeconomic marginalization, induction into America's criminal justice system, and premature death.

31 Though America claims a separation between church and state, there is presently a massive push to Christianize public education (K-12 and colleges and universities) to parallel conservative evangelical messaging around whiteness, gender, heteronormativity, etc. The forty-fifth POTUS is especially attractive to white evangelicals because he represents ultimate gatekeeping of the patriarchy and an allegiance to "true" manhood, "the one true" God, and country. An underpinning magnetism of the forty-fifth POTUS's ultranationalism is not only the belief that white traditionalist cisgender hetero/sexual/sexist men are superior but also that Western civilization needs saving and a reordering that resembles early colonial America more closely. This includes power over women, Black folks, and everyone else. That said, "true" manhood notes white supremacist heteropatriarchal masculinity whereas "real" manhood, which I'll engage in chapter 4, articulates Black men's quest for humanity, power, citizenship, patriarchal rights, and political power through aspirational black patriarchy. These objectives are inherent in "true" manhood. Additionally, "real" manhood for Black men is limiting and oppressive to Black folks. I discuss this further in *Loving Black Boys*.

32 See Doug Mills, "Trump and Allies Forge Plans to Increase Presidential Power in 2025," *New York Times*, July 17, 2023, https://www.nytimes.com/2023/07/17/us/politics/trump-plans-2025.html; Heritage Foundation, *Mandate for Leadership: The Conservative Promise* (Project 2025: Presidential Transition Project) (Washington, DC: Heritage Foundation, 2023).

33 Christian fascism isn't a matter of one bad apple or simple difference of opinion. An authoritarian nationalistic right-wing Christian government is about white supremacist capitalist heteropatriarchal dominance. It has roots in settler colonialism and empire. Normalizing colonialism, slavery, antiblackness, segregation, white supremacy, and discrimination is a matter of life or death. Having a government, court system, and police force structured in white supremacist capitalist patriarchy is a matter of life or death. Changing history to suggest North American slavery wasn't so bad (DeSantis) is a matter of life or death. Teaching that women and girls are second class, to be dominated, and/or that rape and domestic violence are reasonable forms of engagement is a matter of life or death. Not having access to reproductive justice and/or choice is a matter of life or death. Not having entitlements, health care, or a living wage are matters of life or death. Merging the state with right-wing theological beliefs is a matter of life or death. Taking away LGBTQ+ rights and protections that support their humanity and quality of life is a matter of life or death. Demonizing and sexualizing Black women and girls is a matter of life or death.

34 Given the velocity of antiblackness, harm, and trauma associated with this name, and more, the daily threat of his reign, and not to mention the "baby 45s" he's inspired, I prefer the representative "forty-five."

35　Heather Cox Richardson, "July 17, 2023 (Monday) A story in the New York Times today by Jonathan Swan, Charlie Savage, and Maggie Haberman outlined how former president," Facebook, July 18, 2022, https://www.facebook.com /heathercoxrichardson/posts/823987069096527.

36　I maintain the quotes around *Christian* here and throughout this book to follow the citation where the phrase is introduced but also to note the irony of a democracy that touts religious pluralism and separation between church and state being heavily influenced by conservative Christian evangelicals who in fact seek to make America a Christian nation. I use other descriptive terms in later chapters without quotes, however—*Christian heteropatriarchal order, evangelical Christian nationalism,* and *white Christian supremacist capitalist heteropatriarchal power.* I reserve quotes for when engaging democracy.

37　See George Schroeder, "Seminary Presidents Reaffirm BFM, Declare CRT Incompatible," *Baptist Press*, November 30, 2020, https://www.baptistpress.com/resource -library/news/seminary-presidents-reaffirm-bfm-declare-crt-incompatible/.

38　See Ruth Graham and Elizabeth Dias, "Southern Baptists Vote to Further Expand Restrictions on Women as Leaders," *New York Times*, June 14, 2023, https://www .nytimes.com/2023/06/14/us/southern-baptist-women-pastors-ouster.html.

39　Graham and Dias, "Southern Baptists Vote to Further Expand Restrictions on Women as Leaders."

40　Raboteau, *Slave Religion.*

41　Robert Downen, Lise Olsen, and John Todesco, "Abuse of Faith: Investigation Reveals 700 Victims of Southern Baptist Sexual Abuse over 20 Years," *Houston Chronicle*, February 9, 2019, https://www.houstonchronicle.com/news/investigations /article/Southern-Baptist-sexual-abuse-spreads-as-leaders-13588038.php.

42　Kate Shellnutt, "Paige Patterson Fired by Southwestern, Stripped of Retirement Benefits," *Christianity Today*, May 30, 2018, https://www.christianitytoday.com/news /2018/may/paige-patterson-fired-southwestern-baptist-seminary-sbc.html; Gregory Tomlin, "Patterson: Women Are Treasured by God, Have High Calling," *Baptist Press*, October 25, 2004, https://web.archive.org/web/20070927235849/http://www .bpnews.net/bpnews.asp?ID=19402.

43　Tamura Lomax, "Looking for Justice for Black Women and Girls: The Black Church, Jezebel, and Aspirational Black Capitalist Patriarchy," Berkley Center for Religion, Peace and World Affairs, April 8, 2021, https://berkleycenter.georgetown .edu/responses/looking-for-justice-for-black-women-and-girls-the-black-church -jezebel-and-aspirational-black-capitalist-patriarchy.

44　Stuart Hall, ed., *Representation: Cultural Representations and Signifying Practices* (London: Sage, 2003), 237.

45　Patricia Hill Collins, *Black Feminist Thought: Knowledge, Consciousness, and the Politics of Empowerment* (New York: Routledge, 2000), 7 (italics mine).

46　Audre Lorde and James Baldwin, "Revolutionary Hope: A Conversation between Audre Lorde and James Baldwin," *Mosaic Literary Magazine*, no. 39 (Fall 2016): 43, ProQuest.

47　June Jordan, *Some of Us Did Not Die* (New York: Basic/Civitas Books, 2002).

48 This takes nothing away from what it means to those Black and brown folks who've made it home. Nor does it mean to diminish the good Daddy hoped to do through the cross-country move.

49 Tamura Lomax, "Prolegomenon: 'Hoeism or Whatever': Black Girls and the Sable Letter B," in *Jezebel Unhinged*, ix–xviii.

50 In *Black Culture and Black Consciousness*, Lawrence Levine writes, "There was much these whites had to learn if they were to communicate with the freedmen—not only new words, expressions, and pronunciations, but new rules of grammar as well. Slaves and freedmen frequently used a zero copula and eliminated an explicit predicating verb in certain constructions." Concurrently, Black Language, which comes out of slavery and black culture, constructed its own rules for the verb *be*. That said, we've always had different rules of grammar, and these rules are in fact "proper" and legitimate. They're also mimicked by nonblack cultures. This isn't a compliment but rather a critique of continued cultural disciplining, erasure, problematizing, gentrification, and theft.

51 I struggled with using the word *friends* here. It feels odd, given the experience. Yet I don't and didn't consider them my enemies or mere acquaintances. We were friends as we understood it at the time. We did things together, spent the night at each other's houses, ate together, and otherwise, despite moments of antiblackness and misogynoir.

52 I'm drawing on Zakiyyah Iman Jackson's essay "Losing Manhood: Animality and Plasticity in the (Neo)Slave Narrative," *Qui Parle: Critical Humanities and Social Sciences* 25, no. 1–2 (2016): 95–136, www.jstor.org/stable/10.5250/quiparle.25.1-2.0095.

53 In *Where Do We Go from Here—Chaos or Community?*, Martin Luther King Jr. writes: "The White liberal must see that the Negro needs not only love, but justice. It is not enough to say, 'We love Negroes, we have many Negro friends.' They must demand justice for Negroes. Love that does not satisfy justice is no love at all. It is merely a sentimental affection, little more than what one would love for a pet. Love at its best is justice concretized. Love is unconditional. It is not conditional upon one's staying in his place or watering down his demands in order to be considered respectable." See Martin Luther King Jr., Vincent Harding, and Coretta Scott King, *Where Do We Go from Here—Chaos or Community?* (Boston: Beacon Press, 2010).

54 Joan Morgan, *When Chickenheads Come Home to Roost: A Hip-Hop Feminist Breaks It Down* (New York: Simon and Schuster, 1999), 62.

55 See chapter 1.

56 The irony requires explanation. As Charles H. Long writes in *Significations: Signs, Symbols, and Images in the Interpretation of Religion* (Philadelphia: Fortress Press, 1986), black religion is a significant way Black folks come to terms with their ultimate reality in the world. More, the historic Black Church must be held in tension with and distinct from white churches and white theology. My longing for my old church after moving to Mill Valley highlights this contrast. Although it wasn't a black liberationist church, it was still black culturally. Additionally, seminaries and schools of theology/divinity schools are distinct. First, seminaries are often stand-alone institutions. Some emphasize practical ministry for a specific denomination. Others are

more academic. Schools of theology and/or divinity schools typically exist within a larger university and are known for their academic rigor, research, and cross-disciplinary training. Students may go on to do either practical or academic work. Some hold that schools of theology are more academically demanding. Others posit that it all depends. I found my experience to be both practically and academically rewarding and difficult. I chose to do a PhD in religion after completing my master of divinity and master of theology (two separate degrees). Second, schools differ based on theological affiliations, beliefs, faculty, and so on. The school of theology (I also refer to it as a divinity school) I attended and where I placed emphasis on "Black Church studies" was theologically opposed to the seminary in Mill Valley where we lived. For example, the school of theology offered a critical research lens toward the study of religion whereas the seminary in California taught fundamentalist views, for example, the inerrancy of the Bible. It also used the Bible to support sexism, homophobia, and otherwise. My school of theology took a critical and historical approach to the Bible as a text among other texts, was open and affirming in terms of genders and sexualities, and taught feminist, womanist, black liberationist, and queer theologies. On the first day of class, a biblical studies professor threw the Bible in the trash as an illustration of how we'd be unlearning and questioning Christian dogma. Another distinction was the embrace of CRT-aligned theologies (black liberationist and womanist). During my first convocation, a Black man and faculty member preached how he "loved Nat Turner" and his racialized theology of justice. I wouldn't be a black feminist today had I not gone to my divinity school. It was in that space that my religious purview and interpretation of justice were deepened and expanded. At the same time, I would've likely not gone to graduate school if my father had not modeled that for me.

57 See womanist theology. See also Tamura Lomax, "Changing the Letter: Toward a Black Feminist Study of Religion," in *Jezebel Unhinged*, 82–107.

58 A theology based in black freedom and social movements, such as the civil rights and Black Power movements, that believes racism is bad/sin/evil, God is on the side of the oppressed, and that Jesus was and is the great liberator. See James Cone, *Black Theology and Black Power* (Maryknoll, NY: Orbis Books, 1969).

59 Lorde and Baldwin, "Revolutionary Hope," 48.

60 See the introduction to this book.

61 I engage this in chapter 4. For now, the Proverbs woman is an ideal Christian woman.

62 The Southern Baptist Convention was founded in 1845 to safeguard the institution of slavery, racial segregation, and the Confederacy. In line with the forty-fifth POTUS, who issued an executive order stating critical race theory was "anti-American," Southern Baptist seminary presidents issued a similar statement in the *Baptist Faith and Message*. In a riposte, "Is It Time for Black Christians to Give Up on the SBC?," Corrie Shull writes, "At this point, it is clear this is who the SBC is. The SBC remains committed to the very racism and hatred that instigated its founding. At every turn, the SBC resists opportunities to evolve on issues of race and gender in order to authentically follow the revolutionary Jesus Christ of Nazareth—who welcomed the stranger, made space for women and demonstrated what it is to honor the rich tapestry of ethnicities and identities with which God has created

humanity." For more, see Schroeder, "Seminary Presidents Reaffirm BFM, Declare CRT Incompatible"; Yonat Shimron, "Southern Baptist Seminary Presidents Nix Critical Race Theory," *Religion News Service*, December 1, 2020, https://religionnews .com/2020/12/01/southern-baptist-seminary-presidents-nix-critical-race-theory/; and Corrie Shull, "Is It Time for Black Christians to Give Up on the SBC?," *Baptist News Global*, December 8, 2020, https://baptistnews.com/article/is-it-time-for-black -christians-to-give-up-on-the-sbc/.

63 "The Nashville Statement," drafted in 2017 during the annual Southern Baptist conference, offers stances on gender, marriage, patriarchal gender roles, "biblical" manhood and womanhood, chastity, sexuality, opposition to LGBTQ+ sexualities, adultery, fornication, and otherwise, and was signed by more than 150 evangelical leaders and posted online.

64 bell hooks, *Feminism Is for Everybody: Passionate Politics* (London: Pluto Press, 2000).

65 This is the part where it's incorrectly noted that black feminism is antiblack and a version of white feminism. This is false. Black feminism comes out of Black women's and girls' ongoing struggle for freedom and empowerment since captivity. And because of this, it's inherently intersectional as it notes the struggles between race, class, gender, and so on. This is the foundation for building emancipatory communities. Also, while it responds to white racism, it is irreducible to that. More, it's for the emancipation of all Black peoples in the diaspora.

66 In *The Souls of Black Folk*, W. E. B. Du Bois states, "The problem of the Twentieth Century is the problem of the color-line." This line and line of thought undergird both twentieth-century black social movements and black academic specialization, for example, black studies. The role of the latter is critical inquiry, theorizing, and opposition, which speaks to the particularity of Black folks in the diaspora. But as Sojourner Truth, Anna Julia Cooper, Ella Baker, Audre Lorde, June Jordan, Toni Cade Bambara, and so many others teach us, the problems of the color line, of blackness specifically, move across and between genders, sexualities, socioeconomic classes, abilities, et cetera. Black women like Beverly Guy-Sheftall, Gloria T. Hull, Barbara Smith, Barbara Christian, and others also made this plain. Christian specifically asked, "But Where Do Black Women Belong—Black Studies or Women's Studies?," noting that Black women are raced, classed, and gendered at the same time, and more, that there's something distinct about the space we take up. That said, the issue of particularity *within* particularity is historic, ongoing, and necessary, not divisive.

67 Combahee River Collective, "The Combahee River Collective Statement," Yale University American Studies, August 13, 2022, https://americanstudies.yale.edu/sites /default/files/files/Keyword%20Coalition_Readings.pdf.

68 June Jordan, "Resolution #1,003," in *Haruko/Love Poems*, ed. June Jordan and Adrienne Rich (New York: High Risk Books, 1994).

69 Martin Luther King Jr. refers to the world house as a beloved community where we learn to live with each other in peace and with love rooted in justice. World citizenship noted a society where everyone was somebody, valued, equal, and welcome. King saw equity and inherent worth as a moral right. Of course, as Ella Baker and others note, his sex and gender politics failed to match these ideas. I use it more inclusively.

70 Darlene Clark Hine argues Black/African enslaved women resisted breeding through abstinence, abortion, and death. See Darlene Clark Hine, *Hine Sight: Black Women and the Re-construction of American History* (Bloomington: Indiana University Press, 1994). Additionally, Rose Williams, a slave in *The American Slave, Texas Narratives*, recounts resisting rape and breeding at age sixteen by kicking her husband, Rufus, while wielding a fire poker, and threatening to "bust his brains out" and "stomp on them" when he crawled into bed to breed with her. As I write in *Jezebel Unhinged*, Williams asserts, "De lawd have to forgive dis cullud woman, but he have to 'scuse me and look for some others for to 'plenish de earth" (27). See "Image 184 of Federal Writers' Project: Slave Narrative Project, Vol. 16, Texas, Part 4, Sanco-Young," Library of Congress, accessed July 31, 2023, https://www.loc.gov/resource/mesn.164/, 183. See also George P. Rawick, ed., *The American Slave, Texas Narratives*, vol. 5, pt. 4 (Westport, CT: Greenwood Press, 1977), 178. It should also be noted that Thomas A. Foster makes the case that both Rose and Rufus were victims of rape in *Rethinking Rufus: Sexual Violations of Enslaved Men* (Atlanta: University of Georgia Press, 2019). Rose was a victim twice over—to Rufus, whom she called a bully and absolutely didn't like, and to their slaver, William Black. Rufus was a victim to the slaver as he didn't consent to be with Rose. Neither Rose nor Rufus wanted to be together, let alone be breeders within the slave system. Though Rose was eventually forced to give in to being raped, she resisted and refused to marry once free. See also Tera Hunter, *To 'Joy My Freedom: Southern Black Women's Lives and Labors after the Civil War* (Cambridge, MA: Harvard University Press, 1997).

71 I'm not even sure I heard the word *feminism*, black or otherwise, before college. I was introduced to black feminist literature in divinity school/seminary. It's where I learned to theorize what I'd already been feeling but didn't have language for.

4. EMANCIPATING PROVERBS 31

1 "Knuck If You Buck" by Crime Mob is a southern rap song that refers to self-protection, preservation, and fighting.

2 Jakes's use of "real" in his sermon underscores why this book is necessary as well as my critique of the term in this book. I write in the notes to the introduction, though the deployment of "real" means to work against antiblack dehumanization in America, and thus, on one hand, hopes to establish humanity, legibility, and political rights, it ultimately traffics in heteropatriarchy, homophobia, misogynoir, and transantagonism. I assert throughout this text that there's no one or more or less "real" way to be human or express gender or identity. See also T. D. Jakes, "Real Men Pour In," YouTube, accessed August 4, 2022, https://www.youtube.com/watch?v=4fTg4FHSSQY.

3 Tamura Lomax, *Jezebel Unhinged: Loosing the Black Female Body in Religion and Culture* (Durham, NC: Duke University Press, 2018).

4 Jakes is emphasizing a certain group of Black cisgender men. Not all Black men ascribe to or support his interpretation of "real" men. I emphasize *Black* men because although Jakes denies the existence of the Black Church and claims universality (as in he leads a universal church for all people) and a mixed audience, his church,

theology, membership, preaching, style, etc. are either black or predominantly black. Jakes's messaging on "real" manhood and womanhood directly aligns with and draws from black cultural narratives on the same. It's not a universal message. It's a black message to Black people. Jakes's leaning toward universality highlights capitalistic aims and a desire for the largest platform and audience possible.

5 I discuss this at length in *Jezebel Unhinged*. It's the Black Church's version of distinctions between "hos" and "housewives." Jakes and others mass-mediate this binary. *Jezebel Unhinged* takes the entire paradigm to task.

6 Lomax, "Whose 'Woman' Is This? Reading Bishop T. D. Jakes's *Woman, Thou Art Loosed!*," in *Jezebel Unhinged*, 130–68.

7 I've discussed the dovetailing between aspirational black patriarchy and the black messiah elsewhere. Jakes markets both. We don't need a black messiah. We need Black folks loving each other and collectively building emancipatory sanctuaries. See also Princeton Theological Seminary, "Dr. Tamura Lomax | The Dr. Martin Luther King Jr. Lecture," YouTube, accessed August 7, 2023, https://www.youtube .com/watch?v=_TlMdOvdwZk.

8 This references the Adam and Eve story in Genesis in the Christian Bible where Adam and Eve are said to be the first humans in the creation narrative. They're placed in the Garden of Eden to care for the land and are told that they can eat fruit from any of the trees except the tree in the middle of the garden that gives knowledge of what's good and what's bad, or else they'll die. A snake appears and influences Eve to try the fruit on the forbidden tree of life, as the fruit will make her like God. Desirous of wisdom, Eve eats the fruit and gives some to Adam, who eats it as well. The snake and all other snakes, Eve and all other women, and the ground are then cursed by God. Women are cursed with painful childbirths and patriarchy ("you will be subject to him"). And because Adam listened to Eve (patriarchal misbehavior), men will have to work hard for a living to make the ground produce the necessities for survival. Because of this, Eve and women are culturally blamed for sin. Simultaneously, Jakes is arguing that Adam shouldn't have listened to Eve or "eaten out of her hand" in the first place because he's a man. Jakes preaches, "Self-esteem is compromised when you ask your wife for lunch money." In this way, sin also came into the world because Adam broke the gender hierarchy, which Jakes refers to as "divine order" (also, Christian patriarchal order). Consequently, any relations or relating outside of heteropatriarchal order is a sin according to Jakes. Women are inherently and permanently subject to men. Otherwise, they're out of order with God and sinful. This sermon also establishes how women are subject to men sexually, how childbirth is a duty, and how love and sexual relations are between women and men only. For more, see Jakes, "Real Men Pour In."

9 Jakes says when God created the earth, he used it as a womb because he "injected his seed in the womb of the earth" and "used his word as sperm." In the same way, God made Eve from Adam's rib but gave her a womb, giving her the duty to birth and nurture children. See Jakes, "Real Men Pour In."

10 This is interesting to think about in terms of Patrice from *P-Valley*, discussed in chapter 2. She's invested in "real"/Proverbs 31 heteropatriarchal ideal womanhood as

evidenced in her badgering of Mercedes. However, Patrice is also unabashedly committed to gaining state power and will fight dirty with men for it.

11 This is the crux of Jakes's Father's Day sermon. See Jakes, "Real Men Pour In."

12 Jakes is double speaking both economically and sexually. As I've written elsewhere, he has a range of books and sermons about how women are "receivers" and men are "plugs." When "plugs" "receive," they break "divine order" and become women.

13 This reference contradicts Jakes's concern about disposability. It's clear he's attempting to show black male strength by drawing on white heteropatriarchal images of muscular Christianity and black hypermasculinity. The issue is, according to the Bible, Jesus died a brutal death at the hands of the state due to bogus charges. It seems counterproductive to use such a harmful representation for Black men.

14 As argued in chapter 3, significant to neofascism in America is the alliance between white conservative politicians and white Christian nationalists, which rejects democracy; dissent; race, sex, sexual, gender, and religious equity; and anything that resists or challenges male dominance (feminism, LGBTQ+, etc.). Male headship in the household, community, institutions, and governing structure is an expression of power. Everything hinges on the powerful heroic male warrior of the superior race and religion and their vision of the society and world. Thus, the significance of theologizing and politicizing the existence of only two genders, heteropatriarchal normativity, and the "nuclear" family. Women are subservient, female leadership is sign of weakness and ultimately unacceptable, and LGBTQ+ individuals are completely disparaged in this kind of society.

15 What I'm noting here is that some of the things Jakes supports are essential to American neofascism: political and religious conservatism, which centers male dominance and the heroic male warrior; heterosexism; heteronormativity; and heteropatriarchy. Some will claim that he doesn't support sexism because he supports women ministers and leaders. I have a different reading of that, which is detailed in *Jezebel Unhinged*. Jakes supports women leading within the patriarchy. Patriarchy is still the guiding hermeneutic. Simultaneously, however, I would argue that Jakes doesn't support racial inequity, the silencing of dissent, extreme hatred (though theological conservatism, disdain, marginalization, and villainy lead to hate), white supremacist superiority or nationalism, the rejection of democracy, or violence. Jakes seems to be aware of and concerned about what the conservative right's outright rejection of democracy could mean. What I hope to convey is how these seemingly harmless or biblically sound building blocks—heteropatriarchy and heterosexism—also underline vicious structures of dominance that injure us. Too often we recognize fascism by envisioning Hitler or the forty-fifth POTUS while ignoring the conventional steps taken to get to the places they've guided us.

16 I don't do this work here. However, there's something to further explore in terms of Jakes's humble messiah posture. I mention it in *Jezebel Unhinged*. Jakes refers to himself as a servant of God speaking God's message. Yet, he often slips up (or not) about the rules and/or final word in *his* "house" (the church, businesses, etc.). He's the boss. See The Lions Den, "Oprah's Next Chapter with Bishop T. D. Jakes," YouTube, https://www.youtube.com/watch?v=N9UOnHAKg3M.

17 Evangelical sex and gender ideology is supported by various texts throughout the Bible, such as the Adam and Eve creation story inferred by Jakes. See also Lomax, "Looking for Justice for Black Women and Girls."

I first use aspirational black capitalist patriarchy in the essay "Looking for Justice for Black Women and Girls: The Black Church, Jezebel, and Aspirational Black Capitalist Patriarchy" for the Berkley Forum on The Black Church in American Public Life, cosponsored by the Center on African-American Religion, Sexual Politics and Social Justice at Columbia University. The essay was requested in response to the PBS special "The Black Church: This Is Our Story, This Is Our Song," released in February 2021, highlighting the historical and contemporary significance of black churches in America. In it, I define aspirational black capitalist heteropatriarchy as "a particular allegiance to the accumulation of Black cisgender heteronormative male power and status that is both power/less in the face of white supremacy and power/full intracommunally, which sanctions and looks away from sexism, sexist stereotyping, sexual shaming, homophobia, transantagonism, and rape culture." It's committed to an accumulation of capital and sex and gender sociopolitical power. For more, see Tamura Lomax, "Looking for Justice for Black Women and Girls: The Black Church, Jezebel, and Aspirational Black Capitalist Patriarchy," Berkley Center for Religion, Peace and World Affairs, April 8, 2021, https://berkleycenter .georgetown.edu/responses/looking-for-justice-for-black-women-and-girls-the-black -church-jezebel-and-aspirational-black-capitalist-patriarchy.

Additionally, *friendly fascism* refers to how totalitarian governments often begin through palatable appeals to normative forms of domination and oppression.

18 Sundown towns are predominantly white antiblack communities, municipalities, local governments, and police that practice discrimination and intimidation. A sundown country reflects the potential for widespread antiblack racial violence and governing in the current political economy. The argument I'm making here is that enough sundown towns, states, and otherwise might force Black folks into a make-shift sanctuary for the sake of survival and community. Historically, slave plantations had some collectivity. There were still intracommunal differences, betrayals, and violences, however. Notwithstanding, the structure of slavocracy oppressed everyone, requiring alternative ethics for living. I'm also noting white supremacist capitalist patriarchal violence has a way of uniting Black folks contemporarily. We saw this in the Riverfront brawl in Montgomery, Alabama, in August 2023 when a group of white people beat a Black riverboat cocaptain trying to do his job. In this case, Black people—foot soldiers and supporters from afar in social media—united across genders, identities, and sexualities. I want to suggest that aspirations for black heteropatriarchy may take a back seat to collective organizing and aims in some cases against white supremacy. Notwithstanding, history shows this is still shaky when it comes to sex, gender, and capital. I'm not certain harms or injustices done to individual or collective Black cisgender women or LGBTQ+ folks would ignite a similar response. #Sayhername exists due to the lack of collective care and organizing for Black women and girls killed by the state. Silence is even louder when violence is intracommunal. For example, the rapper Tory Lanez was sentenced to ten years in prison for shooting Megan Thee Stallion less than forty-eight hours

after the Montgomery brawl. Yet, some of those who'd just united for the brawl were divided and angry with Megan, who'd initially decided against involving the legal system to protect Lanez, despite suffering bullet wounds. I write more about this in the coda and *Loving Black Boys* (forthcoming), but the pressure for Black women and girls to #protectblackmen is a one-way street. In the end, Megan was called a liar, was shamed, and otherwise, and notably by Black men—and women. Additionally, I'm also not certain über-rich Black people like Jakes would give up aspirations for black capitalist heteropatriarchy for local resistance activities or revolution if there was a lifeline to still collect on patriarchal and/or capitalist privileges.

19   In this dystopian television series, heteropatriarchal men, fringe groups, and para-militaries run wild under the protection of the Constitution and religion.

20   Jakes isn't just a preacher of prosperity gospel. He leads a multitiered profit-generating business as well as a faith-based initiative and has a $1 billion ten-year partnership with Wells Fargo Bank. I wouldn't be surprised if he has his sights set on owning his own bank in the future, especially since he's tossed the mic (preaching) to his daughter, Sarah Jakes Roberts. See also, "1-on-1 with Bishop TD Jakes," *ABC News*, accessed August 7, 2023, https://abcnews.go.com/Nightline/video/1-1 -bishop-td-jakes-99686580.

21   Lomax, *Jezebel Unhinged*, 163.

22   Chatty Passenger, "James Baldwin and Nikki Giovanni 'A Conversation.' Full Broadcast Video," YouTube, accessed August 8, 2023, https://www.youtube.com/watch?v =y4OPYp4sotc.

23   Stuart Hall, ed., *Representation: Cultural Representations and Signifying Practices* (London: Sage, 2003).

24   I argue in *Jezebel Unhinged* that though Jakes may have an international multiethnic audience, he reserves his criticisms specifically for Black people, and namely Black women.

25   This isn't to suggest that Jakes or others are chasing whiteness or white men. I don't think this is the goal. Neither do I believe this is the case for all Black men. Yet there are some Black men (and women) who hope to access powerful capitalist domination, and white men happen to provide an example of what that looks like.

26   In *Representation*, Stuart Hall argues, though everyone is caught up in the circularity of power, because no one can stand wholly outside its operation, we don't experience its force on equal terms.

27   Lomax, "Whose 'Woman' Is This?"

28   On June 24, 2022, five days after Jakes's Father's Day sermon, the US Supreme Court overturned *Roe v. Wade*, the landmark decision that made abortion a federal right in the United States. With the constitutional right to abortion gone, a decision that had been leaked in May 2022, abortion rights have been consequently rolled back in many states, making it so abortions are largely inaccessible. Right-wing conservative politicians and evangelicals celebrated the demise of women's right to have abortions as a spiritual and moral victory. Elizabeth Dias, "For Conservative Christians, the End of Roe Was a Spiritual Victory," *New York Times*, June 25, 2022, https://www .nytimes.com/2022/06/25/us/conservative-christians-roe-wade-abortion.html; Daniel Silliman, "Goodbye Roe v. Wade: Pro-Life Evangelicals Celebrate the Ruling They've

Waited For," *Christianity Today*, June 24, 2022, https://www.christianitytoday.com/news/2022/june/roe-v-wade-overturn-abortion-supreme-court-ruling-pro-life.html.

29 Zillah Eisenstein, "Newest Misogyny/ies," *Logos: A Journal of Modern Society and Culture*, Spring 2023, https://logosjournal.com/2023/newest-misogyny-ies/.

30 There's so much to sit with here, especially when thinking about the Christocentric pressure on Black women and girls to carry fetuses to term, despite poverty, illness, sexual abuse, age, and otherwise. Patrice forced Mercedes to have Terricka as a teenager for this very reason. I've seen this scenario play out countless times in my personal experience. Even Jakes's daughter had her first baby at fourteen years of age, despite her father preaching chastity. Jakes says he cares about the person and personal empowerment, but what of increasing rates of poverty and death for Black mothers? What of sexual violence for poor Black girls? See also Eisenstein, "Newest Misogyny/ies."

31 "Interview with T. D. Jakes," CNN *Larry King Live*, November 17, 2009, http://edition.cnn.com/TRANSCRIPTS/0911/17/lkl.01.html.

32 North American slave archives provide a range of firsthand accounts of violences against pregnant Black women and girls, including and well beyond Mary Turner, a pregnant slave who spoke out against the hanging of her husband, and was thus hanged, burned naked, shot multiple times, and cut open shortly after on May 18, 1918. Her dead fetus, one month shy of being born, lay dead on the ground beneath her, stomped to death with his head crushed open. See also *partus sequitur ventrem* in terms of slave paternal rights.

33 While *Roe* is a defining issue today for the conservative religious right, they generally focused on racism and sexism prior to establishing the Moral Majority in 1979. Abortion and *Roe* didn't become an organizing agenda until the late 1970s and the feminist movement. Prior to that, uniform opposition didn't exist.

34 Though Jakes invited Beto O'Rourke, who supports abortion, to his church, and posits pro-life is irreducible to the fetus in the womb, he's still antichoice. See also "T. D. Jakes in the Midst of Racial Turmoil: You Can't Be Pro-Life Just in the Womb," press release from Guardian Client Newsrooms, June 10, 2020, https://newsrooms.guardian.agency/ph/news/t.d.-jakes-in-the-midst-of-racial-turmoil-you-cant-be-pro-life-just-in-womb; Emma Green, "T. D. Jakes on How White Evangelicals Lost Their Way," *Atlantic*, May 31, 2021, https://www.theatlantic.com/politics/archive/2021/05/td-jakes-pastor-white-evangelicals/619035/.

35 "Interview with T. D. Jakes."

36 During the 2020 presidential election the forty-fifth POTUS targeted aspirational black capitalist heteropatriarchal rappers like Kanye West, Ice Cube, Lil Wayne, and others to gain their support in increasing his share of black votes, to which they agreed, despite MAGA's racist, sexist, classist, and otherwise platform. While on *The View*, 50 Cent revealed he was offered a half million dollars to stump for the forty-fifth POTUS. See also Green, "T. D. Jakes on How White Evangelicals Lost Their Way."

37 The Grio, "Bishop T. D. Jakes on Leadership, Voting, Trump," YouTube, accessed August 7, 2023, https://www.youtube.com/watch?v=TR05_WSDnls.

38 The increased support of the forty-fifth POTUS by Black men is slight but noteworthy. While Black men may hope to align with or feel empowered by his version

of heteropatriarchal imperial power, they stand to lose the most from a second presidency. The forty-fifth POTUS promises a more racially conservative America with a MAGA Supreme Court, complete immunity for police, and the reinstatement of stop and frisk if he's elected again. Part of the uptick in support among Black men has to do with a rejection of feminism, women's rights, LGBTQ+ rights, and queer and women leaders. Yet some of it is due to abandonment by the Democratic Party, which has negated their needs for jobs with living wages, safety, equitable education, fair housing, health care, and otherwise. Notwithstanding, the forty-fifth POTUS offers little more than lip service, a macho performance, and indications of further oppression through lessened resources, military campaigns, and deportation.

39 James Cone, *Black Theology and Black Power* (Maryknoll, NY: Orbis Books, 1969), 105.

40 The number of Black people who identify as Republican is small in comparison to those who vote Democrat. Black political conservatism, largely linked to black religious conservatism, is expressed through ideas on morality, family values, heterosexism, the black "nuclear" family, abortion, and hard work. Of particular import is the relationship between family values and the black "nuclear" family, heterosexism, and aspirational black patriarchy, and how each feeds widely circulated ideas on "real" black manhood and womanhood. These ideas aid in shaping Black Church conservatism and black religious discourses on abortion. It's believed that life begins at conception, and the "nuclear" family represents black power and humanity. Black Christian conservatism needs deeper discussions about black life and death, however—for example, Black women's and girls' cyclical poverty, access to health care, health inequalities, death rates, lack of childcare, lack of reproductive justice, historical lack of bodily autonomy, lack of safety, postpartum death rates, and on and on. In 2020, a selection of Black ministers wrote an open letter to Rev. Raphael Warnock, junior US senator from Georgia, during a potentially life-altering Senate race, urging him to change his stance on abortion. Yet, there was next to nothing to say about Black women dying in labor, children in cages at the border, the execution of Brandon Bernard, or many of the other black genocidal atrocities during this time. Perhaps we missed those open letters to the forty-fifth POTUS. For more on the Black Church and abortion, see Sheila Poole, "Black Ministers Urge Warnock to Change Abortion Rights Stance," *Atlanta Journal-Constitution*, December 11, 2020, https://www.ajc .com/news/black-ministers-send-open-letter-to-warnock-asking-him-to-change-pro -choice-stance/LWFRQI5AEFHW3KNCNMJZMGF7TY/. See also John Flea, Laura Gifford, Marie R. Griffith, and Lerone A. Martin, "Evangelicalism and Politics," *American Historian*, accessed November 29, 2020, https://www.oah.org/tah/issues/2018 /november/evangelicalism-and-politics/; Molly Worthen, "Can Black Evangelicals Save the Whole Movement?," *New York Times*, April 20, 2019, https://www.nytimes .com/2019/04/20/opinion/sunday/black-evangelicals-diversity.html.

41 For example, patronymics, citizenship, political power, equal rights, property rights, and fair and accessible upward mobility, capitalist accumulation, and wealth building. In *Slave Religion: The "Invisible Institution" in the Antebellum South* (New York: Oxford University Press, 1978), Albert J. Raboteau outlines how some slaves agreed to Christian baptism because they believed it would free them and grant them citizenship and rights. However, slavers had no intention of freeing slaves. Slavers and

clergy hoped baptism and catechism would make better and more obedient slaves. They made laws explicitly establishing that Christian conversion had nothing to do with freedom from slavery and that slaves were to obey their slavers as well as the law. This justified and sanctioned a range of violences, including rape, breeding, and beatings, against slaves.

42 I visited Kehinde Wiley's exhibit titled *An Archaeology of Silence* while writing this book. Wiley posits that there's an archaeology of silence on black death by the state in America, which needs unearthing, exposing, speaking, and undermining through a counternarrative in order to face the humanity of those lost and the fury of those who cause black death. Similarly, I'm arguing there's an archaeology of silence on violences against Black LGBTQ+ folks in the Black Church, communities, and otherwise, which requires a loud excavation and analysis of artifacts and remains.

43 When talking to Larry King, Jakes posits, "I am not supportive of gay marriage. But I . . . I don't think that that's the real issue here. I don't think that that should stop them from serving 68,000 people who are homeless or hungry or maybe gay or disenfranchised. I know in our church, when we start feeding the hungry, we don't ask them about their sexuality. We don't ask them about their faith. We don't ask them the color of their skin. When we work with people who are infected by the virus HIV, we don't ask them how they got it. It's irrelevant." It's imperative to pause here. Sexuality is irrelevant to Jakes in terms of serving certain needs. Serving "the needy" is a noble Christian duty. Marrying them is another story. Jakes asserts, "When you really love people and you want to serve people, sometimes you can have the principles, but you cannot let your adherence to the principle become stronger than your love for people. . . . And I'm against abuse to gay people and the . . . the hate crimes and so many things that we can agree on. I think the problem now is that we exacerbate what we don't agree on rather than focusing on what we can agree on." Yet, by stating homosexuality is condemned by scripture and that he's against marriage equality, Jakes is practicing and encouraging ill and unequal treatment. It's worth mentioning that his son Jermaine Jakes was arrested for soliciting sex from a male officer several years ago. See "Interview with T. D. Jakes"; The Lions Den, "Oprah's Next Chapter with Bishop T. D. Jakes."

44 HuffPost Live, "Bishop T. D. Jakes on the Black Church's Shifting Stance on Homosexuality," YouTube, accessed August 7, 2023, https://www.youtube.com/watch?v=F5MRhqSK8Ts&t=1s.

45 The quotes around "black church" are worth noting again because Jakes resists the notion there's a Black Church and that he's a part of it, despite history and all he's gained from it culturally, traditionally, economically, and otherwise.

46 I added this text exactly as written, as I believe there's unspoken emphasis in the line breaks. T. D. Jakes Ministries, "My comment on HuffPo TV drifted into issues of the Supreme Court ruling and changing the world through public policy verses personal witness," Facebook, August 9, 2015, https://www.facebook.com/bishopjakes/posts/10153758229753322.

47 I write in *Jezebel Unhinged* that Jakes prefers a neoliberalist emphasis on self-transformation, hard work, the free market, and personal responsibility because it allows him to negate and absolve social conditions and structural violences,

and therefore depoliticize history, thus appealing and marketing to nonblack conservatives.

48 Too Short. See chapter 3.

49 This is the work I do in *Loving Black Boys* (forthcoming).

50 The Proverbs 31 woman and Mary, the mother of Jesus, serve as exemplars for biblical womanhood. In *When Momma Speaks: The Bible and Motherhood from a Womanist Perspective* (Louisville, KY: Westminster John Knox Press, 2016), Stephanie Buckhanon Crowder argues that Mary serves as "an example of God's possibility" for Black women (82).

51 Proverbs 31:10–31.

52 I discuss Jakes's discourse on femininity in "Whose 'Woman' Is This?"

53 *Softness* refers to feminine ideals around aesthetics, dress, attitude, octave, humility, vulnerability, and so on. The issue is not with softness, however defined, as a choice. It's with softness as a heteropatriarchal requirement of "real" womanhood and thus a prison for what a woman or girl should be. It should be noted that "softness" was also vital to the nineteenth-century cult of domesticity/"true" womanhood, which held that women were naturally soft, weak, and delicate.

54 A major distinction here is that the Black Church, Jakes, et al. emphasize heterosexual marriage.

55 jesshilarious_official, "Who tf stands up for US?," Instagram, July 22, 2023, https://www.instagram.com/reel/CvAUewgRbx1/.

56 Ts Madison, "Addressing the 'Jess Mess' #JessHilarious," YouTube, accessed August 7, 2023, https://www.youtube.com/watch?v=MBzzmI2EEa0.

57 Black slave women were also de/mis/gendered, which led to violent treatment.

58 I write the following in *Jezebel Unhinged:*

> Biblical and cultural jezebel rose up on North American plantations alongside the Black Church and black desire for full humanity. The virtuous woman of Proverbs 31—who gets up at the crack of dawn to work all day in the public sphere, take care of the home, shop, sew, cook, plant, purchase property, trade goods, feed the poor, speak wisdom, and praise the Lord while following instructions and refusing idleness, complaining, and sleep, all while dressed in fine clothing, and while making sure her lamp does not go out at night—presents an opportunity for nobility and humanity that is inaccessible to the jezebel trope. Though Black women and girls may not control pornotropic gazing, they may resist the metanarrative. The virtuous woman of Proverbs 31 is particularly significant because, unlike the Victorian ideal, her attributes are applicable to all women. And though she works like an indentured servant, caring for home, community, and personal flair, the virtuous woman turned supermothering, deeply religious mythical figure turned black lady at least makes dignity seem attainable. . . . It should make sense, then, that Black Church sermons often juxtapose theologies of virtue and ideologies of innate promiscuity, untrustworthiness, and immorality. (50)

Increasingly, younger generations of Black women and girls are claiming their right to sexual decision-making and pleasure outside of marriage and are rejecting historical scripts that mark them as whores, hos, jezebels, etc. Notwithstanding, policing continues. Social media recently suggested a Facebook post for me, which included a picture of Savannah James at a basketball game that read, "No twerking, no Nakedness on IG. No looking for attention. Just cooling in the back raising her kids living a good life. This is what a wife looks like. . . . . . . Savannah James. . . . . . ."

59 Tamura Lomax, "Black Bodies in Ecstasy: Black Women, the Black Church, and the Politics of Pleasure: An Introduction," *Black Theology: An International Journal* 16, no. 3 (2018): 189–94, https://doi.org/10.1080/14769948.2018.1492298.

60 Keri Day, "'I Am Dark and Lovely': Let the Shulammite Woman Speak," *Black Theology: An International Journal* 16, no. 3 (2018): 207, https://doi.org/10.1080/14769948 .2018.1492300. See also Brittney Cooper, "How Sarah Got Her Groove Back, or Notes toward a Black Feminist Theology of Pleasure," *Black Theology: An International Journal* 16, no. 3 (2018): 195–206, https://doi.org/10.1080/14769948.2018.1492299.

61 Toni Cade Bambara, ed., *The Black Woman: An Anthology* (New York: Washington Square Press, 2005), 5–6.

62 Michele Wallace, *Black Macho and the Myth of the Superwoman* (New York: Dial Press, 1979).

63 The insistence on submission and second classness for women and girls means to silence demands for rights and equity, and that their sociopolitical and socioeconomic needs be met, each of which is seen as senseless, impractical, nasty, and unnatural.

64 Baldwin and Giovanni discuss this as well. While Giovanni pushes for partnership, accountability, and love with Black men, Baldwin notes Black men have it hard in the world and thus don't need things to be hard at home. It's interesting watching someone with otherwise radical politics still maintain the patriarchy, which Baldwin does in this footage. See Chatty Passenger, "James Baldwin and Nikki Giovanni."

65 Too many sexual partners, which applies only to women and girls.

66 Making men comfortable and happy refers to ensuring sexual availability, making sure the home is clean, food preparation and serving, providing childcare, running errands, personal beautification, and more. It notes the one-sided expectation of women to do whatever it takes to make men's life easier and pleasant, despite women having their own work, duties, needs, and otherwise. This is also known as the "second shift"—women's unpaid work at home, including caring for men and children and domesticity.

67 This is gendered. No one demands that Black cisgender heterosexual men be sweet in their day-to-day dealings with all women to get basic respect or to get things done. Additionally, the level of sweetness required of women and girls extends further than love relationships and/or being respectful. It's about dominion and subjection.

68 Proverbs 31:1–9.

69 Wil Gafney, "Commentary on Proverbs 31:10–31," *Working Preacher*, September 4, 2015, https://www.workingpreacher.org/commentaries/revised-common-lectionary /ordinary-25-2/commentary-on-proverbs-3110-31-4.

70 Wilda C. Gafney, *Daughters of Miriam: Women Prophets in Ancient Israel* (Minneapolis: Fortress Press, 2008), 157–65.

71 Gafney writes, the Queen Mother commands the king to "speak on behalf of the voiceless and transient, to open his mouth and judge righteously on behalf of the poor and oppressed." Gafney, *Daughters of Miriam*, 158.

72 Gafney asserts the Queen Mother offering prenuptial counsel may be a widow as there is no mention of a spouse. *Ba'al* vv. 11 and 28 is "lord" or "master" indicating hierarchy, not husband.

73 (*shalal*) vv. 11. See Gafney, *Daughters of Miriam*, 158–59.

74 Gafney asserts this is in keeping with the martial aspect of *chayil*. Gafney, *Daughters of Miriam*, 158–59.

75 In verse 15, *tereph* means prey, which Gafney says is often mistranslated to mean food. Gafney, *Daughters of Miriam*, 158.

76 Gafney posits, "The activity of 'strengthening one's arms' is a martial one; it is preparatory for combat or hunting." Gafney, *Daughters of Miriam*, 159. In "Commentary on Proverbs 31:10–31," she notes:

> Proverbs 31:10 has been translated in many ways: *Who can find a virtuous woman?* (King James Version) *A good wife who can find?* (Revised Standard Version) *A capable wife who can find?* (New Revised Standard Version). There are two primary issues in translation that shape the interpretation of the text. The first is the status of the woman since Biblical Hebrew does not have separate words for "woman" and "wife." (All wives are women but not all women are wives meaning that *isshah* can always be translated "woman" but not always "wife" which must be inferred.) The text never uses the common word for husband (*ish*), but a more hierarchal term, master/lord, (*ba'al*) perhaps owing to its royal context. The second issue is the character of the woman, which is the heart of the piece. . . . What is that essential character trait? A few more translations might help. Early English translations included "strong" (Wycliffe) and "honest faithful" (Geneva). The Douay Bible preserves the (Latin) Vulgate and (Greek) Septuagint manuscript tradition with "valiant" while the New English Septuagint has "courageous." The Greek text has *andreian*, "manly." What all these translations are struggling with is the original Hebrew word, *chayil*, with a primary meaning ranging from "military might/power" to "(physical) strength." Its plural form designates warriors or an army.

77 See Gafney, "Commentary on Proverbs 31:10–31."

78 Gafney, "Commentary on Proverbs 31:10–31."

79 In "Commentary on Proverbs 31:10–31," Gafney argues:

> Other language in the text also points to her physical strength. Verse 11 says she provides her lord (also "master" or more rarely "husband") with "spoil" as in spoils of war taken by military might and, v 15 says that she rises while it is night to take "prey," both physical feats of strength and skill but significantly softened in most translations. A second word for physical strength occurs in verses 17 and 25. The emphasis on physical strength extends to metaphorical strength as a secondary virtue along with but not in place of physical prowess. . . . The descriptive rhetoric culminates in verses 29–31. What makes her a woman of warrior strength? Verse 29 reveals that other women have indeed demonstrated warrior strength using the same word, *chayil*. But the woman the Queen Mother describes exceeds and excels them all.

80 Katherine Steinly, "The Woman of Strength," Academia.edu, August 13, 2022, https://www.academia.edu/14274366/The_Woman_of_Strength_Proverbs_31_10_31.

81 Landowning in North America is foremost a violent and exploitative practice against Indigenous populations and was historically deployed to decide who could and couldn't vote. The people who own the most land also own the power.

82 Optimus Fine @sunnydaejones, "TD Jakes and all the other Black mega pastors spent 20 years," Twitter, July 22, 2023, https://twitter.com/sunnydaejones/status /1550550265417326593.

83 Cheryl Kirk-Duggan, "Rethinking the 'Virtuous' Woman (Proverbs 31): A Mother in Need of Holiday," in *Mother Goose, Mother Jones, Mommie Dearest: Biblical Mothers and Their Children*, ed. Cheryl Kirk-Duggan and Tina Pippin (Leiden: Brill, 2010), 97–112.

84 Some may read this as privileged because I'm a Black cisgendered heterosexual married woman. I'm in no way against heterosexual marriage. I hold that everyone who wants marriage should have access to it, and those that don't shouldn't be pressured to participate in it. Many Black cisgender heterosexual women and girls desire love, marriage, children, and so on. We need additional black feminist works on the nuances of love and relationships with Black men and boys, however. We need discourses that engage what love might look like beyond patriarchal constructs. I also write this knowing full well that some Black women want their knight in shining armor while others see the latter as patriarchal. Some others may want their knight in shining armor to have radical politics and to partner. Others may want to be chased and/or taken care of. Some want to at least have a level of partnership that allows for comfort, support, and rest. We need ways of talking through and to these realities that engage Black women and girls across genders and sexualities as powerful choosing subjects rather than objects waiting to be selected.

5. ORDINARY OR INSURGENT?

1 June Jordan, "The Creative Spirit: Children's Literature," in *Revolutionary Mothering: Love on the Front Lines*, ed. Alexis Pauline Gumbs, China Martens, and Mai'a Williams (Oakland, CA: PM Press, 2016), 12.

2 Barrett self-identifies with Scalia's textualism and originalism.

3 Stephanie Mencimer, "Amy Coney Barrett Is the Least Experienced Supreme Court Nominee in 30 Years," *Mother Jones*, October 23, 2020, https://www.motherjones .com/politics/2020/10/amy-coney-barrett-is-the-least-experienced-supreme-court -nominee-in-30-years/.

4 Ice Miller Legal Counsel, "Myra C. Selby," accessed August 31, 2022, https://www .icemiller.com/people/myra-c-selby/.

5 The Associated Press, "A Look at Judge Amy Coney Barrett's Notable Opinions, Votes," *AP News*, October 11, 2020, https://apnews.com/article/race-and-ethnicity -donald-trump-confirmation-hearings-discrimination-amy-coney-barrett -4380ef16b3da79836151bcaaa7eda224; Beth Reinhard and Alice Crites, "'People of Praise Leaders Failed Me': Christian Group Tied to Justice Amy Coney Barrett Faces Reckoning over Sexual Misconduct," *Washington Post*, June 11, 2021, https:// www.washingtonpost.com/investigations/2021/06/11/people-praise-barrett-sexual

-misconduct/; Stephanie Kirckaessner, "Legal Claims Shed Light on Founder of Faith Group Tied to Amy Coney Barrett," *Guardian*, June 6, 2022, https://www .theguardian.com/world/2022/jun/06/people-of-praise-accused-child-abuse-amy -coney-barrett.

6 Zillah Eisenstein, "Towards an Abolitionist Feminism," *Feminist Wire*, May 15, 2015, https://thefeministwire.com/2015/05/towards-an-abolitionist-feminism/.

7 The indictment and live updates on forty-five's bid to overturn the 2020 presidential election can be found in "Trump and 18 Allies Charged with Racketeering in a Bid to Overturn the 2020 Election: Live Updates," NPR, August 14, 2023, https:// www.npr.org/live-updates/trump-news-indictment-georgia-election. For more on the dismantling of affirmative action, see Nina Totenberg's essay "Supreme Court Guts Affirmative Action, Effectively Ending Race-Conscious Admissions," NPR, June 29, 2023, https://www.npr.org/2023/06/29/1181138066/affirmative-action -supreme-court-decision. She writes, "In a historic decision, the U.S. Supreme Court on Thursday effectively ended race-conscious admission programs at colleges and universities across the country."

8 Kathleen Ronayne and Michael Kunzelman, "Trump to Far-Right Extremists: 'Stand Back and Stand By,'" *AP News*, September 30, 2020, https://apnews.com /article/election-2020-joe-biden-race-and-ethnicity-donald-trump-chris-wallace -0b32339da25fbc9e8b7c7c7066a1db0f.

9 As mentioned previously, racism, sexism, and Christian hypermoralism were pivotal to both the North American plantation economy and the violences, sexual and otherwise, against Black/African slaves. Breeding/rape was a tool for maintaining slavocracy. Black/African slave women were reduced to sexual labor during slavery and shamed for said labor using the Christian Bible. Albert J. Raboteau, in *Slave Religion: The "Invisible Institution" in the Antebellum South* (New York: Oxford University Press, 1978), notes how white Christian ministers and missionaries often preached messages about sexual purity to the slaves. The contradiction led them to ask if they could bring their masters before the church for rape and breeding. To protect white Christianity, slavery, and white people, rape and breeding were seen as the slaves' fault, though they had no choice in the matter. Some made the choice to abort, however.

10 America isn't a Christian nation. The First Amendment to the US Constitution notes religious freedom. Yet, many of the authors were Christians who held both slaves and considered religion necessary for maintaining moral virtue. The Declaration of Independence appeals to "the laws of Nature and Nature's God" and asserts that "all men" had basic rights "endowed by their Creator." Religion has long been political. And politics in America are fundamentally religious. Today, white evangelical Christianity, which justified empire, colonization, slavery, and Christian nationhood, is a decreed part of the American government, shaping who belongs; laws; politics; education; social policies on abortion, marriage, welfare, and guns; and how we think and talk about race, sex, and class. Black women and girls, enslaved and free, have suffered immensely under this arrangement from rape-ability and forced breeding during slavery to varying forms of violence, forced pregnancies, unconsented sterilization, stereotyping, the lack of health/care, and more after slavery.

11 While I'm emphasizing the work of mothers, this job is for all caretakers.

12 Jamilah Lemieux, "White women, don't think the Charlottesville photos let you off the hook for even a second," Twitter, August 12, 2017, https://twitter.com /jamilahlemieux/status/896372757012893696.

13 Christina Caron, "Heather Heyer, Charlottesville Victim, Is Recalled as 'a Strong Woman,'" *New York Times*, August 13, 2017, https://www.nytimes.com/2017/08/13/us /heather-heyer-charlottesville-victim.html.

14 The Barretts, Karens, and Miss Anns of the world are seminal to safeguarding morals, privilege, and position and keeping nonwhite folks in line, each of which is a virtue of Western civilization and empire. Within this paradigm, blackness serves as a threat to white supremacy, virility, and patriotic manhood. The use of the state to control Black folks is a moral and civic duty, even if (in some cases, especially if) it leads to black genocide or hostile and abusive environments. I write about the significance of race, gender, and the "nuclear" family in *Jezebel Unhinged: Loosing the Black Female Body in Religion and Culture* (Durham, NC: Duke University Press, 2018):

> In *Race and the Education of Desire: Foucault's History of Sexuality and the Colonial Order of Things* (1995), historian and anthropologist Ann Laura Stoler posits that the work of empire was constructed through depictions of European-ness and respectability codes defined against the colonized. Many of these depictions involved sexual, marital, and household management as well as clear distinctions between employer-servant relations. Women were expected to safeguard morals and prestige, as men were deemed more susceptible to moral turpitude. Stoler notes that it was the work of widely disseminated photographs and postcards that made these arrangements appear effortless and natural, particularly as Europeans were often situated occupying position and privilege, as servants awaited orders from their masters. Stoler argues that the assertion of European supremacy in terms of patriotic manhood and racial virility was not only an expression of imperial domination, but a defining feature of it. (113)

15 "President Donald Trump on Charlottesville: You Had Very Fine People, on Both Sides | CNBC," YouTube, November 28, 2020, https://www.youtube.com/watch?v =JmaZR8E12bs.

16 Hopefully, I've made the case that I understand "femininity" to be meaningful as well as socially constructed and therefore fluid. It becomes harmful when deployed as static and oppressive, for example, proof of womanhood, biological, binary, or inherently delicate, submissive, soft, weak, or otherwise. On black genocide, see James Baldwin, "On Being White . . . and Other Lies," *Essence*, April 1984, 90–92, ProQuest, or Anti-Racism Digital Library, https://sacred.omeka.net/items/show/238.

17 Angela Y. Davis, "Women and Capitalism: Dialectics of Oppression and Liberation," in *The Black Feminist Reader*, ed. Joy James and T. Denean Sharpley-Whiting (Malden, MA: Blackwell, 2000), 146–75.

18 I will return to Christocentric "real" womanhood later in the chapter. However, it is more than being a biological woman as argued in tensions between Black cisgender and transgender women in chapter 4. In many cases, it includes, and at times requires, marriage, as articulated by Jakes.

19 Despite being a proud "pussy grabber," being ableist, being charged with sexual assault, and more.

20 The ties between white women, evangelicalism, Republican conservatism, racism, and sexism are unexceptional. For more, see Robert Chao Romero, "Whiteness, Social Identity, and American Evangelicalism: An Analysis of the 2020 Presidential Election," Missio Alliance, November 20, 2020, https://www.missioalliance.org/whiteness -social-identity-and-american-evangelicalism-an-analysis-of-the-2020-presidential -election/; Christopher Mathias, "Trump Has Appointed 2 White Nationalists to Government Roles since Losing the Election," *HuffPost*, November 19, 2020, https://www .huffpost.com/entry/trump-appoints-white-nationalists-darren-beattie-jason-richwine _n_5fb6eedbc5b67f34cb398973; and Anthea Butler, *White Evangelical Racism: The Politics of Morality in America* (Chapel Hill: University of North Carolina Press, 2021).

21 Mackenzie Ryan, "'Better Martyrs': The Growing Role of Women in the Far-Right Movement," *Guardian*, August 12, 2023, https://www.theguardian.com/world/2023 /aug/12/conservative-women-tradwife-republican.

22 Cheryl I. Harris, "Whiteness as Property," *Harvard Law Review* 106, no. 8 (1993): 1707–91, https://harvardlawreview.org/print/no-volume/whiteness-as-property/.

23 See Reinhard and Crites, "'People of Praise Leaders Failed Me'"; Kirckaessner, "Legal Claims Shed Light on Founder of Faith Group."

24 "READ: Amy Coney Barrett's Opening Statement in Her Confirmation Hearing," NPR, October 11, 2020, https://www.npr.org/sections/live-amy-coney-barrett -supreme-court-confirmation/2020/10/11/922453657/amy-coney-barretts-opening -statement-in-her-confirmation-hearing.

25 The "strong black woman" trope is running rampant here.

26 Alan Fram and Jonathan Lemire, "Trump: Why Allow Immigrants from 'Shithole Countries'?," *AP News*, January 12, 2018, https://apnews.com/article /immigration-north-america-donald-trump-ap-top-news-international-news -fdda2ff0b877416c8ae1c1a77a3cc425.

27 166 Cong. Rec. S6588 (daily ed. October 25, 2020).

28 "Report on the Nomination of Ketanji Onyika Brown as an Associate Justice of the Supreme Court of the United States," Lawyers Committee for Civil Rights under Law, accessed August 15, 2023, https://www.lawyerscommittee.org/wp-content /uploads/2022/03/REPORT-ON-THE-NOMINATION-OF-JUDGE-KETANJI -BROWN-JACKSON-AS-AN-ASSOCIATE-JUSTICE-OF-THE-SUPREME-COURT -OF-THE-UNITED-STATES.pdf; Ann E. Marimow and Aaron C. Davis, "Potential Pick Ketanji Brown Jackson Would Make History as First Federal Public Defender on Supreme Court," *Washington Post*, February 11, 2022, https://www.washingtonpost.com /politics/2022/02/11/ketanji-brown-jackson-supreme-court-defender/?=undefined; Ann E. Marimow and Matt Viser, "Biden's First Slate of Judicial Nominees Aims to Quickly Boost Diversity in Federal Courts," *Washington Post*, March 29, 2021, https:// www.washingtonpost.com/local/legal-issues/biden-judicial-nominees-ketanji—brown -jackson/2021/03/29/38efad34-7773-11eb-8115-9ad5e9c02117_story.html.

29 Marimow and Viser, "Biden's First Slate of Judicial Nominees."

30 In *Kindred* (Garden City, NY: Doubleday, 1979), Octavia Butler asserts the past provides intel on the future, allowing us to look honestly at the webs of power, remember

all the ways we survived, and collectively reimagine and build a more ethical future. The reader may need clarity about the interchange between "worldmaking" and national crises. The United States isn't the world. In fact, it's small in comparison to other countries. Yet, its impact isn't inconsequential. It aids in the metanarrative and treatment of Black people globally. Worldmaking here matters. More, I project world-making as not so much going out and changing the world but a cooperative continuity of radical strategies toward that end to ultimately make small and large differences count. In that way, everyone can participate in maintaining the world as is or making it more emancipatory. There are already plenty of folks doing the former.

31 See Kimberlé Crenshaw, "Demarginalizing the Intersection of Race and Sex: A Black Feminist Critique of Antidiscrimination Doctrine, Feminist Theory, and Antiracist Politics," *University of Chicago Legal Forum* 1989, no. 1 (1989): 139–67; Raboteau, *Slave Religion.*

32 Barrett described the murder of George Floyd as deeply personal and the use of the N-word as bad but not impacting or socially abusive, suggesting racism is a private and/or personal matter and unrelated to sociopolitical systems and structures of violence.

33 See Clarence Thomas's use of the court and gifts. See the forty-fifth POTUS's use of the office. See also Baldwin, "On Being White . . . and Other Lies" on moral corruption. Additionally, the merging of military and Christianity is particularly evident in the song "Onward, Christian Soldiers," written by Sabine Baring-Gould in 1865 and later adopted by the Salvation Army. In my youth, it was a favored Vacation Bible School processional in my black Southern Baptist church. Black children and adults would march into the church sanctuary holding a Christian flag on one side and the American flag on the other. The idea was that we were soldiers for Christ willing to go to war in the name of Christian sovereignty and order. This messaging rings true today. However, in this context, I mean to note the current conflation of Christian supremacy with white supremacy evidenced between the support of the forty-fifth POTUS and white evangelicals.

34 The forty-fifth POTUS referred to Black Lives Matter as disgusting, threatening, and terroristic on multiple occasions.

35 We'll have to see if John Peter's black masculinity yields any traditional heteropatriarchal benefits.

36 Hortense Spillers's essay "Mama's Baby, Papa's Maybe: An American Grammar Book," in *Black, White, and in Color: Essays on American Literature and Culture* (Chicago: University of Chicago Press, 2003), 203–29, is a good place to begin when thinking about slave women, motherhood, breeding, the marketplace, and gendered stereotypes. Jennifer C. Nash articulates unmothering as the theft and loss of children to the slave trade in *Birthing Black Mothers* (Durham, NC: Duke University Press, 2021). Saidiya Hartman posits that the market and thus the stamp of commodity haunted the maternal line through pregnancy and childbirth. Melissa Harris-Perry asserts that the depiction of Black women and girls as sexually insatiable "breeders" suited the slave system but not the free state, which employed involuntary sterilization, pressure to submit to long-term birth control, restriction of state benefits, and policies that vetoed access to reproductive justice.

The stereotyping of Black/African slave women and girls during slavery is important for understanding how they're viewed within the political economy as well as social policy. Harris-Perry posits that welfare policy is intimately linked in the American imagination with Black women's sexuality and the belief that Black women and girls are sexually immoral and have a propensity to produce multiple children with multiple sexual partners that the state must care for through tax-supported welfare programs at a higher rate than for others. This notion comes from historical breeding practices, which blamed slave women (rather than rapists, slavers, and the slave structure) for their station. Also, because black female sexuality, a benefit to the slave economy, was redefined as a malignancy, something to be "cut out and controlled in order to protect the public," in freedom, poor Black mothers were seen as unworthy of welfare aid and vulnerable to forced sterilization and abortion.

Concomitantly, they were blamed for their poverty (due to myths around inherent laziness) rather than structural disenfranchisement, the lack of child and familial care, and the strain on women-headed households, all of which constructed a permanent economically alienated intergenerational black underclass. The Black children, divested from social services and exposed to cyclical poverty, came to represent crime. Thus, the neo-eugenicist push for sterilization and other forms of state-sanctioned genocide were seen as ways to decrease crime. And Black mothers, despite class, were seen as abominable. Saidiya Hartman explores this idea with regard to North American enslaved Black women in her texts *Scenes of Subjection: Terror, Slavery, and Self-Making in Nineteenth Century America* (New York: Oxford University Press, 1997) and *Lose Your Mother: A Journey along the Atlantic Slave Route* (New York: Farrar, Straus and Giroux, 2008). And see Melissa Harris-Perry, *Sister Citizen: Shame, Stereotypes, and Black Women in America* (New Haven, CT: Yale University Press, 2011).

37 Keri Day takes up the conservative political ideology and platform, "family values," and welfare reform, and how they were reimagined through a merging between the sexualization of Black women and girls, the evangelical Christian right, the political right, culture, and the law in *Unfinished Business: Black Women, the Black Church, and the Struggle to Thrive in America* (Maryknoll, NY: Orbis Books, 2012).

38 Though there are clear socioeconomic difficulties, I'm thinking about the demonizing and shaming of Black teen mothers, which typically doesn't apply to Black teen fathers.

39 The belief is that children who grow up without fathers in the home will be automatically prone to pathology, drugs, poverty, incarceration, et cetera. While Black men and boys are also subject to poverty, incarceration, and otherwise, single fathers are not viewed the way unmarried mothers are in terms of passing down pathology to their children. Single fathers are applauded for stepping in and up.

40 The issues with these stereotypes are numerous. See chapter 4 and my note on Michele Wallace's *Black Macho and the Myth of the Superwoman* (New York: Dial Press, 1979) and Day, *Unfinished Business*.

41 I didn't initially stay home to mother. After my six-week maternity leave, I went back to paid work for one month. I hated it, and I missed baby Lee something terrible. Not to mention, none of my clothes fit, my breasts were constantly leaking and sore, and the job that I left was not the job I returned to. While I was on leave, the company gave my role to a white woman who wanted to reap the benefits of my years of

labor. I was in banking at the time and had taken a historically unproductive branch and made it one of the top-producing locations in the city, allowing for financial and other rewards. To accommodate the white woman seeking my branch, I was stuffed into a random role and office doing a job I never signed up for and wasn't good at. If not illegal, this was sexist, racist, and unethical, at best. I lasted a month in the new role. During this time, my spouse talked his job into giving him paternity leave, which wasn't standard corporate practice yet, because he wanted time to bond with baby Lee. He loved it. I cried every time they visited me. When at home, baby Lee began preferencing his father and not wanting to breastfeed. I'm forever thankful for our parental partnership. However, I didn't calculate it to include Lee's rejection of me and breastfeeding. Simultaneously, we didn't want baby Lee in daycare and could afford for one of us to be at home. Ultimately, it was me. My husband made nearly double my salary and was on the fast track in his job whereas I'd reached a ceiling.

42 My spouse loved to cook and to care for baby Lee in the evenings; it was a badge of honor and source of pleasure. When baby Lee cried at night and wanted to be comforted by being held and walked around the house, my husband got up and did that. When we started graduate school a year later and I cried because we had to leave baby Lee in daycare, my spouse took him every day while I waited at home for him to come back and pick me up for class. When I couldn't bear seeing needles poke baby Lee's newborn flesh at doctors' visits, my partner took the lead as I waited nervously at home. And during those difficult years when I was a doctoral candidate about to lose my mind and soul, my husband was daddy and othermother.

43 bell hooks, *Salvation: Black People and Love* (New York: Harper Perennial, 2001), 151.

44 Mark Anthony Neal, *New Black Man* (New York: Routledge, 2015), 102.

45 "Safely" and "properly" note at least three concerns: slain Black boys, heteronormativity, and absent Black fathers. Black mothers became symbolic of the "breakdown of the Black family structure" and lack of "moral codes" after slavery. Historical narratives around pathology, coupled with cultural tales about Black mothers' alleged inability to raise Black sons without Black fathers dovetail with anxieties around (1) state-sanctioned violence against Black men during slavery, which took away paternal rights; (2) state-sanctioned violence against Black men in freedom, which forced them out of the home; and (3) state-sanctioned violence against Black men and boys, causing death. This places a heavy burden on Black mothers raising Black sons.

46 Hunter Ashleigh Shackelford, "To Black men at [Black Lives Matter] protests that say 'black queens, protect our children from this violence,'" Facebook, May 1, 2015, https://www.facebook.com/hunterashleighshackelford/posts/10204201647392725.

47 Dani McClain, "As a Black Mother, My Parenting Is Always Political," *Nation*, March 27, 2019, https://www.thenation.com/article/archive/black-motherhood -family-parenting-dani-mcclain/.

48 Black people, identities, sexualities, genders, and otherwise were queered/othered and de/mis/gendered outside of heteronormativity during colonialism. In the essay "Punks, Bulldaggers, and Welfare Queens: The Radical Potential of Queer Politics?," Cathy J. Cohen writes that state-sanctioned white supremacist heteropatriarchy; slavery and its sexual politics, rape, lynching, terrorism, breeding, and broken kinships; the prohibition of marriage; the regulation of sexual relationships; forced

sterilization; and otherwise reinterpreted black sex in general as deviant, pathological, morally deficient, reckless, and nonnormative, placing Black folks, in slavery and freedom, outside of heteronormativity. This isn't to say Black folks aren't heterosexual. It's to say our sexual lives were queered/placed outside of normativity during colonization. Of course, Black people live out a range of sexualities and explorations on a continuum. However, heteronormativity isn't a real thing for anyone because there isn't a standard sexuality. See Cathy J. Cohen, "Punks, Bulldaggers, and Welfare Queens: The Radical Potential of Queer Politics?," GLQ: A Journal of Lesbian and Gay Studies 3, no. 4 (May 1997): 437–65. See also Spillers, "Mama's Baby, Papa's Maybe."

49 #Protectblackmen is used in a few ways, including meaning to protect Black cisgender men and boys from white supremacist capitalist heteropatriarchy; protect Black cisgender men and boys from the police; protect Black cisgender men and boys from white supremacist capitalist violence; protect Black cisgender men and boys from white vigilante violence; protect Black cisgender men and boys from feminism; protect Black cisgender men and boys from accountability from Black women (see Megan Thee Stallion); and protect Black cisgender men and boys from being feminine, queer, and otherwise. I write the following in Loving Black Boys (forthcoming): "Black girls learn early that it's our duty to fight against black cisgender heterosexual male oppression, to #protectblackmen and boys from the various societal ills harming them, and to selflessly help build the aspirational black capitalist heteropatriarchal world [they've] imagined—even when these efforts lack reciprocity and/or reduce Black women and girls to support and/or sexual roles. Indeed, Black women and girls have been socialized to believe Black men and boys have it worse than us and that our freedom is bound up with their taking up their rightful place in the heteropatriarchy." Yet, #protectblackmen and boys could be useful if explored more inclusively and wholistically to engage collective Black endangerment and alienation. As I assert, "Much of which happens by the state. Some of which happens at our hands."

50 Black baby boys enter a peculiar life of double meanings, between monsters and kings (or crises and solutions), with the latter serving as a black cultural counter to the former. I was lauded for the opportunity of raising "future kings." I also get what the countercultural language on Black/African royalty intends to do.

51 Baldwin, "On Being White . . . and Other Lies."

52 I define hostagacy as a governing structure that allows for and relies on whole populations of hostages (slaves) to work (slavery).

53 The history of white motherhood during North American slavery and its role in reproducing and maintaining colonizing violences, for example, breeding, rape, and other abuses against women and girls, may be a good place to start.

54 Caitlin Dickerson, "U.S. Expels Migrant Children from Other Countries to Mexico," New York Times, October 30, 2020, https://www.nytimes.com/2020/10/30/us/migrant -children-expulsions-mexico.html.

55 See prayer breakfasts for forty-five, grabbing women "by the pussy," and sexual assault charges.

56 This isn't to negate the history of abortion or infanticide for Black mothers, and especially during slavery. Slave mothers sometimes killed their babies to keep them

from going into slavery. For some, this was seen as the highest form of love because death was preferable to slavery. Some might even say that this was in fact reproductive justice. We see this in the film *Beloved* (1998). Notwithstanding, what I hope to do here is expand these ideas. For more on slave women, sex, breeding, pregnancies, abortive measures, and reproductive justice, see Darlene Clark Hine, *Hine Sight: Black Women and the Re-construction of American History* (Bloomington: Indiana University Press, 1994).

57 This book is about black girlhood to black mothering. This chapter presents a particular focus on Black mothers. However, I deploy *people* here because I want to highlight all who mother, which is irreducible to sex or gender. At one point in my own history, I referred to my spouse as father and mother. This was during my PhD program, where I was largely absent. In chapter 2, I also refer to Uncle Clifford on *P-Valley* as an othermother. Mercedes notes Uncle Clifford as being better to her and more mothering to her than her own mother. Some might wonder why use the word *mothering* at all. Why not just *parents* or *caretakers*? Because some of us (the author included) use *mother* to define ourselves, however we might define and/or realize this role. The point isn't traditionalism or binaries. I'm absolutely not a traditional mother. My views of sex, gender, and roles are fluid. My role with my children is best understood through the radical black feminist politics I gave them, despite whatever they decide to do with them. This is how I chose to mother.

58 Jordan, "Creative Spirit," 12.

59 Alexis Pauline Gumbs, "m/other ourselves: a Black queer feminist genealogy for radical mothering," in *Revolutionary Mothering: Love on the Front Lines*, ed. Alexis Pauline Gumbs, China Martens, and Mai'a Williams (Oakland, CA: PM Press, 2016), 20.

60 Gumbs, Martens, and Williams, *Revolutionary Mothering*, 148.

61 Patricia Hill Collins, "The Meaning of Motherhood in Black Culture and Black Mother-Daughter Relationships," *Sage* 4, no. 2 (Fall 1987): 3–5.

62 Collins, "Meaning of Motherhood in Black Culture," 4.

63 I affirm that this is a designation that one must consent to. Not all want to mother or othermother or to have their labor defined in this way.

CODA

1 The View, "Ajike "AJ" Owens' Mother Speaks Out on Daughter Being Fatally Shot by Neighbor | The View," YouTube, accessed August 23, 2023, https://www.youtube .com/watch?v=oiICDafx6b8; Rebekah Riess, "Florida Woman Accused of Fatally Shooting Her Neighbor through a Door Pleads Not Guilty," *CNN*, July 11, 2023, https://www.cnn.com/2023/07/11/us/susan-lorincz-not-guilty-plea-florida-neighbor -shooting/index.html; Jennifer Henderson and Jamiel Lynch, "Florida Woman Who Fatally Shot a Black Neighbor Admitted Hurling Racial Slurs at Victim's Children in the Past, Affidavit Says," *CNN*, June 9, 2023, https://www.cnn.com/2023/06/09/us /ajike-owens-shooting-death-neighbor-florida-friday/index.html.

2 The View, "Ajike "AJ" Owens' Mother Speaks Out."

3 The View, "Ajike "AJ" Owens' Mother Speaks Out."

4 James Baldwin, "On Being White . . . and Other Lies," *Essence*, April 1984, 90–92, ProQuest, or Anti-Racism Digital Library, https://sacred.omeka.net/items/show/238.

5 Audre Lorde and James Baldwin, "Revolutionary Hope: A Conversation between Audre Lorde and James Baldwin," *Mosaic Literary Magazine* no. 39 (Fall 2016): 42–52.

6 I note the irony and power of self-naming here.

7 Mankaprr Conteh, "Megan Thee Stallion Will Not Back Down," *Rolling Stone*, June 15, 2022, https://www.rollingstone.com/music/music-features/megan-thee -stallion-new-album-1366025/.

8 James Queally, "Megan Thee Stallion Takes the Stand in Tory Lanez Trial with Support from Demonstrators," *Los Angeles Times*, December 13, 2022, https://www .latimes.com/california/story/2022-12-13/megan-thee-stallion-takes-the-stand-in -torey-lanez-trial.

9 Jon Blistein, "Megan Thee Stallion to Face Tory Lanez in Shooting Trial Today: 'I Want Him to Go to Jail,'" *Rolling Stone*, December 12, 2022, https://www.rollingstone .com/music/music-news/megan-thee-stallion-said-alleged-tory-lanez-shooting -1234644649/.

10 Queally, "Megan Thee Stallion Takes the Stand."

11 Queally, "Megan Thee Stallion Takes the Stand."

12 June Jordan, "Resolution #1,003," in *Haruko/Love Poems*, ed. June Jordan and Adrienne Rich (New York: High Risk Books, 1994).

13 Italics note plurality.

14 Italics note plurality.

15 Emphasis is placed on cisgender Black boys, however, given that I'm writing about my sons.

16 Whereas Martin Luther King Jr. spoke about a revolution of racial values, bell hooks reminds us that such a revolution includes intracommunal sex and gender healing based in love ethics. She posits that Black men save themselves when they learn the art of loving and allow themselves to grieve and heal from the loss of the patriarchy never attained. We shouldn't have to develop elaborate schemes to protect daughters from Black boys and men. We should raise Black boys to men to participate in building a more emancipatory society. This calls to mind all the rules that we give to girls to protect them from boys, rules I too was raised with. I'm also thinking about the annual prom pictures of Black dads with guns, their daughters, and their male prom dates. How often are these fathers hoping to protect their daughters from their younger or current selves? The threat of additional violence toward Black boys from Black men isn't a solution.

17 This in no way means Black mothers are perfect. I'm highlighting the role of mothers in imparting information. In her book *When Momma Speaks: The Bible and Motherhood from a Womanist Perspective* (Louisville, KY: Westminster John Knox Press, 2016), Stephanie Buckhanon Crowder asserts that much of the thinking in children comes from mothers, grandmothers, and othermothers imparting spiritual values and moral wisdom across generations. This isn't universal or totalizing. Present and willing fathers also play a role in character building. However, this is often seen as women's work, especially during the early years of a child's life. Crowder asserts that mothers were central to and valued in familial life in West Africa but were commodified in slavery. She writes, "Slavery uprooted what had been some West African ideas of the mother as the central force in tribe or nation building.

Since the worth of women rested not in their maternal duties but in the fiscal possibilities, plantation life served to destroy communal mothering practices and accountability. By forcing women to focus on surviving rape while trying, without much success, to keep and to nurture their children, slavery took motherhood from being a social staple of the African American community and made it a reflection of individualism at the hands of monetary gain" (7). I hold that while there were extreme limitations placed on mothering, Black/African, slave and free, mothers and othermothers found a range of subversive ways to still impart culture, politics, character, and so on in their children. Several slave testimonies and other accounts speak to this. For example, both Harriet Jacobs and Frederick Douglass talk about the significance of their grandmothers.

18 Alexis Pauline Gumbs, "m/other ourselves: a Black queer feminist genealogy for radical mothering," in *Revolutionary Mothering: Love on the Front Lines*, ed. Alexis Pauline Gumbs, China Martens, and Mai'a Williams (Oakland, CA: PM Press, 2016), 19–23.

19 My view of Christianity is influenced by the freedom fighters on North American plantations. My theology is one of love and justice, with a passionate and unapologetic loathing for oppression, including evangelical and theological misogynoir. I maintain a political theology of rebellion against anything that seeks to oppress Black people and am critical of ideas that center notions of hypermoralism, empire, supremacy, Christian piety, or Christian patriarchal order. Ergo, what is "unvirtuous" and "sinful" for me are efforts that enable black oppression and genocide. What is "good" centers the freedom, power, and well-being of the collective. Concomitantly, I hold a genderless vision of God.

20 Black feminist mothering understands that black humanity is interdependent. As Gumbs posits, mothering is "all day long and everywhere when we acknowledge the creative power of transforming ourselves, and the ways we relate to each other. Because we were never meant to survive and here we are creating a world full of love" (preface to Gumbs, Martens, and Williams, *Revolutionary Mothering*, xvii).

21 Black feminist mothering makes room for a range of identities and calls for an openness to healing and subversion, which includes but moves beyond gender and sexuality. It's for the nurturing of nontoxic futures over and against patriarchal and essentialist prisons. It also understands gender is learned in communities that give meaning and take meaning away. The hope is that Black people are freed to be whatever life-giving expression of humanity they want to be and that the latter is valued because it is so.

22 April Baker-Bell, *Linguistic Justice: Black Language, Literacy, Identity, and Pedagogy* (New York: Routledge, 2020).

Bibliography

Bailey, Moya. *Misogynoir Transformed: Black Women's Digital Resistance*. New York: New York University Press, 2021.

Baker-Bell, April. *Linguistic Justice: Black Language, Literacy, Identity, and Pedagogy*. New York: Routledge, 2020.

Baldwin, James. "On Being White . . . and Other Lies." *Essence*, April 1984. Anti-Racism Digital Library. https://sacred.omeka.net/items/show/238.

Bambara, Toni Cade, ed. *The Black Woman: An Anthology*. New York: Washington Square Press, 2005.

Butler, Anthea. *White Evangelical Racism: The Politics of Morality in America*. Chapel Hill: University of North Carolina Press, 2021.

Butler, Octavia E. *Kindred*. Garden City, NY: Doubleday, 1979.

Césaire, Aimé. *Discourse on Colonialism*. New York: Monthly Review Press, 2000.

Coates, Ta-Nehisi. *Between the World and Me*. New York: Spiegel and Grau, 2015.

Cohen, Cathy J. "Punks, Bulldaggers, and Welfare Queens: The Radical Potential of Queer Politics?" *GLQ: A Journal of Lesbian and Gay Studies* 3, no. 4 (May 1997): 437. Ebsco.

Collins, Patricia Hill. *Black Feminist Thought: Knowledge, Consciousness, and the Politics of Empowerment*. New York: Routledge, 2000.

Collins, Patricia Hill. "The Meaning of Motherhood in Black Culture and Black Mother-Daughter Relationships." *Sage* 4, no. 2 (Fall 1987): 3–5.

Cone, James. *Black Theology and Black Power*. Maryknoll, NY: Orbis Books, 2008.

Cooper, Brittney. "How Sarah Got Her Groove Back, or Notes toward a Black Feminist Theology of Pleasure." *Black Theology: An International Journal* 16, no. 3 (2018): 195–206. https://doi.org/10.1080/14769948.2018.1492299.

Crenshaw, Kimberlé. "Demarginalizing the Intersection of Race and Sex: A Black Feminist Critique of Antidiscrimination Doctrine, Feminist Theory, and Antiracist Politics." *University of Chicago Legal Forum* 1989, no. 1 (1989): 139–67.

Crenshaw, Kimberlé. "Mapping the Margins: Intersectionality, Identity Politics, and Violence against Women of Color." *Stanford Law Review* 43, no. 6 (1991): 1241–99. doi:10.2307/1229039.

Crowder, Stephanie Buckhanon. *When Momma Speaks: The Bible and Motherhood from a Womanist Perspective*. Louisville, KY: Westminster John Knox Press, 2016.

Davis, Angela Y. "Rape, Racism, and the Myth of the Black Rapist." In *Women, Race, and Class*, 172–201. New York: Vintage, 1983.

Davis, Angela Y. "Women and Capitalism: Dialectics of Oppression and Liberation." In *The Black Feminist Reader*, edited by Joy James and T. Denean Sharpley-Whiting, 146–82. Malden, MA: Blackwell, 2000.

Day, Keri. "'I Am Dark and Lovely': Let the Shulammite Woman Speak." *Black Theology: An International Journal* 16, no. 3 (2018): 207–17. https://doi.org/10.1080/14769948.2018.1492300.

Day, Keri. *Unfinished Business: Black Women, the Black Church, and the Struggle to Thrive in America*. Maryknoll, NY: Orbis Books, 2012.

Du Bois, W. E. B. *The Souls of Black Folk*. Greenwich, CT: Fawcett, 1961.

Eisenstein, Zillah. "Newest Misogyny/ies." *Logos: A Journal of Modern Society and Culture*, Spring 2023. https://logosjournal.com/2023/newest-misogyny-ies/.

Fanon, Frantz. *Black Skin, White Masks*. New York: Grove Press, 1967.

Foster, Thomas A. *Rethinking Rufus: Sexual Violations of Enslaved Men*. Atlanta: University of Georgia Press, 2019.

Gafney, Wil. "Commentary on Proverbs 31:10–31." *Working Preacher*, September 2015. https://www.workingpreacher.org/commentaries/revised-common-lectionary/ordinary-25-2/commentary-on-proverbs-3110-31-4.

Gafney, Wilda C. *Daughters of Miriam: Women Prophets in Ancient Israel*. Minneapolis: Fortress Press, 2008.

Gilman, Sander L. *Difference and Pathology: Stereotypes of Sexuality, Race, and Madness*. Ithaca, NY: Cornell University Press, 1985.

Glaude, Eddie S., Jr. *African American Religion: A Very Short Introduction*. Oxford: Oxford University Press, 2014.

Gumbs, Alexis Pauline. "m/other ourselves: a Black queer feminist genealogy for radical mothering." In *Revolutionary Mothering: Love on the Front Lines*, edited by Alexis Pauline Gumbs, China Martens, and Mai'a Williams, 19–31. Oakland, CA: PM Press, 2016.

Gumbs, Alexis Pauline, China Martens, and Mai'a Williams, eds. *Revolutionary Mothering: Love on the Front Lines*. Oakland, CA: PM Press, 2016.

Hall, Stuart, ed. *Representation: Cultural Representations and Signifying Practices*. London: Sage, 2003.

Harris, Cheryl I. "Whiteness as Property." *Harvard Law Review* 106, no. 8 (1993): 1707–91. https://harvardlawreview.org/print/no-volume/whiteness-as-property/.

Harris-Perry, Melissa. *Sister Citizen: Shame, Stereotypes, and Black Women in America*. New Haven, CT: Yale University Press, 2011.

Hartman, Saidiya. *Lose Your Mother: A Journey along the Atlantic Slave Route*. New York: Farrar, Straus and Giroux, 2008.

Hartman, Saidiya. *Scenes of Subjection: Terror, Slavery, and Self-Making in Nineteenth-Century America*. New York: Oxford University Press, 1997.

Higginbotham, Evelyn Brooks. *Righteous Discontent: The Women's Movement in the Black Baptist Church, 1880–1920*. Cambridge, MA: Harvard University Press, 1993.

Hine, Darlene Clark. *Hine Sight: Black Women and the Re-construction of American History*. Bloomington: Indiana University Press, 1994.

hooks, bell. *Black Looks: Race and Representation*. Boston: South End Press, 1992.

hooks, bell. *Communion: The Female Search for Love*. New York: Harper Perennial, 2002.

hooks, bell. *Feminism Is for Everybody*. London: Pluto Press, 2000.

hooks, bell. *Salvation: Black People and Love*. New York: Harper Perennial, 2001.

hooks, bell. *We Real Cool: Black Men and Masculinity*. New York: Routledge, 2004.

hooks, bell. *The Will to Change: Men, Masculinity, and Love*. New York: Atria Books, 2004.

Hunter, Tera. *To 'Joy My Freedom: Southern Black Women's Lives and Labors after the Civil War*. Cambridge, MA: Harvard University Press, 1997.

Jackson, Zakiyyah Iman. "Losing Manhood: Animality and Plasticity in the (Neo)Slave Narrative." *Qui Parle: Critical Humanities and Social Sciences* 25, no. 1–2 (2016): 95–136. www.jstor.org/stable/10.5250/quiparle.25.1-2.0095.

Jordan, June. "The Creative Spirit: Children's Literature." In *Revolutionary Mothering: Love on the Front Lines*, edited by Alexis Pauline Gumbs, China Martens, and Mai'a Williams, 11–18. Oakland, CA: PM Press, 2016.

Jordan, June. "Resolution #1,003." In *Haruko/Love Poems*, edited by June Jordan and Adrienne Rich. New York: High Risk Books, 1994.

Jordan, June. *Some of Us Did Not Die*. New York: Basic/Civitas Books, 2002.

Kendall, Mikki. *Hood Feminism: Notes from the Women That a Movement Forgot*. New York: Viking, 2020.

King, Martin Luther, Jr., Vincent Harding, and Coretta Scott King. *Where Do We Go from Here—Chaos or Community?* Boston: Beacon Press, 2010.

Kirk-Duggan, Cheryl. "Rethinking the 'Virtuous' Woman (Proverbs 31): A Mother in Need of Holiday." In *Mother Goose, Mother Jones, Mommie Dearest: Biblical Mothers and Their Children*, edited by Cheryl A. Kirk-Duggan and Tina Pippin, 97–112. Leiden: Brill, 2010.

Levine, Lawrence. *Black Culture and Black Consciousness: Afro-American Folk Thought from Slavery to Freedom*. New York: Oxford University Press, 1977.

Lomax, Tamura. "Black Bodies in Ecstasy: Black Women, the Black Church, and the Politics of Pleasure: An Introduction." *Black Theology: An International Journal* 16, no. 3 (2018): 189–94. https://doi.org/10.1080/14769948.2018.1492298.

Lomax, Tamura. "The Black Church Movement Profile Is Dead: The Audacious Absurdity of Transgressive Imagination between 'The American Dream' and the Nightmare." In *Moved by the Spirit: Religion and the Movement for Black Lives*, edited by Christophe D. Ringer, Teresa L. Smallwood, and Emilie M. Townes, 117–34. Lanham, MD: Lexington Books, 2023.

Lomax, Tamura. *Jezebel Unhinged: Loosing the Black Female Body in Religion and Culture*. Durham, NC: Duke University Press, 2018.

Lomax, Tamura. "Looking for Justice for Black Women and Girls: The Black Church, Jezebel, and Aspirational Black Capitalist Patriarchy." Berkley Center for Religion, Peace, and World Affairs, April 8, 2021. https://berkleycenter.georgetown.edu /responses/looking-for-justice-for-black-women-and-girls-the-black-church-jezebel -and-aspirational-black-capitalist-patriarchy.

Lomax, Tamura. *Loving Black Boys: A Black Feminist Bible on Racism and Revolutionary Mothering*. Durham, NC: Duke University Press, forthcoming.

Lomax, Tamura. "Theorizing the Distance between Erotophobia, Hyper-moralism, and Eroticism: Toward a Black Feminist Theology of Pleasure." *Black Theology: An International Journal* 16, no. 3 (2018): 263–79. https://doi.org/10.1080/14769948.2018.1492305.

Long, Charles H. *Significations: Signs, Symbols, and Images in the Interpretation of Religion*. Philadelphia: Fortress Press, 1986.

Lorde, Audre. "Age, Race, Class, and Sex: Women Redefining Difference." In *Sister Outsider: Essays and Speeches*, 114–23. Berkeley: Crossing Press, 2007.

Lorde, Audre. "Uses of the Erotic: The Erotic as Power." In *Sister Outsider: Essays and Speeches*, 53–59. Berkeley: Crossing Press, 2007.

Lorde, Audre, and James Baldwin. "Revolutionary Hope: A Conversation between Audre Lorde and James Baldwin." *Mosaic Literary Magazine*, no. 39 (Fall 2016): 42–52. Ebsco.

McGuire, Danielle L. *At the Dark End of the Street: Black Women, Rape, and Resistance—a New History of the Civil Rights Movement from Rosa Parks to the Rise of Black Power*. New York: Vintage, 2011.

Miller-Young, Mireille. *A Taste for Brown Sugar: Black Women in Pornography*. Durham, NC: Duke University Press, 2014.

Morgan, Joan. *When Chickenheads Come Home to Roost: A Hip-Hop Feminist Breaks It Down*. New York: Simon and Schuster, 1999.

Morgan, Joan. "Why We Get Off: Moving towards a Black Feminist Politics of Pleasure." *Black Scholar* 45, no. 4 (Fall 2015): 36–37.

Morrison, Toni. "Home." In *The House That Race Built: Original Essays by Toni Morrison, Angela Y. Davis, Cornel West, and Others on Black Americans and Politics in America Today*, edited by Wahneema Lubiano, 3–12. New York: Vintage, 1998.

Mustakeem, Sowande' M. *Slavery at Sea: Terror, Sex, and Sickness in the Middle Passage*. Urbana: University of Illinois Press, 2016.

Nash, Jennifer C. *Birthing Black Mothers*. Durham, NC: Duke University Press, 2021.

Nash, Jennifer C. *The Black Body in Ecstasy: Reading Race, Reading Pornography*. Durham, NC: Duke University Press, 2014.

Neal, Mark Anthony. *New Black Man*. New York: Routledge, 2015.

Owens, Leslie Howard. *The Species of Property: Slave Life and Culture in the Old South*. New York: Oxford University Press, 1976.

Raboteau, Albert J. *Slave Religion: The "Invisible Institution" in the Antebellum South*. New York: Oxford University Press, 1978.

Rawick, George P., ed. *The American Slave, Texas Narratives*. Supplement, no. 2, vol. 7, pt. 6. Westport, CT: Greenwood Press, 1977.

Sharpley-Whiting, T. Denean. *Pimps Up, Ho's Down: Hip Hop's Hold on Young Black Women*. New York: New York University Press, 2008.

Shurden, Walter B. *Struggle for the Soul of the SBC: Moderate Responses to the Fundamentalist Movement*. Macon, GA: Mercer University Press, 1994.

Spillers, Hortense. "Mama's Baby, Papa's Maybe: An American Grammar Book." In *Black, White, and in Color: Essays on American Literature and Culture*, 203–29. Chicago: University of Chicago Press, 2003.

Stoler, Ann Laura. *Race and the Education of Desire: Foucault's History of Sexuality and the Colonial Order of Things*. Durham, NC: Duke University Press, 1995.

Wallace, Michele. *Black Macho and the Myth of the Superwoman*. New York: Dial Press, 1979.

White, Deborah Gray. *Ar'n't I a Woman? Female Slaves in the Plantation South*. New York: Norton, 1999.

Index

kinship: Black girls and, 35; black mothering vs., 11
Kirk-Duggan, Cheryl, 117

landownership, power and, 149, 195n81
Lanez, Tory, 47, 150–53, 187n18
Lemieux, Jamilah, 124
Levine, Lawrence, 181n50
LGBTQ rights: Black Church opposition to, 99–103; Black men's opposition to, 103–5; violence involving, 191n42; white evangelical opposition to, 98–99
Lil Wayne, 189n36
Linguistic Justice: Black Language, Literacy, Identity and Pedagogy (Baker-Bell), 21
literacy, black feminism and, 20–21
Lomax, Lee, 1, 12–13, 132–34, 154–55, 200n41
Lomax, Seth, 1, 12–13, 64–65, 138, 154–55, 175n2
Lomax, Tamura: androgynous stage in life of, 58; autobiographical letter to Black girls, 25–35; family life recalled by, 25–27, 68–74, 78–80, 112–17, 177n16, 178n19; father (Daddy) recalled by, 42, 68–74, 78–86, 116–17; kitchen fire experienced by, 63–65; mother (Momma) recalled by, 28, 42, 59–61, 69, 72–73, 78, 85–86, 89, 112–17, 131–32, 141, 177n16; OCD experienced by, 64–65, 175n3; pregnancy and motherhood for, 131–39, 154–55, 200n41; rape experienced by, 57–58; sexual violence experienced by, 57–60, 175n58
Long, Charles H., 181n56
Long Walk Home, A, 169n1
Lorde, Audre: Baldwin dialogue with, 17–18, 56–57, 175n60; as black feminist, 87, 89, 149; on Black girls, 84, 175n60; on black mothering, 140–42; on heteropatriarchal evangelicalism, 80; on survival, 163n34; on white racism, 174n51
Lorincz, Susan, 146–48, 152
"Losing Manhood: Animality and Plasticity in the (Neo)Slave Narrative" (Jackson), 15
love ethics: Black girls and, 34–35; black sovereignty and, 21, 165n59; cultivation of, 12, 164n38; justice and, 81, 181n53; patriarchal constructs of, 195n84; patriarchy and, 97
Loving Black Boys: A Black Feminist Bible on Racism and Revolutionary Mothering (Lomax),

13, 73, 162n22; black communal refuge and, 22; black liberation in, 171n12; black mothering in, 146, 164n31; Black women and girls and, 202n49; capitalist heteropatriarchy and, 15–17; collective black endangerment and, 150; husband terminology in, x; sanctuary discussed in, 153–54; survival framework in, 163n34; victim blaming in, 187n18

Maddox, Jack, 54–55
Maddox, Rosa, 54–55
"Mama's Baby, Papa's Maybe: An American Grammar Book" (Spillers), 69, 199n36
manhood, Black Church heteropatriarchal framing of, 6–13, 93–97, 161nn21–22
Marin City, California, 178n22
marriage: Black girls' passage to, 7–8, 60–62; patriarchal constructs of, 195n84; weaponization of cisgender heterosexual marriage, 133
Martin, Trayvon, 147
masculinity: capitalist heteropatriarchy and, 164n36; sexual violence and, 167n7
McClain, Dani, 136–37
McConnell, Mitch, 120–21, 128
McDade, Tony, 101
"Meaning of Motherhood in Black Culture and Black Mother-Daughter Relationships, The" (Collins), 143
Meek Mill, 56
Mencimer, Stephanie, 120
#MeToo movement: Black Church rejection of, 51–52; Black women and girls and, 51–56; rape culture and, 269n1
Miller-Young, Mireille, 47–48
Mill Valley, California, Lomax's experiences in, 70–74, 81–83, 85–86
misogynoir: of Black boys and men, 81–83; in Black Church, 2, 48–51, 158n6; Black girls' navigation of, 56–62, 173n36; foundational role of, 161n15; heteropatriarchal normativity and, 18–19
"Mississippi Goddam" (Simone), 145–47
Mock, Janet, 158n5
Moral Majority, 99, 107, 189n33
Morgan, Joan, 62, 82
Moynihan, Daniel Patrick, 133
Mustakeem, Sowande M., 53–54

www.ingramcontent.com/pod-product-compliance
Lightning Source LLC
Chambersburg PA
CBHW031930120525
26572CB00023B/227